THE
HISTORY OF
AUSTRALIA

ADVISORY BOARD

THE
HISTORY OF
AUSTRALIA

Frank G. Clarke

The Greenwood Histories of the Modern Nations
Frank W. Thackeray and John E. Findling, Series Editors

Greenwood Press
Westport, Connecticut • London

Library of Congress Cataloging-in-Publication Data

Clarke, F. G. (Francis Gordon), 1943–
   The history of Australia / Frank G. Clarke.
      p.   cm.—(The Greenwood histories of the modern nations, ISSN 1096–2905)
   Includes bibliographical references and index.
   ISBN 0–313–31498–5 (alk. paper)
   1. Australia—History.   I. Title.   II. Series.
DU110.C53   2002
994—dc21   2001054704

British Library Cataloguing in Publication Data is available.

Library of Congress Catalog Card Number: 2001054704
ISBN: 0–313–31498–5
ISSN: 1096–2905

First published in 2002

Greenwood Press, 88 Post Road West, Westport, CT 06881
An imprint of Greenwood Publishing Group, Inc.
www.greenwood.com

Printed in the United States of America

The paper used in this book complies with the
Permanent Paper Standard issued by the National
Information Standards Organization (Z39.48–1984).

10 9 8 7 6 5 4 3 2 1

Contents

Series Foreword

The Greenwood Histories of the Modern Nations series is intended to provide students and interested laypeople with up-to-date, concise, and analytical histories of many of the nations of the contemporary world. Not since the 1960s has there been a systematic attempt to publish a series of national histories, and as series editors, we believe that this series will prove to be a valuable contribution to our understanding of other countries in our increasingly interdependent world.

Over thirty years ago, at the end of the 1960s, the Cold War was an accepted reality of global politics, the process of decolonization was still in progress, the idea of a unified Europe with a single currency was unheard of, the United States was mired in a war in Vietnam, and the economic boom of Asia was still years in the future. Richard Nixon was president of the United States, Mao Tse-tung (not yet Mao Zedong) ruled China, Leonid Brezhnev guided the Soviet Union, and Harold Wilson was prime minister of the United Kingdom. Authoritarian dictators still ruled most of Latin America, the Middle East was reeling in the wake of the Six-Day War, and Shah Reza Pahlavi was at the height of his power in Iran. Clearly, the past thirty years have been witness to a great deal of historical change, and it is to this change that this series is primarily addressed.

With the help of a distinguished advisory board, we have selected

nations whose political, economic, and social affairs mark them as among
the most important in the waning years of the twentieth century, and
for each nation we have found an author who is recognized as a spe-
cialist in the history of that nation. These authors have worked most
cooperatively with us and with Greenwood Press to produce volumes
that reflect current research on their nation and that are interesting and
informative to their prospective readers.

The importance of a series such as this cannot be underestimated.
As a superpower whose influence is felt all over the world, the United
States can claim a "special" relationship with almost every other nation.
Yet many Americans know very little about the histories of the nations with which the United States relates. How did they get to be the
way they are? What kind of political systems have evolved there? What
kind of influence do they have in their own region? What are the dominant political, religious, and cultural forces that move their leaders?
These and many other questions are answered in the volumes of this
series.

The authors who have contributed to this series have written comprehensive histories of their nations, dating back to prehistoric time in some
cases. Each of them, however, has devoted a significant portion of the
book to events of the past thirty years, because the modern era has contributed the most to contemporary issues that have an impact on U.S.
policy. Authors have made an effort to be as up-to-date as possible so
that readers can benefit from the most recent scholarship and a narrative
that includes very recent events.

In addition to the historical narrative, each volume in this series contains an introductory overview of the country's geography, political institutions, economic structure, and cultural attributes. This is designed
to give readers a picture of the nation as it exists in the contemporary
world. Each volume also contains additional chapters that add interesting and useful detail to the historical narrative. One chapter is a thorough chronology of important historical events, making it easy for
readers to follow the flow of a particular nation's history. Another chapter features biographical sketches of the nation's most important figures
in order to humanize some of the individuals who have contributed to
the historical development of their nation. Each volume also contains a
comprehensive bibliography, so that those readers whose interest has
been sparked may find out more about the nation and its history. Finally,
there is a carefully prepared topic and person index.

Readers of these volumes will find them fascinating to read and useful in understanding the contemporary world and the nations that comprise it. As series editors, it is our hope that this series will contribute to a heightened sense of global understanding as we enter a new century.

Frank W. Thackeray and John E. Findling
Indiana University Southeast

Preface

Australian history has been written for over two centuries, beginning with European explorers and colonists attempting to convey something of the complexity of the strange upside-down world they encountered in the Southern Hemisphere. Their descendants who have been born and brought up there continue to try to explain their country, its peoples, and its power, to themselves as much as to others. In many ways, Australia defies description, and its history both before and after the arrival of Europeans is rich and multilayered. It is the oldest country, because unlike most of the world it underwent very little alteration during the last ice age, and its surface has been comparatively unchanged by volcanic activity. Its native peoples did not write but had evolved a highly specialized way of life that permitted them to exist in, understand, and manage their own countries for millennia before the arrival of the whites. Modern Australia has its foundations in these two cultural strands, and the unresolved tensions between them continue to bedevil a community that still has not attained a reconciliation between black loss and disempowerment and white obduracy and refusal to acknowledge the reality of invasion and theft. These tensions also underlie the writing of Australian history and affect the way in which historians interpret their data. I have striven for balance and objectivity and to avoid unfairness and bias. To the degree that I have succeeded, this volume will annoy those who hold to a more partisan and inflexible position at either end of the interpretive spectrum. Australian history has become one battleground in the culture wars currently dividing Australia.

Simply stated, my intention in this volume is to provide a snapshot of Australia's history from the arrival of human beings through current times. If that alone were not evidence of an unattainable ambition, I also have attempted to discern and describe recurring themes and some of the overriding cultural ideas that have impacted upon Australian developments since 1788. Much generalization and compression have been necessary to achieve this within the word limitations imposed by a single volume, and I have used a roughly chronological approach to contextualize the material. The unequal distribution of population, with the vast majority living along the eastern seaboard, has led to a similarly unequal historical treatment, with the history relating more to the eastern side of Australia than to the largely empty interior or the vast under-populated area of Western Australia. If the gaps and deficiencies provoke a search for more detail and whet the appetite for greater knowledge, this book will have done its job.

I wish to thank my friends and colleagues in the Department of Modern History at Macquarie University for their encouragement and support; and also the thousands of undergraduate and postgraduate students whom I have taught over the years for their enthusiasm and passion to find the truth. Individually, I owe a debt to Trevor Mc-Claughlin, Portia Robinson, John Walmsley, and Leighton Frappell, for their good-natured and cheerful support as I tried ideas out on them. I am also indebted to my wife and partner Jan, who has put up with my obsession with Australian history over many years with unfailing good humor, despite the inroads it has made on my time and the absent-minded preoccupation it has produced even when I am physically present. Whatever merits the book possesses belong to these people. Its many shortcomings are decidedly my own responsibility.

Timeline of Historical Events

70,000– 60,000 B.C.E.	Ancestors of Aborigines arrive in Australia
C.E. 1600s	Portuguese, Dutch, and English explorers discover Australia
1770	New South Wales annexed for Britain by James Cook
1772	Western Australia annexed for France by François-Alesno de St. Allouarn
1788	British First Fleet arrives in New South Wales
1803	Van Diemen's Land (Tasmania) settled by British
1829	First Free colony founded by British in Western Australia
1836	South Australia settled by British; Port Phillip District (Victoria) colonized from Van Diemen's Land
1850	Victoria becomes an independent colony
1851	Gold discovered at Bathurst in New South Wales and at Ballarat and Bendigo in Victoria
1854	Peter Lalor leads uprising of gold diggers at the Eureka Stockade in Ballarat against petty officialdom

1855   Responsible Government conferring control over local affairs granted to New South Wales, Victoria, Tasmania, and South Australia

1859   Queensland becomes an independent colony

1861   Anti-Chinese riots at Lambing Flats goldfield in New South Wales; Free Selection legislation in New South Wales to enable acquisition of freehold lands for farming

1863   Northern Territory transferred from New South Wales to South Australia

1877   Palmer River gold rush in Queensland

1879   Meeting of first intercolonial trade union congress in Sydney

1880   The *Bulletin* begins publication

1883   Queensland attempts to annex New Guinea

1889   Henry Parkes's Tenterfield oration rekindles the federation debate

1890   Australasian Federation Conference, Melbourne; Responsible Government granted to Western Australia

1891   Coolgardie and Kalgoorlie goldfields discovered in Western Australia; great strikes in shearing and maritime unions throughout the eastern colonies

1892   Bank and building societies collapse and herald onset of economic depression in the eastern colonies

1894   Women gain the vote in South Australia

1897   First two sessions of Federal Convention

1898   Referendums on federation in New South Wales, Victoria, South Australia, and Tasmania

1899   Referendums on federation; Western Australian women gain the vote; Boer War begins in South Africa

1900   Referendum on federation in Western Australia

1901   Inauguration of the Commonwealth of Australia; first federal elections; implementation of a white Australia policy, an anti-Asian immigration measure

1911   Northern Territory transferred to Commonwealth

1911	Royal Military College of Australia opened at Duntroon
1911	Commonwealth Bank established
1914	Outbreak of World War I; recruitment begins for first Australian Imperial Force (AIF)
1915	April 25 landings at Gallipoli, Turkey, in the struggle to wrest control of the Dardanelles from the Turks
1916	Celebration of first ANZAC Day, in honor of the Australian and New Zealand Army Corps soldiers who landed on the Gallipoli Peninsula in 1915
1919	Prime Minister Hughes attends Paris Peace Conference on 18 January
1921	Election of Australia's first female legislator in Western Australia
1924	Loan Council established
1927	Federal Parliament moves to Canberra
1929	Onset of the Great Depression
1931	Appointment of first Australian-born governor general
1939	Outbreak of World War II; recruitment begins for Second AIF
1941	Pearl Harbor brings America into the war; Australia seeks an American alliance
1947	Government embarks on program of assisted immigration
1949	Great Coal Strike begins
1951	ANZUS Treaty lays the basis of Australia's postwar security
1954	The Petrov Affair and the Cold War
1954	Signing of Southeast Asia Collective Defence Treaty (SEATO) on 8 September 1954
1955	The great split in the Australian Labor Party (ALP)
1964	Australia participates in Vietnam War
1966	Retirement of Robert Gordon Menzies, Australia's longest-serving prime minister
1967	Referendum to recognize Aborigines as Australian citizens

1972   Election of the Whitlam ALP government; principle of equal pay accepted; Australia withdraws from Vietnam

1975   Anti-Discrimination Act passed; governor general dismisses the government for inability to guarantee supply by the passage of its budget through the senate

1983   Election of Hawke/Keating ALP government heralds the beginning of economic rationalization and financial deregulation

1984   Banking system deregulated

1988   Celebration of the bicentenary of White Settlement on 26 January

1992   Mabo Decision by High Court recognizes native title

1993   Land Rights Act gives legislative form to native title

1999   Referendum to become a republic fails

2000   Sydney Olympic Games a huge success

2001   Australia offers the United States of America the fullest military support in the War against Terrorism

1

The Nuts and Bolts of Modern Australia

GEOGRAPHY, CLIMATE, AND POPULATION

Australia is a paradoxical land. It is a modern, industrialized, and technologically advanced nation on a continent that is largely unpopulated. Its 7,682,300 square kilometers (2,966,136 square miles) provide a home for just over 19 million people. Australia is the only island continent and the only continent to be occupied by a single nation in the world. Its population hugs the cities of the seaboard, and the interior is mostly empty. The sparsity of population in the interior is explicable by the latitudes wherein the continent lies. The Australian landmass falls between fifteen and thirty-five degrees of latitude, which is where most of the world's deserts are to be found. Moreover, more than 80 percent of the continent lies in arid or semiarid climatic zones. It has an average annual rainfall of only 465 millimeters (18 inches) and is consequently about one-third dryer than all other continents except Antarctica. Unlike the rest of the world, Australia's climate is not strictly predictable on seasonal lines but is subject to the vagaries of the El Niño phenomenon, with its characteristic cycles of drought and heavy rainfall. Despite its fossil and nutrient-poor soils, it relies on exports of primary produce and minerals to sustain a way of life that is comfortable and affluent for a majority of its people; yet this is achieved at a horrendous cost in environmental damage and destruction of fragile ecosystems. About 70 per-

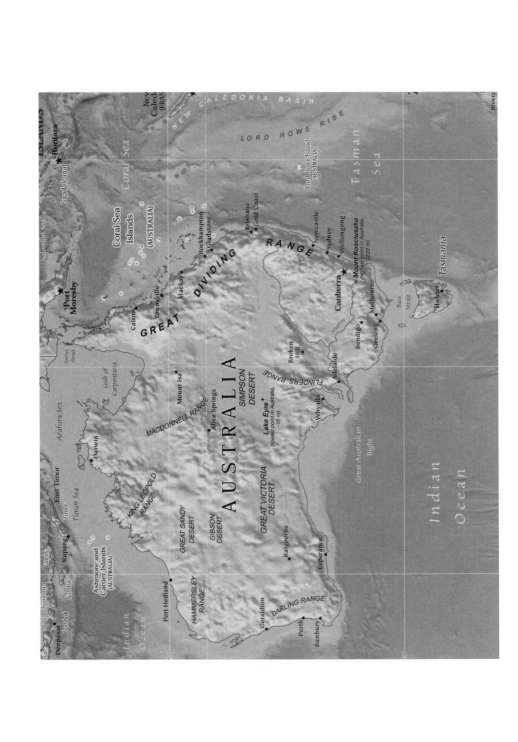

cent of Australia is unfit for any form of agriculture, and much of it can only be used for depasturing limited numbers of sheep or cattle. Australia's very prosperity puts at risk the long-term sustainability of its current way of life, and soil degradation and salinity are making rapid inroads into the country's capacity to provide the agricultural exports that underwrite the affluent lifestyle of its people.

Australia's population has increased steadily by 1 to 2 percent per year over the last ten years, caused by a combination of an excess of births over deaths and a vigorous migration program. As population crowds into the cities and clusters along the coastline, another paradox emerges in that the national cultural stereotype of the rugged and bushbased Australian male is increasingly unrepresentative; but the bush myth has yet to be replaced with an urban counterpart or a beach-based legend with which Australians can identify. Perhaps the reluctance to abandon old shibboleths partly reflects the aging population profile, for Australia is far from the youthful and vigorous community it professes to be, and the inevitable result of low fertility and low mortality rates is a progressive increase in the median age of the community. In 1997, the median age profile was thirty-four years; based on current trends, that will rise to forty to forty-one in 2021 and to forty-four to forty-six years in 2051. Moreover, just as the bush mythology is no longer appropriate for the most urbanized country in the world, so—in its celebration of Anglo/Celtic masculine values—is it similarly inappropriate for one of the most multicultural communities in the world, where women comprise more than half the population. Women and migrants make up an important and culturally neglected majority within the modern Australian community.

CULTURE AND COMMUNITY

Australia prides itself on its friendly, laid-back ethos, and the entire nation basked collectively in the world's approval during the highly successful Sydney Olympic Games in September 2000. Perhaps it has something to do with the climate of the coastal regions of the eastern seaboard, but access to sun and surf in a climate where one can be outdoors in comparatively light clothing twelve months of the year certainly encourages a relatively hedonistic approach to life. So, too, does the tradition of looking to government for the provision of basic social services and welfare. Medicine, education, employment placement, and basic accommodation for those most disadvantaged are still considered to be governmental areas of responsibility in Australia, although both main

political parties have adopted policies of divesting themselves of as much
of this financial burden as they can. Australians still look to government
to protect them from the worst excesses of the market and to underwrite
a way of life that guarantees a minimum standard of living at a level of
modest comfort. Such a mind-set in a congenial climate with an aging
population produces a complacency that renders the community quite
conservative in outlook.

In an environment of reasonable affluence, since the late 1940s Australia has been able to absorb large numbers of immigrants from all parts
of the globe, and today the nation is one of the most multicultural communities in the world. Since 1945, almost 5.7 million people have settled
in Australia, and today nearly one in four members of the community
was born overseas. Over 30 percent of new settlers each year in the past
decade have come from Asian backgrounds, and for the past three years
New Zealand has replaced Britain as the largest source birth country of
migrants. At first glance such a migration program might seem opposed
to the innate conservatism of the society, but in fact, the success of the
postwar immigration policy is largely due to a combination of affluence
and complacency. In periods of economic downturn, there has been a
notable rise in hostility to migrants, which dissipates again as the economy picks up. Daily life has been immeasurably enriched by the contributions made by the many migrant communities, and they are all
protected from discrimination under the terms of the federal government's 1975 Anti-Discrimination Act, which makes it illegal to discrim-
inate in any area of life on the basis of color, race, religion, gender, or
country of origin. English is regarded as the national language of Australia, and despite the high number of migrants, in 1996, 85 percent of
the population spoke only English at home and less than 1 percent could
not speak English at all.

Racial harmony, however, has not been achieved with the descendants
of the Aborigines, who make up about 2 percent of the population and
still suffer appalling housing, health, and medical disadvantages that
stem from their role as victims of the original invasion by Europeans in
1788. They lost their countries and received no compensation of any sort
until landmark land rights legislation in 1993. Currently, the Aboriginal
and Torres Straits Islanders Commission (ATSIC) receives over $1 billion
a year to fund programs designed to correct the two centuries of dis-
advantage. Much has been achieved, but much remains to be done. Reconciliation with the indigenous people has become a matter of great
political division in Australia, with the Australian Labor Party (ALP)
prepared to offer an official apology for all the injustices inflicted on

Aboriginal people since 1788 and the Liberal/National Party coalition refusing to make such a symbolic gesture for fear that it would provoke a rash of legal actions from Aborigines and their organizations demanding compensation. ATSIC is also interested in pursuing a treaty with the federal government as part of the reconciliation process, but that, too, has become a highly contested matter.

GOVERNMENT

Australia has a form of government that is derived from the Westminster System developed in Great Britain. The British monarch—known in Australia as the queen of Australia—is the titular head of state and is represented by her designate the governor general. Governors general are chosen for five-year terms by the prime minister of the day, and the position has sometimes been used as a useful form of political patronage. At the federal level, Australia possesses a two-chambered legislature made up of a lower house—the House of Representatives—to which members are elected via an exhaustive preferential voting system to represent individual electorates, and an upper house, the Senate, to which members are elected via a proportional voting system to represent their states. Both chambers have equal powers, except that the Senate cannot introduce money bills; for that reason, governments are made and unmade—and the prime minister and the Leader of the Opposition always sit—in the House of Representatives. Voting is a compulsory duty of citizenship in Australia, and people who fail to vote are fined a small sum as a penalty. The various states and territories roughly replicate these arrangements, with a governor as representative of the monarch, lower chambers known as Legislative Assemblies, and upper houses known as Legislative Councils.

The core of the Westminster System as practiced in Australia is the doctrine known as the separation of powers. Under this doctrine, the civil service and the judicature are kept entirely separate from the world of politics, and career public servants and all court officials and judges have guaranteed career paths irrespective of the political party in office. Positions are not lost when governments change, and no judge or civil servant theoretically can be subjected to political pressure, threats, or intimidation. It was believed that the system made it possible for governments to receive full, frank, and fearless advice, whatever their political outlook. By and large, it has worked well.

Australia has six political parties that have won representation at state and federal levels, these being the Australian Labor Party, the Liberal

Party, the National Party, the Australian Democrats, the Greens, and One Nation. There are a plethora of other smaller political parties and single-issue groups that run candidates at state and federal elections, but they have not broken through to achieve serious electoral significance.

FEDERAL CAPITAL

In 1901, when the six Australian colonies federated to become the Commonwealth of Australia, it was agreed that the site of the new capital should be in New South Wales, but at least 160 kilometers (100 miles) from Sydney. In 1909, a vote of the Federal Parliament chose Canberra. Two years later a territory of approximately 1,500 square kilometers (579 square miles) was excised from New South Wales to become the Australian Capital Territory (ACT), and in 1912, American architect Walter Burley Griffin won an international competition to design the new capital. Griffin moved to Australia to supervise the construction of his design but was forced by the petty obstruction and provincialism of Australian public servants to resign his commission in 1920. National government and administration moved to Canberra in 1927, and the city has continued to expand ever since. The basic design established by Griffin has been retained, and today Canberra is a beautiful garden city on a large artificial lake named after Griffin that is the administrative center of the national government and has become famous for its livability and as the home of important national icons such as the National Gallery, the National Library, the National Museum, the High Court, the National War Memorial, and of course the Parliament House.

In recent times, Australia has become obsessed with the question of national identity and of what it means to be Australian. Older Australians are profoundly troubled by the rapidity of change and the sheer size of the migration program, especially the growing proportion of the population from some sort of Asian background. The influence of Asian criminal gangs has become a growing cause for concern, as has police inability to handle the problems stemming from such gangs beginning their standover tactics and recruitment of new members in the local schools.[1] On the other hand, younger Australians and especially those of school age have been brought up in an ethnically diverse society and appear very comfortable with the direction in which the culture is now traveling. One in every eight inhabitants of Sydney, Australia's largest city, is now of Asian background, and by 2020, on current trends that will become one in every five. Similar ratios apply in the other main cities. A major sea change has occurred since the 1980s, and Australia's relationships within the Asia/Pacific region are recognized now as more important than those with Europe; but underlying all foreign relationships is the centrality of the American alliance as the ultimate guarantee of a numerically small nation's freedom and independence.

2

Aboriginal Australia (c. 65,000 B.C.E.–C.E. Eighteenth Century)

Aborigines, the first Australians, have lived on the continent for at least 60,000 to 70,000 years, and the dating of human remains and artifacts keeps extending the period of time for which evidence of human occupation of Australia can be unearthed. Archaeologists prefer to date occupation from the hard evidence of human bones and tools, but other scientists—using the evidence of carbon deposits in geological core samples and abandoned camp sites—have suggested that the original human occupiers of Australia arrived well over 100,000 years ago. Some Aboriginal spokesmen have even suggested that their people have always been present, and they deny that their ancestors were immigrants.

Until recently, the oldest archaeological sites discovered had been in the south of the continent, but far older sites are being uncovered in the northern regions of Australia, from where most scholars believe the flow or trickle of population worked its way down the face of the country into the southern regions. Aborigines are thought to have found their way here during the period when the southeastern shores of Asia were much closer to Australia and when New Guinea and Tasmania were still part of the Australian landmass.

During this last ice age, the level of the seas around Australia and throughout the Asian region are estimated to have been somewhere between 130 and 200 meters (430 and 666 feet) lower than at present, and the Australian shoreline of that period—with all the evidence of early human arrival—is today well beneath the sea. By walking and by short voyages across the shallow seas, the first native Australians filtered into the large and unpopulated continent's northern regions. Over thousands of years, by natural increase and successive migrations, the people of early Australia finally reached the southern extremity of the continent, now known as Tasmania. When the ice age ended and the seas slowly rose, New Guinea and Tasmania became separated from the mainland of Australia, and this brought an end to the movement of people overland into northern Australia and also into Tasmania. Both mainland Australia and Tasmania then began a long period of isolation from the rest of the world that remained unbroken—as far as we know—until the 1400s, when Indonesian traders and fishermen reestablished contact with the continent and the unique people that had developed during those millennia. When European explorers landed several hundred years after the Indonesians, they, too, were struck by the singularity of the now numerous peoples whom they encountered.

TRIBES AND TERRITORIES

By the time European observers arrived on the scene, Australian Aborigines had developed a fairly rigid pattern of clan and tribal territories, but this might not always have been the case. Obviously, with people moving from the northern regions into new and unoccupied territories farther to the south, the close links between land and tribe so noticeable in the eighteenth and nineteenth centuries must have been nonexistent or considerably more flexible. Nor can it be said that Aboriginal peoples constituted a unified people in any social or political sense, since the small groups were divided by a staggering diversity of languages and customs. Oral communication between natives from different regions was to prove impossible in the nineteenth century, and it seems likely that this differentiation had existed for many thousands of years. For example, on the island of Tasmania there were five distinct languages spoken, all of which were different from one another and none of which had anything in common with languages spoken in the Port Phillip district of the adjoining mainland.

Tribal territorial boundaries must have been more adaptable in the earlier years of occupation than they had become by the time the Europeans arrived. Adjustments would have been necessary to accommodate the migration of clans or tribes moving farther south through the territory of tribes already settled, and those people who lived in the territories now beneath the seas must also have been absorbed into the tribes living in adjacent and unsubmerged lands. It seems a more accurate representation of traditional life in Aboriginal Australia if we think in terms of several hundred independent republics, rather than of a continent occupied by a single Aboriginal nation.

Estimating the size of the Aboriginal populations throughout precolonized Australia has been notoriously difficult, and demographers still are in substantial disagreement. Current opinion is that the Aboriginal population of Australia on the eve of the first European arrivals was probably somewhere between 600,000 and 1 million people. We cannot assume, however, that this was a stable population level for most of the history of black (Aboriginal) Australia. It may well have been that in earlier times, before the desertification of much of inland Australia, far larger populations of Aborigines lived out their lives here. The fossil record of inland regions supports the proposition that there were times when quite large populations of Aborigines lived around a huge inland lake system that provided ample game and plants for food gathering.

Whenever Aborigines arrived in Australia, the fossil records make it plain that they existed for thousands of years alongside a wide variety of now extinct flora and fauna. Giant kangaroos, a species of giant wombat the size of a water buffalo, marsupial lions and tigers, and giant snakes, lizards, and emus are but a few of the species of megafauna for which we have fossil remains. A question that still remains unresolved is the extent of Aboriginal involvement in the disappearance of these animals. Were they, as suggested by some zoologists, hunted to extinction, or did they disappear as a result of some natural calamity or climatic change? Was it perhaps a combination of hunting and the slow process of inexorable climatic change that produced the species loss over the millennia?

The pressure on these giant animals would have been much greater, had Aboriginal numbers just grown geometrically, but if we can judge from practices in the eighteenth and nineteenth centuries, Aborigines consciously managed their population sizes so as to avoid putting undue strain on food supplies or way of life. The population was widely dispersed throughout the continent, and even the inhospitable inland desert regions carried small numbers of Aborigines who were able to live a comparatively comfortable existence in that harsh environment. Along the river systems and in the coastal regions the density of population increased as the fertile land was capable of carrying more people. The balance of population and the capacity of the tribal territory to support the population seems to have been carefully preserved. Unwanted children or children who could not be suckled—a result of multiple births or an infant whose mother had died—were killed. Children were kept on the breast for several years, both for survival and to increase the time between births. An Aboriginal mother could only care for one infant at a time, as she had to participate in the normal food-gathering activities of the tribe and carry her share of the camp materials during seasonal movements. Infanticide was an important mechanism in the overall control of the Aboriginal population. It also seems clear that in some parts of Australia Aboriginal women were able to procure reliable and safe means of birth control; specific plants, for example, triggered spontaneous abortion, and that these were sometimes used to end unwanted pregnancies.

The very nature of the Aboriginal way of life and their traditional economy made managing population size necessary. Women played a vital role in food-gathering activities, and they were unable to enjoy the luxury of full-time mothering. Aboriginal males hunted the larger animals for their meat, and provided fish when these were available, but the women's regular gathering of seeds, fruits, roots, and small animals provided approximately two-thirds of the daily food intake. This was the basis of traditional Aboriginal life. Consequently, anything that affected the activities of the women impacted directly on the general well-being of the tribe and indeed on its ability to survive at all. Too many babes in arms, too many women marrying outside the clan, or too many women being abducted by surrounding tribes—all had profound implications for the long-term ability of the tribe to maintain its population at a level sufficient to secure its survival and its traditional territory.

KINSHIP, RELIGION, AND THE LAND

We do not know at what stage of the occupation of Aboriginal Australia the rigid definition of tribal territories became established. By the time Europeans arrived, these territorial divisions had existed since time immemorial, and tribal lands had become integrated into an intricate and detailed set of religious beliefs and practices that governed all aspects of traditional Aboriginal life. As in so much of Aboriginal Australia, there were significant regional variations, but in general terms Aborigines believed that the physical structure of their tribal territory—its geological features and the plants and animals that existed within the territory— embodied spiritual entities of great antiquity that overshadowed the land and preserved and protected it. Since the land was the physical expression of these spirit ancestors, and since they were also the progenitors of the Aborigines themselves, the land and the people who lived on it were indissolubly connected in a mutually dependent relationship. Aborigines therefore did not own their land in any European sense of that term but instead existed upon it and were responsible for maintaining it as part of their continuing relationship with the spirit presences embodied within it. The land was central to any sense of personal identity, and this must have reinforced the natural human disinclination to move into unfamiliar areas, until over thousands of years it resulted in a culture so closely linked to its geographical territory that it often proved unable to survive when Europeans forcibly transplanted it to other locations.

Aboriginal culture was also nonexpansionist, as the territory of another tribe had little or no significance or meaning to Aborigines in adjoining areas. This meant that wars over land involving the expansion of one tribe's territory at the expense of another's were unknown. Aborigines believed that the spirit ancestors had established the territory within which their successors should live, and they felt no link with or desire to possess the lands of other tribes. This does not mean that conflict between tribes was nonexistent. Indeed, violent clashes were certainly quite common as Aboriginal tribes raided one another for women, sought revenge for earlier raids, or responded to deaths they attributed to sorcery from another tribe. Nevertheless, such conflict did not normally involve the taking of territory. Nor was domestic discord within the clan or tribe unknown, and occasionally an untimely end resulted from such internal family quarrels. By and large, however, traditional Aboriginal society was introverted, peaceful, and possessed of a respect for custom and familiar ways of doing things.

Within the tribal territory there could exist several small groups or clans that moved systematically from place to place in search of food. These clans would periodically come together as a larger unit for the purposes of celebrating an important festival, for trade, for arranging marriages, and for important religious rites and ceremonies. When gathered together in such a way the tribe could number hundreds of people, but the smaller clans or family groups could be as small as one or two dozen. Because of the relationships between the spirit ancestors at the time of creation, nearly every person with whom an Aborigine came in contact during the course of a lifetime would be some sort of relative. This made for strict and involved marriage customs to avoid inbreeding, and traditional Aboriginal law dealt harshly with violation of the marriage laws by banishment from the tribe or by ritual spearing.

Because women were so vital to survival in traditional society, the older, more powerful men of the tribe tended to secure the youngest girls as wives. This was important insurance in a harsh environment, for when a man grew too old to hunt, he could survive on the mainly vegetable foods gathered by his young and vigorous wives. Thus it was quite common in traditional Aboriginal society for very young girls to be given in marriage to comparatively old men, a custom that European observers in the nineteenth century abhorred. Older males typically might have between two and four wives.

Membership in a tribe involved detailed and specific rights and duties. The sharing of resources was one of the primary obligations incurred, and in traditional Aboriginal society, no one was ever alone. Always there were the wider relationships upon which people could depend in times of stress or need. Everything was shared with one's kin, including wives, food, hunting implements and tools, trade goods, and valued ceremonial articles. Such items were freely given as part of a reciprocal system of sharing that reinforced familial bonds. Individual acquisitiveness was not an admired character trait, and loyalty to clan and tribe overrode individual advancement.

TRADITIONAL ECONOMY

Aborigines did not exist in a state of introverted self-absorption, and just as the clans that made up a tribe or language group met together periodically, so, too, did tribes in adjoining territories come together at certain times for the purposes of trade and religious ceremonies. The extent of the trading network can be gauged by the finds archaeologists have made of materials thousands of kilometers away from their place of origin. Pearl shells are the best-known items of this type, but other artifacts introduced by Indonesian fishermen in the extreme north have also been found far inland, and stone implements have been unearthed at considerable distances from the area in which the stone was quarried. Some tribes with special skills in the manufacture of boomerangs or ceremonial belts of human hair supplied these items to other tribes that did not manufacture them for themselves. Such specialization also occurred for more obvious geographic reasons, as the ceremonial clays and ochres did not occur naturally in all parts of Australia, and the stone preferred for spearheads and seed grinding was also restricted to a number of limited locations. The tribes in these areas were in a strong position to trade advantageously with those in less-well-endowed areas.

The traditional economy of Aboriginal Australia, however, was not centred on trade but, rather, was structured on subsistence husbandry that was delicately attuned to the breeding cycles of food animals and the seasonal variations in vegetation. For a long time it was assumed by scholars that this way of life could accurately be described with the label "hunter-gatherer," and Aborigines were depicted as a passive species that wandered the countryside utilizing the bounty of nature without changing the environment. This romanticized vision led to a twentieth-century revival of the myth of the noble savage, in which the Aborigine was said to have lived an idyllic existence in harmony with nature and in an unchanging world.

FIRE-STICK FARMING

Recently a more realistic assessment has begun to prevail under the terms of which Aborigines are viewed as being far from passive in the management of their territory. The more information about traditional Aboriginal life becomes known, the clearer it becomes that Aborigines practiced a form of animal and agricultural husbandry more accurately described as fire-stick farming than as hunter-gathering. What emerges is that Aborigines were anything but the passive exploiters of nature. They managed their tribal territories very carefully and in so doing exploited to the limits of their technology the countryside in which they lived, producing irreversible change in the Australian environment.

Perhaps the most noteworthy example of the means by which such change was brought about is the way Aborigines used fire. Early European navigators repeatedly commented on the fires they saw burning as they approached the coastline of Australia, and the smoke was visible far out to sea. While a number of such bushfires could well have been caused by random lightning strikes, they cannot all be explained this way. Moreover, the evidence of early European settlers throughout Australia is agreed on the widespread use of fire by the Aborigines as a method of more fully exploiting their tribal territories. Aborigines regularly set fire to the bush in a deliberate attempt to expand the grasslands and to attract the grass-eating animals that provided an important portion of their protein intake. There is also evidence that Aborigines used fire as a hunting technique in order to enclose animals in a confined space where they could be more easily killed. Occasionally, fire became a weapon, and there are many accounts by Europeans of Aboriginal use of fire to kill the settlers' stock and destroy their crops.

When we realize that Aborigines possessed no methods of controlling fires once they had begun or of fighting fires that got out of control, then it becomes obvious that when fires escaped, they burned until it rained or they burned themselves out. Regular burning of this type over thousands of years might well have caused major ecological change, particularly when associated with climatic change of the interior of the continent. We know that inland Australia was once far more fertile, carrying much larger populations of animals and people than it did by the time Europeans arrived. As the climate slowly dried out the interior, regular burning of the bush, accompanied by progressively lower rainfall, would have accelerated the process by which the inland became desert. Eventually a time would occur when the regenerative powers of nature could no longer cope with the twin processes of fire-stick farming and increasing aridity.

As a technique of control and development, the use of fire in those parts of the continent better served by rainfall proved to be very efficient. The wide grasslands burned easily, and the ashes were a good foundation for the new shoots of tender green grass that grew up in the devastated areas, once rain fell. These new grasses encouraged the kangaroos and wallabies to move into the area and enabled the overall populations of such animals to increase. The ecological changes thus produced, therefore, were major and extended beyond the eradication of large areas of closely timbered land and its replacement by open forest and grassland. The Aborigines increased the capacity of the land to support certain favored species of animals and reduced the populations of animals more at home in a closely forested terrain. Fire-stick farming over thousands of years produced a land where fire-resistant species of plants prospered at the expense of species less capable of adapting to regular burning. Prolonged use of fire also robbed the soil of nitrogen and in a time of climatic change in the sparser woodland of the interior encouraged the development of the great inland deserts that we know today. Some of the early explorers and pastoralists recognized the paradox that it was the farming methods of the Aborigines that had been primarily responsible for preparing the country so well for the introduction of their sheep, for it was the grasslands and the open forest areas cultivated over the millennia by the Aborigines that proved most attractive to the colonial sheep farmers of the nineteenth century.

Fire-stick farming is a far from passive existence, and a question often raised in the 200 and more years of European settlement is, Why did the Aborigines never develop any form of tillage or cultivation of cereal grains or fruit? Seeds, grains, and fruits occurred naturally throughout Australia, and Aborigines collected them in season and either ground them into flour for cakes or ate them in their natural state. Yet they never seem to have made any attempt at cultivation of these food items in a systematic way, and we need to understand why. In the north of Australia we do know that Aborigines occasionally accompanied the Indo-nesian fishermen back to their homeland where they would have seen a society based on the cultivation of rice. They would also have encoun-tered the yam as an edible root vegetable, and the coconut, as well as domestic animals like pigs and dogs. Aside from an enthusiastic accep-tance of dogs, the Aborigines never attempted to develop a similar econ-omy by borrowing technology and expertise from the Indonesians. The plants grew well enough in Australia, and Aborigines would harvest and consume them when they found them, but they did not adopt an agrar-ian model.

There are two conjoined reasons for this. First, the Aborigines' long occupation of this country had given them a profound understanding of the vagaries of the El Niño phenomenon and its impact on the climate and rainfall patterns of the continent. The El Niño phenomenon makes rainfall notoriously unpredictable in Australia, and any form of culti-vation that depended on rainfall could not be sustained over the long term. There were periods of drought that went for years on end and would have spelled disaster to a people who had placed their reliance on growing and harvesting crops for their survival. Unlike the predict-able climatic cycles of Europe and North America, where seasonal change and climatic variation are severe but regular, the El Niño cycles are impossible to forecast. Long experience had taught Aborigines that their method of existence worked best in this country.

Second, Aborigines appear to have made a deliberate choice not to embrace the agricultural way of life because of its demands on time and energy. One of the most apparent of the effects of agriculture is the intensity of effort required over long periods to produce any worthwhile result. In the meantime, life somehow has to be supported. It is typical of the agricultural peasant farmer to labor from sunup to sundown in his fields, but Aborigines were able to maintain their way of life without this continuous and backbreaking toil. Several hours of hunting, fishing, and collecting by the clan would usually be sufficient for the supply of that day's foodstuffs.

The remainder of the time was given over to leisure. As long as the population was kept within limits so as not to overstrain existing food supplies, there was no need for Aborigines to change to the far more arduous way of agriculture. It was in maintaining food supplies with a minimum of effort that traditional Aboriginal society most closely ap-proximated the more leisured way of life of today's developed nations. There were places and seasons in Australia where Aborigines were able to sustain a comfortable way of life with an ease that appalled European observers, who tended to equate hard work with godliness. The English explorer William Dampier's dismissive observations in 1688 of coastal Aborigines in the northwest of Western Australia drew attention to their lack of the accoutrements of a "civilized" culture but also commented upon the ease with which the Aborigines were able to feed an entire tribe by merely visiting an elaborate fish trap they had built nearby. When the tide receded, all that was required was for them to walk down to the beach and collect the fish, which were immediately cooked and eaten. This process occurred after each high tide.

Similar observations were made by other Europeans who regarded the Aboriginal disinclination to embrace a life of small-scale farming on a more recognizable European pattern as evidence that an incorrigible laziness lay at the heart of Aboriginal culture. It never seems to have occurred to the Europeans that Aborigines might have assessed and then rejected the model of European- or Indonesian-style agriculture or animal husbandry in favor of their own traditional and comparatively leisured style of living. After more than two centuries of experiencing the ravages inflicted by El Niño on European-style rural production since 1788, there are now many Australians who see the need to look again at a way of life that proved to be sustainable over thousands of years.

INVASION AND THE CONFLICT BETWEEN CULTURES

When contact between the two races did eventually occur, the cultural gap yawned alarmingly between a people who valued a way of life that was nonacquisitive and communal, with few social and political distinctions based on birth or possessions, and a people whose values embraced individual acquisitiveness and a system of preferment favoring those who acquired possessions or were born into the ruling gentry. Since both Aborigines and Europeans rejected one another's cultures as having little to offer, the opportunities for misunderstanding became tragically enlarged. In other parts of the world colonized by the British, the subject races had adopted at least some of the customs and trappings of British civilization. In the Pacific area, for example, the Maori eagerly accepted firearms and participated enthusiastically in trading with the European interlopers. In Australia, however, the British found themselves confronted by Aborigines who were not prepared to alter their traditional way of life beyond the superficial acceptance of iron implements and a fondness for the more portable of European-style foodstuffs like flour, tea, and sugar. Trading between blacks and whites was not usual, and a cultural intransigence marked the attitudes of both peoples to each other. Each felt that the other race was uncouth and did not know how to behave properly or lawfully, and the original dispute over the invasion and the unauthorized occupation by the British of Aboriginal lands quickly developed into a wider cultural conflict of truly tragic consequence in the history of Australia.

The obvious preference of Aborigines for their own culture was interpreted by the British as evidence that Aboriginal culture was irretrievably buried in the Stone Age. This view proved much easier to sustain in Australia, because Europeans were able to settle there without having to adapt to local conditions by accepting Aboriginal food-gathering techniques and climatic coping strategies, as had been necessary when the British settled the North American continent. Settlers therefore saw little or nothing of value in the culture they had come to supplant in this country and imagined that they had nothing to learn from the original inhabitants of their new land. The Aborigines came to be despised as a rural pest, whereas the First Nations of North America and later the New Zealand Maori were admired and feared as brave and noble exemplars of an admirable warrior culture.

Why did the closeness of Aboriginal links with the land escape the notice of early settlers? How did the British come to be so blind as to be unable to recognize that Aborigines were connected with their tribal territories by ties both religious and psychic that were qualitatively different from those of other native peoples whose lands they had taken? It is too easy to escape into the realm of racial stereotyping and cultural defamation at this point and to dismiss the British people as a race of predatory thugs usurping Aboriginal lands, regardless of the consequences of such behavior. The record shows that this would produce a historical distortion out of all contact with reality. The fact is that we are confronted with the problem of explaining how well-intentioned British administrators and statesmen could quite genuinely believe that in Australia Aboriginal links with the land were of such a nature as not to amount to ownership in the eyes of Europeans.

The British regarded Australia as *terra nullius*, a land owned by no one and therefore capable of being claimed by any power that was prepared to utilize the land for farming. This doctrine never meant that the British claimed that the continent was uninhabited. From Dampier's visit onward, European navigators had met with and studied the Aborigines, and in 1770 James Cook had even pronounced them happier than Europeans. The key to understanding the British official view lies in the criteria generally accepted throughout Europe in the eighteenth and early nineteenth centuries of what constituted an effective occupation by a nation of its territories. In this question, the primacy accorded to agriculture was paramount. European jurists agreed that God had intended that humankind should populate the earth, but how was an increasing population to be fed except through agriculture? As the population of the world increased, more and more land would be needed for agriculture in order to maintain the increase, and when agricultural nations became too confined at home, they had a right to move into parts of the world where the land was not being tilled for crops and to appropriate that "wasteland" for their own use. A way of life such as that of Australia's Aborigines was believed to be against God's will because hunting animals and gathering fruits and seeds involved too great an expanse of territory. It was agriculture that gave a nation title to its territory, and the lack of agriculture similarly was taken to show that the land, although it might be occupied, was not owned by the occupiers if they merely wandered over the surface of the country and did not exploit it in recognizably European ways. Wherever the British encountered native peoples who engaged in agriculture, they went through a treaty signing protocol that recognized that ownership of the land lay in the hands of those who farmed it. North America and New Zealand are cases in point. Australia became an exception to this practice because Aborigines already knew that agriculture was an insecure basis for a long-term sustainable lifestyle in a country so at the mercy of El Niño.

Thus it was that when Europeans came to settle Australia, they were sent by a government that firmly believed that the Aborigines did not own their lands and that therefore treaties of occupation with the native inhabitants of the continent were not necessary to secure title. The way of life that had evolved over more than 60,000 years of unbroken occupation in Australia was not recognized as constituting an effective ownership of the continent. The Aboriginal rejection of agriculture as a way of life meant that they were regarded as nomadic occupiers of the country but not its lawful possessors. Herein can be found the seeds of more than two centuries of conflict between blacks and whites in Australia, concerning who owned the country then and who owns the country now. And flowing from that is the question of whether any form of legal or moral obligation exists for the descendants of the whites to apologize to and to compensate the descendants of the blacks for the invasion and loss of their country after 1788.

3

European Arrivals and Colonization (Seventeenth Century–1830)

IN SEARCH OF THE GREAT SOUTH LAND

European nations were interested in discovering the Great South Land. *Terra Australis Incognita* (the Unknown South Land) had been the name given to this country of the imagination, and a belief in its existence became a commonplace assumption of most educated Europeans for centuries. Speculation blossomed concerning the value of such a land because of the latitudes in which it was presumed to lie. Scholars surmised that if lands in similar latitudes in known parts of the world were fertile and temperate, then these characteristics would be shared by a land in the same latitudes in the unknown Southern Hemisphere. Moreover, since the time of Marco Polo, European greed had been whetted by rumors of an unknown southern continent of staggering riches. As European nations took increasingly to the sea over the next few centuries in the search for empire, trade, and plunder, Portugal, Holland, Spain, France, and England all made attempts to discover and claim this mysterious southern continent.

The Dutch made a number of landfalls during the seventeenth century and named the continent New Holland, but the English buccaneer William Dampier became the first European to spend a prolonged period and to survive to write about it. His impressions of the western coastline and its people were anything but favorable. He described the land as being dry, sandy, and destitute of water; there were no animals for food, and the sea was not plentifully stocked with fish. The people of the country were so primitive that, in Dampier's view, "they differ but little from Brutes."[1]

A USELESS COUNTRY?

Dampier's voyages served to reinforce the view made public by the Dutch that nothing advantageous was to be gained from New Holland. The sheer size of Australia, however, led some geographers to doubt whether the observations made by explorers were typical of the country as a whole.

The French launched a series of voyages into the Pacific, and their British rivals responded with the incomparable James Cook. It was Cook's first expedition aboard the HMS *Endeavour* that in 1770 finally brought a representative of one of these historic adversaries to the eastern coastline of Australia, and he promptly annexed the territory on behalf of his sovereign King George III under the name of New South Wales. But the French were not too far behind, and in 1772 the explorer François-Alesno de St. Allouarn aboard his ship the *Gros Ventre* made landfall at Turtle Bay on the western coast of Australia and claimed the country in the name of the French monarch, Louis XVI.[2] It appears that both Cook in 1770 and St. Allouarn in 1772 were engaging in preemptive annexations in promising latitudes that were designed to forestall rivals rather than to gain territory for immediate exploitation.

THE ROAD TO BOTANY BAY

The historic rivalry resumed during the American War of Independence, and both nations were seriously weakened by their involvement. Britain suffered calamitous defeat, and France was bankrupted by victory. Following the lost war, Britain moved to reorganize its remaining overseas empire and decided to settle Australia with convicts. Convicts provided an ideal source of human capital for such ventures, and all European colonizing nations used convicts overseas. In law, convicts sentenced to death and then sent to the colonies as exiles were regarded as legally dead. They possessed no rights until the period of transportation had run its course. This made them ideal colonizing material, and if they returned before the period of the sentence had been completed, the original death sentence came into force. Moreover, Britain was still a world power, and British fleets still operated in all the oceans of the world, providing British administrations with a global strategic reach. Such circumstances forced the British government to think globally, and the decision to send a fleet to New South Wales fitted into this wider strategic reassessment. The convicts sent to Australia in the First Fleet were a means to facilitate British expansion, and we should remember that while Australia was settled by the convicts, it was not primarily settled for the convicts.

THE TRANSPORTATION DILEMMA

This is not to deny that the government faced a considerable domestic problem concerning the increasing numbers of criminals condemned to transportation. Britain transported about 1,000 criminals a year to its colonies in North America. Once the Americans refused all further shipments of convicts, the British government elected to house prisoners sentenced to transportation on old unseaworthy ships moored in the Thames and at Portsmouth and Plymouth. These receptacles, known as the hulks, proved to be considerably more than the temporary expedients originally planned, and hulks remained in service until 1868.

As the American war dragged to its conclusion in 1783, rumors concerning the overcrowded conditions aboard the hulks abounded. They were mostly wrong, and convicts on the hulks were in fact well looked after and received adequate medical care and attention, but the rumors caused considerable public unease and created a political problem that could not be ignored.

CAPTAIN ARTHUR PHILLIP AND THE FIRST FLEET

In 1786, the British government recalled one of the Admiralty's most senior spies and a trusted strategic adviser from a clandestine mission in France and appointed him as leader of the expedition and governor of a new convict colony at Botany Bay in southeastern Australia. Captain Arthur Phillip had been employed by the Royal Navy as an intelligence operative for a number of years and possessed extensive knowledge of Spanish capabilities in South American waters. Who better than such a trusted adviser to monitor French and Spanish activities in the Pacific?

The First Fleet under Phillip's command set sail from Portsmouth on its 12,000-mile (19,200-kilometers) voyage to Botany Bay on 13 May 1787. Accompanying Phillip were 443 seamen, 568 male and 191 female convicts (with 13 children), 160 marines, 51 officers and noncommissioned officers (NCOs), 27 soldiers' wives (with 19 children), and 9 members of the governor's personal staff. The lieutenant governor and second-in-charge was Major Ross, the commanding officer of the marines, and Captain David Collins was appointed deputy judge advocate, the colony's foremost legal officer. The spiritual welfare of the new settlers was under the care of the Reverend Richard Johnson, an Anglican chaplain.

In addition to the regular officers of the marines, the expedition also included Lieutenant William Dawes, a man with abilities that would prove useful in working the New Zealand flax plant on Norfolk Island. Among the convicts were hempdressers, rope makers, and weavers, and the equipment carried included a machine for dressing flax with the necessary hackles, combs, pins, and brushes, together with a loom for weaving the flax thread into canvas.

The First Fleet straggled into Botany Bay between 19 and 20 January 1788, but Phillip soon became dissatisfied with the site. He deemed the harbor unsatisfactory and dangerous and the provision of fresh water inadequate. To add a spur to activity, six days after the British arrival, a French expedition under Jean-François de La Perouse also sailed into Botany Bay. Phillip ordered his ships to remove to adjacent Port Jackson, where he had discovered a harbor sufficient in size to permit a large war fleet "a thousand sail of the line" to ride at anchor in the most perfect security.

Perhaps it was also a response to the appearance of the French that Phillip moved quickly to implement his instructions to annex Norfolk Island. Less than three weeks after the first landing at Port Jackson, he sent Lieutenant Philip Gidley King of the Royal Navy to establish a settlement on Norfolk and instructed him to proceed immediately to the cultivation of the flax plant. This marked the first of many such extensions of British territory in the South Seas as Britain attempted to pre-empt real or imagined French threats of settlement.

ESTABLISHING THE COLONY

The limits of the colony were greatly extended with the formal announcement that the longitude of the inland boundary lay at 135 degrees (Greenwich) east, whereas the longitude of Cook's annexation in 1770 had been at 142 degrees (Greenwich) east. These extra 7 degrees of longitude "cribbed" by England in 1788 added a piece of territory more than a thousand kilometers (650 miles) wide to New South Wales.[3] If merely establishing a receptacle for convicts had been the aim of Phillip's expedition, then sufficient space for hundreds of years of convict transportation lay in the area annexed by Cook in 1770. The grab for thousands of square kilometers more in 1788—to which Britain had no valid claim by right of prior discovery—provides further evidence of the imperialist nature of this undertaking. New South Wales in 1788 encompassed approximately half of mainland Australia, and the boundary extended seaward at least to Norfolk Island.

EARLY DIFFICULTIES

Phillip's first task was to ensure the survival of his people. Housing and feeding the populace became the priority, and food shortages constituted a major danger as rations had to be progressively reduced when supply ships failed to appear. The Second Fleet in June 1790 brought some supplies, it is true, but also 733 convicts, nearly 500 of whom were sick.

Providing for these new arrivals plus the existing population put great strain on the colony's limited resources. Gardening and farming proved very unsatisfactory. Furthermore, the agricultural implements—axes, spades, and shovels—proved woefully inadequate, and no plough was to be found in the colony until 1796 when an enterprising John Macarthur imported the first one. In the meantime, the settlers attempted to grow crops on the infertile soils around Sydney with tools that allowed them to use only the first few inches of top soil. There were insufficient stock animals to provide manure to enrich this poor soil, and the labor came from a convict workforce that was characterized by a desire to do as little hard work as possible on the government farms. Agricultural returns were poor, and Phillip had to reduce the rations even further.

The first colonists endured great hardship during these foundation years. The stores were exhausted, winter was approaching, and by 1790 clothing for the convicts and footware for the marines were in desperately short supply. The colony was quite literally in danger of coming apart at the seams. And to make matters worse, the Aborigines were becoming threatening.

ABORIGINAL RESISTANCE

The colonists were aware of their vulnerability to attack, and the Aborigines must have noticed opportunities. Why, then, did they fail to take advantage of their superior numbers? Early in 1789, observers commented on an "extraordinary calamity" among the Aborigines, as colonists began to report in all the coves and inlets around Port Jackson "the bodies of many of the wretched natives of this country."[4]

The disease was quickly identified as smallpox by the colony's surgeons, who also observed the extreme susceptibility of the Aborigines. The death rate among Aborigines in the area during this outbreak has been estimated at around 50 percent.[5] This devastation of the natives of Sydney Cove helps to explain the lack of any large-scale resistance to white settlement. Once the disease had swept through the Aborigines of the Port Jackson region, the dispirited remnants were no longer capable of being more than an occasional nuisance to the spread of settlement. Certainly, they were unable to threaten its survival.

RUM AND THE COLONIAL ECONOMY

By the time illness caused Phillip to leave the colony in 1792 a basic economic pattern based on barter, IOUs, and an unforeseen officers' monopoly of wholesaling had emerged. Because their salaries were paid in sterling and nobody else had any, the officers unexpectedly became the only group capable of purchasing the cargoes of incoming vessels.

Upon Phillip's departure, authority passed automatically to the commanding officer of the local regiment, the New South Wales Corps, who freely granted land to his officers and also generously endowed them with convict laborers and personal servants, all clothed and fed from the government store. Convicts working for these private entrepreneurs soon found themselves offered inducements in the form of spirits, tobacco, sugar, and tea, all of which the officers had begun to import before Phillip's departure. Because of the association of the Corps' officers with the importation and the distillation of spirits, the Corps became known as the Rum Corps, and its coup d'état against Governor William Bligh in 1808 has gone down in history as the Rum Rebellion.

All the early governors confronted the entrenched power of the New South Wales Corps, and essentially they proved unable to cope. The use of rum as a payment for labor was only the most visible difficulty. Rum undermined colonists from unknown convicts to the governors by providing them with an oral anesthetic whereby loneliness, despair, sickness, and a numbing sense of exile could be rendered more bearable or temporarily blotted out. The men and women of the colony sought what comfort they could in those traditional forms of pleasure and relief afforded by alcohol and sex, and a reputation for alcoholic overindulgence and sexual promiscuity became firmly established. In fact, consumption of alcohol on a per capita basis was lower in New South Wales than in England; and many women, far from being prostitutes, made significant contributions to the economic and social life of the colony by running shops, bakeries and inns. Some like Mary Reiby eventually became prominent merchants.[6]

CONVICT TROUBLES

From the early days of settlement, both male and female convicts enjoyed a reputation for laziness and a poor attitude toward work that occasionally became the despair of colonial officials. Many convicts came from environments in the British Isles where work was avoided in favor of crime, and Phillip found such people a most unsatisfactory workforce:

> Experience, sir, has taught me how difficult it is to make men industrious who have passed their lives in habits of vice and indolence. In some cases it has been found impossible; neither kindness nor severity have had any effect; and tho' I can say that the convicts in general behave well, there are many who dread punishment less than they fear labour; and those who have not been brought up to hard work, which are by far the greatest part, bear it badly. They shrink from it the moment the eye of the overseer is turned from them.[7]

Part of the basis for this disapproval lay in fear. The convicts frightened "respectable" people in the colony both by their numbers and by their clannishness. The bulk of the convicts came from the lower levels of British society, and the French Revolution had shown what such people were capable of. An interpreter was frequently needed to translate the deposition of a witness or the defense of a prisoner in the colony's law courts because the convicts spoke a "flash" language or distinct dialect among themselves that was incomprehensible to outsiders.[8] After the failure of yet another rebellion in Ireland in 1798, this problem was compounded by the arrival of hundreds of Gaelic-speaking Irishmen; and the existence of separate languages among the convicts caused considerable unease to settlers and officials who felt threatened by their inability to understand what convicts were saying to one another. Sedition and violence were suspected, and such a view was not entirely wide of the mark as demonstrated by the failed rising of the Irish convicts at Castle Hill in 1804.

FIGHTING OFF THE FRENCH

As the tensions that produced these scenes of domestic unrest and excitement built up in New South Wales, the old enmity between France and Britain once again played a vital part in British expansion in this part of the world. During the time of the first Napoleon, the French demonstrated a continuing interest in Australia. Maps were published in France naming the continent Terre Napoleon and placing the names of the emperor's wife and family on prominent geographical features. In 1803, Van Diemen's Land was annexed to forestall the French, and in 1829 and 1836, the free settlements of Western Australia and South Australia were established for the same reason. These new settlements demonstrated British readiness to preempt a French claim to any part of the Australian continent.

EARLY INDUSTRY: WHALING, SEALING, AND WOOL

In the meantime, the colony of New South Wales was beginning to pay its way. Whaling and sealing provided the first staples from the colony, and exports in these areas were not exceeded in value by wool until the 1830s. Colonial traders like Robert Campbell and the former convict Simeon Lord diversified into shipbuilding and sealing and found that handsome profits could be turned from such ventures. The seal skins and the oil were sold either in China or in the United States, and most of the colonial sealers and whalers established themselves in Van Diemen's Land because of its proximity to the seal rookeries and the southern fisheries. Hobart quickly developed into the most important port for whalers and sealers from all countries in the Southern Hemisphere.

While economic primacy remained with sealing and whaling, the foundations of the wool industry were also laid in these early years. In June 1798, Captain Henry Waterhouse had shipped the first flock of Spanish merinos to New South Wales, and several settlers had purchased stock from this pioneering venture. The Reverend Samuel Marsden had begun selective breeding with some of these sheep the following year, and other colonists, including John Macarthur, were quick to follow suit. The colonial economy continued to grow and diversify over the next few decades, despite all the conflict and political agitation caused by the colorful personalities involved in colonial public life at that time. None came more colorful than the fourth governor, William Bligh.

THE RUM REBELLION

On 8 August 1806, a figure of some notoriety landed at Sydney Cove and assumed the office of governor of New South Wales. William Bligh had demonstrated courage and determination in piloting the loyal crew members of the HMS *Bounty* across half the Pacific following the mutiny and loss of his ship. He had been chosen for the position of governor precisely because of those qualities of strength and self-sufficiency. His personality, however, was defective, and he quickly demonstrated his unsuitability to hold office.

The rough edge of the new governor's tongue was soon felt by people of all ranks and positions in colonial society. When his goods were being unloaded on the Sydney quayside, an old sailor commented admiringly: "By God, I thought I could swear with any man but I give it up to the governor who should have a patent for swearing as he beats every man I ever knew."[9] Bligh described the soldiers of the New South Wales Corps as "wretches" and "gaolbirds" and as virtually indistinguishable from the convicts. He claimed that officers of the Corps were so compromised by their associations with male and female convicts that they could not be trusted with rendering impartial justice in the colony's law courts. Bligh also outraged the sensitivities of the rising John Macarthur by commenting that he believed Macarthur had gained his grant of land by lying to the British authorities, and he intended to ensure that Macarthur did not keep it.

Bligh had come to New South Wales with instructions to prohibit the use of rum as a medium of exchange. Therefore, he attempted to kill two birds with one stone when he tried to bring John Macarthur before the courts for the illegal importation of stills for the manufacture of rum and also charged him with sedition. The response was swift. On 26 January 1808, the soldiers of the New South Wales Corps marched—with fixed bayonets—under the orders of their commanding officer Major George Johnston, to Government House and there placed Bligh under arrest. Major Johnston administered the colony, with John Macarthur as colonial secretary.

THE AGE OF MACQUARIE

The British government was singularly unimpressed by officers who mutinied and overthrew their legitimate superiors. Governor Lachlan Macquarie came as commanding officer of his own regiment, and the New South Wales Corps was shipped out in disgrace. Major Johnston was arrested and sent to England to face court-martial. Despite support from John Macarthur, who traveled to England to give evidence, Johnston was disgraced and cashiered. Macarthur himself was refused permission to return to New South Wales until the end of 1816, which left the business interests of the Macarthur family in the capable hands of his wife Elizabeth, where they prospered exceedingly well.

When Macquarie took office in 1810, the settlement had degenerated into a sorry state:

> I found the Colony barely emerging from an infantile imbecility and suffering from various privations and disabilities, the country impenetrable, agriculture in a yet languishing state; commerce in its early dawn; public buildings in a state of dilapidation and mouldering to decay; the few roads and bridges formerly constructed almost impassable; the population in general depressed by poverty; no public credit, no private confidence; the morals of the great mass of the people in the lowest state of debasement and religious worship almost totally neglected.[10]

EXPANSION AND CONSTRUCTION

Some measure of Macquarie's achievements can be gauged from the basic arithmetic of his period in office. The population had been 11,590 when he arrived and stood at 38,778 upon his departure. Cattle had increased from 12,500 to 103,000, while sheep numbers had risen from 25,900 to 290,000. Land under cultivation had expanded from 7,600 acres (3,040 hectares) to 32,270 acres (13,069 hectares). The area of settlement itself had grown twenty times in size as the governor encouraged a series of land explorations that successfully opened up New South Wales for farming and grazing. Many new towns had been established, and nearly 300 miles (480 kilometers) of roads constructed, not the least important of which lay across the Blue Mountains and unlocked the rich Bathurst Plains to the west. In all, the penetrated area of the mainland increased from 2,500 square miles (647,500 hectares) to 100,000 square miles (25,900,000 hectares) during these years. Sydney itself was drastically altered from a straggling makeshift town to a properly laid-out city with wide straight streets and soundly constructed and attractive public buildings. All in all, Macquarie's time as governor of New South Wales was marked by rapid expansion and construction, and yet these achievements were often accomplished in the teeth of extraordinary opposition from the upper levels of colonial society and from within the ranks of the colonial administration itself. The governor's social policies lay at the heart of this conflict.

Society in New South Wales had become highly stratified, and the normal economic divisions between rich and poor were complicated by another set of divisions between those who had come free to the colony and those who had come out as convicts. The free settlers and their descendants regarded themselves as socially and morally superior to those who had arrived in New South Wales as felons, or whose parents had been felons; and they gloried in the sobriquets of "pure merinos" or "exclusives" or "sterling," in order to distinguish themselves from the criminally tainted "emancipists" or their native-born children the "currency lads and lasses." Macquarie announced his determination to break this caste system in his very first dispatch from the colony, and to this end, he began, over the objections of the exclusives, inviting wealthy emancipists to dine with him at Government House and also making them magistrates.

By the end of the Macquarie period in New South Wales, the convict system had produced a considerable degree of ambivalence toward the colony in the minds of British administrators and observers. On the one hand, they admired the obvious progress so readily apparent by 1821 when New South Wales seemed to be on the threshold of a prosperous and assured future. On the other hand, they also believed that the population of Australia was criminally tainted or corrupted by association with criminals, that the native-born Australians carried hereditary criminality in their blood, and that as a consequence the human breeding stock of the colony was so corrupted and degenerate that several generations of crime-free lives were needed before any native-born Australians should be considered eligible for official positions.

CONVICTS: PUNISHMENT AND REWARD

Convicts were undoubtedly punished in Australia. They endured exile and the loss of liberty. They were subject to the cruelty and whims of brutal overseers, and they were flogged. But corporal punishment—usually by means of the birch—was a widespread phenomenon throughout all levels of British society and had become a commonly accepted form of social discipline. In convict Australia, the wonder is not that so much flogging occurred but that so little actually took place. A statistical breakdown of punishment in Van Diemen's Land, for example, shows that most convicts experienced only one flogging during their sentences.[11] Furthermore, it is clear that convicts and masters accepted flogging as normal, just as it was in England, and convicts did not appear to seethe with resentment and a desire for revenge when their masters resorted to the magistrate and the lash in the face of worker disobedience.[12] There was an important protection for the convicts built into the system in

Australia, in that only a magistrate could order a man flogged, and by Macquarie's time, the maximum number of lashes for unsatisfactory work had been reduced to fifty, and the usual sentence was twenty five.

Rewards were also an inherent part of the system—alcohol and extra rations for serving convicts; and at the end of a sentence of transportation, ex-convicts received a grant of land, together with stock, seed, and provisions for two years, to enable them to establish themselves as peasant farmers. The grants increased in size according to the number of a convict's dependents, who were also supported from "the stores." Most British convicts came from the lower orders, with no possibility of becoming landowners.[13] Moreover, in the British Isles ownership of land carried with it connotations of wealth and social respectability. Many observers were scandalized that the convict system in Australia seemed positively to reward crime rather than to punish it, and by the end of Macquarie's period, it had become an article of faith in official circles in Britain that the governor had erred on the side of leniency, thereby helping to rid a sentence of transportation to Australia of all its terrors. Leniency of treatment in Australia, it was felt, actually undermined the efficacy of British criminal law.

THE BIGGE ENQUIRY

John Thomas Bigge sailed in 1819 to conduct an investigation into the state and condition of New South Wales and to make recommendations regarding its future. He was instructed to keep in mind that the primary function of the Australian settlements was the penal one and that their growth as colonies must remain a secondary consideration.

Bigge outranked Macquarie, and the commissioner and the governor quickly fell out. Within a month of arriving, Bigge had overruled the governor's appointment of the former convict Dr. William Redfern to the magistracy, and it was not long before he had demonstrated that his sympathies clearly lay with the exclusives. He supported with enthusiasm John Macarthur's view that the future of the colony lay in the production of wool for British manufacturers and recommended that land policy in New South Wales should change in favor of large proprietors with capital who would invest it in producing wool. He believed that the convicts, former convicts, and the native-born could improve their characters as shepherds in the outback rural districts. The new system would amply repay Britain in a very few years with such abundant supplies of fine wool at so cheap a price as to give British wool manufacturers a virtual monopoly in the marketplace. The convict system would become cheaper, and the sentence of transportation would regain its salutary terror.

MACQUARIE'S FAREWELL

Macquarie returned to England in February 1822. He went with the warm affection of the emancipists and the native-born, who appreciated all that he had tried to do for them. He also went as a failure. Bigge's reports attacked Macquarie for being too lenient and a poor administrator; and the man who is known to history as the father of Australia became a victim of Colonial Office disloyalty and the vicious enmity of the exclusives. Macquarie died brokenhearted in July 1824 after fruitlessly trying to defend himself against the calumnies of the Bigge reports. His passing was greatly regretted by the emancipists and native-born in New South Wales, who realized that an era had ended and that they stood on the threshold of a major change in direction.

NEW SOUTH WALES IN TRANSITION

Changes in direction, however, do not appear overnight, and the rest of the 1820s marked a long transitional period as British policies moved inexorably to implement Bigge's recommendations and to produce a type of plantation economy in New South Wales. Governor Thomas Brisbane was instructed to limit land grants to emancipists according to the means they possessed of doing justice—without support from the stores—to a grant of land. The next governor, General Ralph Darling, received instructions that made no mention of land grants to ex-convicts. Thenceforth, land would be issued to private persons in direct proportion to the amount of capital they had to invest. Moreover, an absolute minimum land grant size of 320 acres (129.6 hectares) was introduced, to qualify for which the prospective grantee needed to possess £250 ($500) of capital. This effectively placed the ownership of land beyond the reach of ordinary emancipists and the lower orders.

A clear social and political policy began to emerge during the 1820s that encouraged the perpetuation in New South Wales of traditional English estimations of the inherent value in landownership, accompanied by an apparently deliberate attempt to create artificially a colonial equivalent of the British landed gentry. At the same time, and not unconnected with this reevaluation, the British government also resolved to extend privileges to the growing free population in the settlement by establishing a Legislative Council to be appointed by the governor to advise him.

The settlements in Van Diemen's Land became a separate colony, and civil judges replaced military judges in the colonies' law courts, though trial by jury continued to be withheld from such "morally tainted" populations.

The convict and emancipist portion of the population grew rapidly. Between 1821 and 1830, 21,780 felons had been transported to New South Wales and an additional 10,000 to Van Diemen's Land. This numerically significant group was soon to enjoy the leadership of an inspirational native-born Australian, William Charles Wentworth, and the outlet of their very own newspaper—partly owned by Wentworth—the *Australian*. They were to show, as the decade unfolded, a self-awareness and a pride in their new home. They refused to become the submissive serfs the exclusives desired, and they were responsible for the emergence of a concept destined to exercise remarkable influence in Australian social and political life from then on: the idea that every white man in Australia was entitled to a "fair go." Birth or station in life did not affect this most basic of human entitlements. Secretaries of state, governors, and all those in positions of authority in the colonies could talk all they liked about the privileges afforded by wealth and status, but the colonists began to believe that they too had a privilege in this new land—the right to equal opportunity. This belief became intertwined with a further conviction that the land of Australia rightfully belonged to the native-born and to the convicts who had pioneered it and that they should enjoy the fruits of it over and above the free immigrants with capital. W.C. Wentworth articulated this view in the *Australian* in 1826:

> Every young man in the Colony ought to be able to look forward with certainty to the prospect of having his own farm; of being able to settle upon it, as soon as he arrives at years of maturity. He can, on leaving his parental roof, commence in the world with much less capital, and yet with a greater prospect of success than the emigrants.[14]

In this, Wentworth was reinforcing an assertion he had made earlier in the month when he published an "Address of Welcome to Governor Darling" and drew the governor's attention to the resentment felt by the native-born when they saw grants of land "which they consider their own as it were by natural inheritance" being lavishly bestowed upon strangers with money.[15]

Wentworth and his partner Dr. Robert Wardell had provided this rising emancipist consciousness with a focus and an outlet in 1824 when they established the *Australian*. Governor Brisbane permitted the newspaper to remain in existence as an interesting experiment. In time, Brisbane's successor Ralph Darling would find good cause to regret this liberality.

GOVERNOR DARLING

All that, however, lay in the womb of time when Darling assumed office in New South Wales in December 1825. For a period he enjoyed a honeymoon with both emancipist and exclusive factions and wrote to reassure the Colonial Office that the free newspapers of New South Wales—now including the *Monitor*, owned and edited by Edward Smith Hall—presented no threat to public order. In less than a year Darling began to have second thoughts. The newspapers, particularly the *Monitor* and the *Australian*, took every opportunity to attack the exclusives and the governor and to hold them up to ridicule.

Personal relations between Darling and the editors worsened, and the tirade of abuse leveled against government officials and the exclusives only served to push the governor further into sympathy with them. This became particularly obvious when Darling himself came under attack for inhumanity and undue severity in his treatment of two soldiers of the 57th Regiment, Joseph Sudds and Patrick Thompson.

When Sudds and Thompson committed a theft in 1826 so that they might become convicts and stay in the colony rather than leave when their regiment was rotated out in the usual way, Darling resolved to make an example and publicly expelled them from the regiment in heavy irons. But Sudds died a few days later, and the symbolic punishment of military defaulters became a different symbol altogether. The *Australian* and the *Monitor* presented the incident as a martyrdom, inflicted by those who believed that the only way to deal with the lower orders was by severity and harshness. That Darling was uninformed that Sudds was sick tended to be ignored, and Darling was maligned by Wentworth as a coldhearted monster who might well find himself facing a charge of murder.

LAND POLICY TROUBLES

While the attacks on Darling came to a head over the case of Sudds and Thompson, there is little doubt that the emancipists and their supporters would have attacked him anyway because of his implementation of the new policies flowing from the Bigge reports. The aspect that most displeased the emancipist faction was the policy restricting grants of land to those possessing large amounts of capital. Emancipist resentment of this alteration in priorities surfaced earlier in 1825 with the arrival in New South Wales of representatives of the Australian Agricultural Company. The huge grant of up to a million acres (400,000 hectares) given to the company inflamed the emancipists. Darling just happened to be in office when the new policies began to bite, but whoever had been the governor at the time would have come under heavy attack. The Sudds and Thompson case, therefore, provided no more than a pretext to legitimize the attacks on Darling launched by Wentworth and Hall on behalf of the emancipist faction in New South Wales.

The *Monitor* and the *Australian* took the lead in attacking Ralph Darling thereafter. Darling prosecuted A.E. Hayes, the new editor and proprietor of the *Australian*, and succeeded in having him jailed for libel. Hall soon joined his fellow editor in prison. To the governor's chagrin, but to the delight of their supporters, both men continued to publish their newspapers from jail and subjected every action of Darling's to critical inspection. Darling's readiness to identify with the exclusives and his isolation from the wider colonial society did not go unremarked in Britain, and in March 1831, he received notification that he was to be relieved.

The recall was greeted by scenes of unfeigned delight among the emancipists, and their newspapers rejoiced at the discomfiture and departure of a man they had come to regard as a tyrant. W.C. Wentworth threw a large party to celebrate the victory, and while the band played "Over the Hills and Far Away," more than 4,000 emancipists and supporters guzzled gin and beer and ate gargantuan quantities of roast mutton and roast beef on the lawns of Wentworth's property at Vaucluse. The guests did not note that Wentworth was already beginning to display a liking for the trappings of wealth and social position or that these gave him more in common with the exclusive view of the world than their own. A time would come, in the not-too-distant future, when he, like Darling, would be reviled as a man who sought to deny a fair go to those less well situated than himself.

VAN DIEMEN'S LAND AND SWAN RIVER

Between 1824 and 1836, Van Diemen's Land was administered by Lieutenant Governor George Arthur, who presided over an administration renowned for its severity and close supervision. Arthur shared the military background of Ralph Darling and implemented policies that were just as unpopular, yet the small size of the island colony permitted Arthur to take personal control of every aspect of administration in a way Darling was unable to do in New South Wales. The outcome was that Arthur succeeded where Darling failed. Arthur drove the single hostile newspaper out of business by publishing an official newspaper in opposition. He established a convict system that became the envy of New South Wales officials because of his personal control over each and every step in a convict's passage through the system. Good conduct brought graduated relaxation of discipline, but poor conduct resulted in a descent through ever harsher levels of punishment until the unfortunate felon ended up in the hell of the colonies of secondary punishment at Macquarie Harbour and Port Arthur. Only a small percentage of prisoners ever served time in such places; nonetheless, they became bywords for horror and brutality, and Arthur believed that their existence provided an incentive to convicts to behave.

In 1829, the first free colony in Australia was founded at Swan River in Western Australia. It was to be an agricultural colony with no convicts or paupers, financed by a wide range of middle-class investors. Land in the new colony was granted free of charge in direct proportion to the amount of capital or property a settler invested. All items of property were considered appropriate for valuation as investment capital, whether or not they were useful for agricultural pursuits, and the records of the colonial secretary's office in Western Australia show that some settlers absurdly overvalued their possessions to obtain larger grants, and some laborers likewise. One gentleman valued two sporting rifles at £600 ($1,200), while laborers attempted to include the value of their clothing and any personal goods they brought with them. One man claimed a wheelbarrow wheel as a capital investment; another attempted to value a rabbit as livestock. The regulations provided for a land grant in the ratio of one acre (0.4 hectares) for 1/6d. (d. = pence $.15) worth of capital. This was extremely generous, and as a result, a number of large and uneconomic grants were made to individuals who proved unable to work them, while others who might have made the land productive were forced to take inferior grants without adequate water or access to market. Some of those unfortunate enough to have come to the colony as workers starved to death.

TIDES OF CHANGE

The unpopular and conservative Darling was replaced by a liberal in Major General Richard Bourke, and the system of land alienation in all three Australian colonies was to be fundamentally recast yet again. Great changes were afoot. Commissioner Bigge had at least possessed the advantage of time actually spent in Australia. The new voice came appropriately perhaps from Newgate Prison and from an individual who was destined never at any time in his life to set foot on Australian soil. Nevertheless, Edward Gibbon Wakefield was to bring about a major change in British colonial practice. Wakefield's contribution to Australian development lay in the area of ideas, and his opinions reflected the concerns of his contemporaries and articulated them in a way that was both stimulating and attractive. His views on the social and economic conditions in England and the way in which a revised system of colonization could benefit both mother country and colonies were to prove enormously influential in the decades to come.

WAKEFIELD

Edward Gibbon Wakefield was an adventurer sentenced to three years of jail for abducting an heiress. British prisons at this time—for those who had money—were places of ease and comparative comfort, and Wakefield read widely. As a result he developed an interest in Australia and in the possible future open to his fellow convicts who were awaiting transportation there. He became increasingly engrossed by the subject and developed the basic corpus of ideas that underlay his subsequent theories of colonization. In 1829, the *Morning Chronicle* newspaper published a series of letters that purported to be from a settler in New South Wales. They were fictions produced by Wakefield to test his theories and were published later that year in London under the title *A Letter from Sydney the Principal Town of Australasia*. Here and in his later publications Wakefield set out his analysis of the problems facing England and his proposals for solving them.

According to Wakefield, Britain suffered from an overabundance of capital that kept interest rates too low for those who wanted to live on investment income and an oversupply of laborers that kept wages at or below subsistence level and encouraged radicalism among the lower orders. On the other hand, the colonies were crying out for investment capital and for laborers. What was needed was a method of shifting the capital and labor to the Australian colonies, where they would be gainfully employed. English investors would earn a safe return, and workers would enjoy immeasurably better living standards and a surety of employment.

In *A Letter from Sydney*, Wakefield argued that the current system of land disposal was wasteful, and he proposed a new systematic method of land purchase, the proceeds of which were to be used to pay the passages of laborers from England. Thus the more land sold, the more laborers would flow into the colony. Land would gain an intrinsic value in Australia where it had hitherto been considered valuable only insofar as it could be exploited. By manipulating the purchase price, the authorities could ensure a "sufficient price" whereby land was always priced beyond the reach of immigrant workers who would therefore be forced to work for the landowners until they had saved sufficient to purchase land for themselves. Land in the colonies would become what it already was in Britain, a measure of social and economic status, and the important British social distinctions between owners of property and nonowners would be reproduced in Australia. A dangerous tendency toward egalitarianism in colonial life would be thereby corrected, and British investment and emigration would be attracted by the new opportunities in Australia.

By 1831, the Wakefieldian system and a new governor in New South Wales heralded the opening of an era of innovation and development throughout the Australian colonies.

4

Riding on the Sheep's Back (1831–1855)

Edward Gibbon Wakefield's proposals received a partial application by the Colonial Office in the Ripon Regulations of 1831, which provided for the sale by auction of crown lands in New South Wales and Van Diemen's Land and stipulated that part of the money thus produced should create a fund with which to defray the costs of carrying free British emigrants to the colonies. The new system was intended to rationalize British land and emigration policies in Australia, and it represented an important change of emphasis in British policy, as an interlocking system of land sales and emigration had not hitherto been tried. The Ripon Regulations made waste (unused by Europeans) or crown lands in Australia available for purchase with a minimum reserve price of 5s. (s. = shilling) an acre ($.50 for 0.4 hectares). Revenue thus gained was earmarked to subsidize free pauper emigration to Australia.

REVISING THE LAND SYSTEM

The 1820s had been a decade of great pastoral expansion in Australia, and colonial exports of wool to the mother country had become increasingly important. In 1821, the year the first commercial export of wool was sent to England, the clip amounted to only 1.754 million pounds (79,632 kilograms). In 1830, 2 million pounds (900,000 kilograms) of wool were sent to the United Kingdom, and exports rose steadily so that by 1850 Australia was sending an annual wool clip of just under 40 million pounds (18 million kilograms) to Britain, which at that time accounted for more than half of the country's entire import of wool.[1]

It is against this backdrop that British attempts to revise the land system in Australia should be viewed. In some respects, British policies seemed to be out of touch with the economic realities in Australia in the years between 1831 and 1855, and there appeared to be an unrealistic preoccupation with agricultural development despite the obvious and increasing importance of wool. The settlements of Western Australia and South Australia were both projected as agricultural colonies, and much of the official and the private propaganda encouraging the lower classes to emigrate to Australia stressed the agricultural rather than the pastoral potential of the Australian colonies.

Domestic conditions in Britain undoubtedly help to explain why Englishmen tended to associate the future of Australia so perversely and resolutely with cultivation. What could lower-class emigrants do in Australia, where there was little industry to offer factory jobs, but farm on their own account? Britain had little experience with a pastoral model like Australia's, and the possibilities of jobs in the wool industry did not impinge on the consciousness of most commentators, who also reacted against the horrors of industrialization by idealizing and romanticizing the way of life lived in the rural districts of preindustrial England. The ideology of yearning to return to a golden age of individual self-sufficiency based on farming could no longer be achieved in the British Isles, but it might still be attainable in the Australian colonies. The cult of virgin lands provided Britain with a psychological and emotional frontier of its own to match the attractions of the American West.

Moreover, as a corollary to the feeling that cultivation represented a superior way of life, many Englishmen believed that pastoral occupations—generally termed *squatting* in Australia—led inexorably to moral degeneration, especially when the labour force was comprised of convicts and former convicts. The widespread dispersal of a morally corrupt population across the Australian bush was a cause for much concern, and the slaughter of Aborigines on outback sheep stations lent weight to such views. Throughout the 1830s and 1840s Wakefield and Colonial Office functionaries under the influence of his ideas continued to reiterate the warning that if Australian colonists turned their energies to pastoral rather than agricultural pursuits, the inevitable result would be the establishment within a few generations of "a race approaching to barbarism."[2]

THE RIPON REGULATIONS

Land policy, drawn up in London in such a climate of opinion, often proved hopelessly out of touch with colonial realities in Australia. The Ripon Regulations were expressly designed to concentrate settlement into compact agricultural communities, and as early as 1831—the year of their implementation—Governor Darling pointed out to the Colonial Office that it was already impossible to prevent settlers from sending their sheep and cattle beyond the formal boundaries of the settled districts. By 1835 the problem of regulating the massive expansion of the pastoral industry faced Governor Richard Bourke and could no longer be delayed. It had already become obvious that pastoral expansion into the interior of New South Wales was both inevitable and necessary if the colony was to continue to prosper. The Ripon Regulations certainly succeeded in providing a revenue, just as Wakefield had predicted, but they failed as a mechanism for concentrating population.

The potential for massive profit in moving flocks of sheep onto crown lands that cost the owner of the sheep nothing and therefore tied up no capital proved to be too alluring, and in 1835, Bourke estimated that over 1 million sheep were engaged in unauthorized grazing on crown lands in New South Wales. The flock owners just moved their sheep to a vacant area of crown land and squatted on it by allowing their sheep to indulge in free-range grazing. Already such squatters were hundreds of kilometers beyond the boundaries of formal settlement, and Bourke recognized the impossibility of stemming this flow of men and animals. He could, however, attempt to come to terms with it and regulate and supervise what he could not halt. Failure to do so would have amounted to an abdication of the crown's authority over all the lands beyond the official boundaries.

Conditions in the frontier districts demanded that the governor act quickly to establish government authority. The stock and property of the squatters were under threat from the depredations of lawless vagabonds and outlaws called bushrangers who infested the pastoral districts and harassed the flocks of the larger sheep men. The inability of the colonial government to ensure the protection of the squatters from bushrangers and Aborigines led to a resort to vigilante violence on the frontier, and the *Sydney Gazette* drew attention to the increasing lawlessness: "In every part of the country squatters without any reasonable means of maintaining themselves by honesty, have formed stations, and evidently pursued a predatory warfare against the flocks and herds in the vicinity."[3]

BOURKE'S ACT

In 1836, the Legislative Council of New South Wales passed Bourke's Act to restrain and regulate the occupation of crown lands. Commissioners of Crown Lands were appointed who were also salaried or stipendary magistrates. Their job was to protect crown lands from unauthorized occupation, to enforce the rule of law, to keep the peace between settlers and Aborigines, and keep track of convicts and those on probation known as "ticket-of-leave convicts" in the frontier districts. In addition, the act provided that any respectable colonist beyond the formal limits of settlement could legally graze his stock over as much land as he pleased upon payment of a £10 ($20) annual license fee. The commissioners were to be assisted by a small force of police and were to arbitrate between pastoralists who disagreed over rights to a particular run and remove unlicensed intruders on crown lands. As a result of this act, respectable persons could now legally occupy crown lands, and the principal settlers of the colony quickly took advantage of the situation and invested considerable capital in squatting.

It is important to note that the decision taken by Bourke ran counter to official British policy on crown lands in Australia, yet the imperial government approved the device the following year. The explanation for this inconsistency lies in a quirk of British law that maintains that possession of a tract or piece of land for a prolonged period of time eventually confers ownership on the possessor. Known as "possessory title," this maxim placed at risk crown ownership of land in the squatting districts. Bourke's Act provided security and a measure of protection for pastoralists if they took out a license, but the very taking of the license effectively marked their recognition of the crown's right to issue the license, and therefore of the crown's ownership of the crown lands. It was an urgent necessity for Bourke to obtain such an acknowledgment, but it highlights a great contradiction between policy and practice in the area of crown lands' control in Australia. At the very time when a new colony designed specifically to implement Wakefield's vision of a concentrated agricultural utopia was being founded in South Australia, the British authorities approved a colonial act that gave both encouragement and legal sanction to squatters to occupy thousands of hectares of land—right up to the borders of the new colony—in clear violation of policy and prevailing ideology.

The Ripon Regulations also had important effects in the smaller colonies of Van Diemen's Land and Western Australia. In the island colony, the amount of usable crown land that remained ungranted by 1831 was quite small. Thus the revenue potential of the new system for Van Diemen's Land was nowhere near as great as for the mother colony of New South Wales. The import of this situation was that the island colony did not possess the means to pay its own way when the British authorities began to cut back on expenditure of British revenues on the convict system and colonial administration and to levy those costs against local revenues raised in each colony. But the impact on Western Australia was even more damaging. The application of the Ripon Regulations to the fledgling colony produced economic collapse and disaster. Under the regulations, crown land was to be sold at auction for a minimum reserve price of 5s. an acre ($.50 for 0.4 hectares) and the revenue used to pay the passages of laborers to work the properties. In Western Australia, however, the original land grants had been so large, and the population so small, that land on the private market was selling for a fraction of the new set price. Consequently, very little new land was sold, very little revenue was raised, and therefore no new laborers could be brought to the colony. Without labor the colony could not develop, and without development the land price remained obdurately below the set price. When in 1842 the official reserve price for land in the Australian colonies was raised to £1 an acre ($2 for 0.4 hectares), the gap between the price of land on the official and the private markets yawned as widely as ever. The colonists, unable to bring labor into the colony from England, decided that the only way they could break out of this impasse was to follow the successful pattern set by New South Wales, and in 1847 they set aside their scruples and petitioned the British government to make Western Australia a convict colony.

EDUCATING THE RISING GENERATION

In New South Wales, the liberal Richard Bourke turned his attention to the question of educating the native-born. What sort of education would be best suited to the progeny of convicts, former convicts, and lower-class free immigrants? The sons of the exclusives usually were sent home to England to be educated as befitted the next generation of the ruling class, and many sent their daughters as well. Could a system of education be devised that would counteract the tainted bloodlines of the colony and the baleful influence of convictism? British education theorist Dr. Thomas Arnold, the headmaster of Rugby School, had no illusions that education might become a social corrective for inherited criminality:

> If they will colonise with convicts, I am satisfied that the stain should last, not only for one whole life, but for more than one

generation; that no convict or convict's child should ever be a free citizen; and that, even in the third generation, the offspring should be excluded from all offices of honour or authority in the colony.[4]

In 1835, Secretary of State for the Colonies Lord Glenelg wrote to Richard Bourke of his belief that "in no part of the World, is the general Education of the People a more sacred and necessary duty of the Government than in New South Wales."[5] This prejudice against the children of the colony rose from British perceptions that in colonizing with criminals the mother country had mortgaged the long-term future of Australia. Education at government expense was to be encouraged for colonial children at a time when such expenditures were not acceptable in Britain itself. The depth of British concern can be gauged from governmental involvement in an age of educational laissez-faire.

Bourke attempted to introduce a secular form of education into New South Wales modeled on the Irish National System. Briefly, the government would bear the costs of providing a nondenominational Christian education that stressed moral training in Christian ethics; and at the same time, opportunities would be provided for instructors of the different Christian sects in the colony to impart their own sectarian teaching to the children of their particular flock. All denominations were to be afforded equal access to the children of their persuasion, but aside from this, the children were to receive a common education.

To his surprise and alarm Bourke found that this reasonable and tolerant attempt to highlight the common ground between the various religious groups in the colony led to an outbreak of sectarian prejudice from the Anglican and Presbyterian clergy directed at the equal treatment afforded to the Roman Catholics. Christian charity was the one thing apparently lacking in this bruising confrontation between conflicting religious denominations in New South Wales. Bourke's proposed rationalization of education into a single nondenominational system collapsed in the face of the intemperate ranting bigotry of Anglican leader Bishop William Grant Broughton and Presbyterian leader Reverend John Dunmore Lang who cooperated together against Bourke in a "No Popery" campaign. Bourke found himself reduced to the inefficient, expensive, and unwieldy stratagem of subsidizing the schools of all the denominations irrespective of their enrollments and effectiveness.

SETTLING SOUTH AUSTRALIA

Cumbersome expedients seem to have been characteristic of British policy in Australia during the 1830s, and the settlement of South Australia in 1836 proved no exception. Established by an act of the Imperial Parliament two years earlier, and designed as a test case for Wakefieldian colonization theories, the new colony possessed one of the clumsiest administrative setups ever foisted upon a new settlement. A joint-stock company known as the South Australian Company—and comprising investors anxious to test Wakefield's colonization blueprint—and the British government agreed after a series of compromises to establish a new colony in that part of New South Wales that is now known as South Australia. The outcome of their negotiations was a strange hybrid of a colony. It was to be a crown colony with a governor appointed by the British government; but the South Australian Association was to appoint a board of commissioners to supervise the sale of land and to control the land fund. They would be represented in the colony by a resident commissioner who would accompany the first governor to the colony in 1836 and divide the administration with him.

The first governor, John Hindmarsh, and the first commissioner, James Hurtle Fisher, failed to agree on nearly everything, and each disagreement was treated as a trial of strength. Government was impossible and administration degenerated into a series of childish altercations, while migrants flooded into the colony, land speculation flourished, and farming languished. The colony, which was to receive no convicts, rode on the back of a wave of capital importation, as each wave of immigrants indulged in an orgy of land buying from settlers in the previous wave. Metropolitan land values in the capital Adelaide soared, but in four years only 443 acres (179 hectares) of farmland actually came into production. In the years 1838 and 1839, for example, exports from the colony earned £22,500 ($45,000), while colonists splurged £505,200 ($1,000,400) on the purchase of imported goods. Such a situation could not continue indefinitely.

A new governor, George Gawler, was dispatched to South Australia, and he combined the functions of resident commissioner with his vice-regal position in an obvious attempt to overcome the administrative imbroglio. Gawler found the colony in a sorry state when he arrived, with,

[s]carcely any settlers in the country, no tillage, very little sheep and cattle pasturing, and then only by a few enterprising individuals risking their chance as squatters. The population shut up in Adelaide existing principally upon the unhealthy and uncertain profits of land jobbing; capital flowing out for the necessities of life to Sydney and Van Diemen's Land almost as fast as it was brought in by passengers from England.[6]

The governor's method of dealing with this situation was to spend money lavishly on public works to provide employment for the laborers and to reorganize the survey office in an effort to hasten its activities and get would-be farmers away from the temptations of land speculation in Adelaide and onto their farms. To finance this program of recovery Gawler drew bills or wrote checks on behalf of of the South Australian Commissioners in London. The bills were dishonored, and ultimately the British government ended the Wakefield experiment, took over the bankrupt colony's debts, and sent in an efficient administrator in Sir George Grey with firm instructions to reform and retrench. Grey's arrival coincided with a severe colonial recession, the effects of which were felt throughout Australia, and he ruthlessly cut back on public works, forcing the laborers to leave for other colonies or to go out into the bush looking for work on the farms now at last beginning to come into production. Convict and former convict stockmen from New South Wales established an overland stock route to the new colony and taught the inexperienced settlers the techniques of survival in Australian conditions. Sheep flocks increased; a large migration of religious refugees from Germany occurred; wheat began to be exported to the other colonies; and in 1846 copper mines were discovered, which boosted the colony's export earnings. Slowly South Australia dragged itself from the debit to the credit side of the ledger, and it formed an important part of a thriving intercolonial trading network that included New South Wales, New Zealand, and Van Diemen's Land as the 1840s progressed.

PORT PHILLIP: A SUBIMPERIAL EXPANSION

At the same time as the South Australian colony was being founded from England, the colony of Van Diemen's Land engaged in a venture of subimperial expansion in its own right. Originally settled from the colony of New South Wales, Van Diemen's Land's expansion into the Port Phillip district of southern New South Wales during the 1830s demonstrates the dynamic and expansionary forces engendered in the environment of colonies of settlement. New Zealand also felt the effects of energetic subimperialism from New South Wales, as private entrepreneurs like W.C. Wentworth and bible-toting missionaries like the Reverend Samuel Marsden turned their attention to that green and fertile land. In both cases, the expansionary stimulous was economic, and informal settlement took place in advance of formal recognition from the mother country.

In New South Wales, reports from exploring expeditions had aroused considerable interest in the grazing potential of the colony's southern region. By the early 1830s, a few overlanders from further north were pushing into the Port Phillip area in search of squatting territory. But the main impetus for settlement of the area came from a group of businessmen in Van Diemen's Land who found themselves restricted by the unavailability of further grazing land and government attempts to make them purchase their holdings after the implementation of the Ripon Regulations. They came together in the Port Phillip Bay Association and determined to move their flocks across to the mainland where pastoralism could be pursued without the interference of the Ripon Regulations. John Batman, as the representative of the group, negotiated a series of treaties and land cessions from the Port Phillip Aborigines, which threw into question the whole subject of landownership in Australia. Did it rightfully belong to the Aborigines, or was it—as the lawyers maintained—the property of the crown?

BATMAN'S "TREATIES"

For a small collection of mirrors, tomahawks, shirts, and several hundredweight of flour, Batman claimed to have purchased extensive areas of land from the Aborigines on behalf of the association. These proceedings caused considerable alarm to the authorities both in Sydney and in Britain. Governor Bourke issued a proclamation in which he stated that Batman and the other squatters in the Port Phillip Bay region were illegally trespassing on crown lands, and in Britain, Secretary of State Lord Glenelg rejected out of hand the view that Aborigines possessed any right to dispose of their land:

> It is indeed enough to observe, that such a concession would subvert the foundation on which all Proprietary Rights in New South Wales at present rest, and defeat a large part of the most important Regulations of the local Government.[7]

Any recognition extended to Batman's treaties could have had catastrophic effects on the administration of land policy throughout Australia. It would have amounted to an admission by the British authorities that land in Australia was not the property of the crown but belonged to the natives. It would thus have constituted an admission that since 1788 the British had been freely disposing of an estate that did not belong to them. For these reasons there was no question of the treaties being accepted. The implications were too overwhelming to contemplate.

Settlers flowed into the newly opened district, and in 1836, London agreed to recognize the inevitable and acceded to requests to allow a formal status to the embryo colony. The site for the principal city was chosen and named Melbourne in honor of Viscount Melbourne, the British prime minister at the time. Captain William Lonsdale was appointed magistrate to superintend the tiny settlement, and in 1839, Charles La Trobe became resident superintendent of the Port Phillip district, a role he fulfilled until 1850 when the position was transformed, and he became the first lieutenant governor of the new colony of Victoria, as the Port Phillip district then became.

THE PASTORAL BOOM

All this expansionary activity took place as a consequence of the pastoral boom that lasted throughout the 1830s. Colonists and their flocks established a presence at this time that dramatically expanded the area of effective settlement and consequently placed enormous strains on the administration of New South Wales. Settlement expanded northwards into what was to become the colony of Queensland as well as into central New South Wales, and all Bourke could do was to attempt to license the squatters. He was forced to recognize that he was powerless to prevent pastoral expansion as long as a sure market and limitless supplies of capital were to be found in Britain. In many ways this inability to control events was characteristic of the British authorities from the 1830s onward, and we find them consistently accepting, albeit with reluctance, that the inhabitants of New South Wales, and to a lesser extent those of the smaller colonies, could no longer be coerced into settlement patterns they did not desire, no matter how favorably these might recommend themselves to British armchair theorists back home. The pastoral boom showed this to be so, and the gold rushes proved it beyond doubt.

CONVICTS RECONSIDERED

As the tide of free immigration flowed into Australia after 1831, and as it became apparent that the revenue from sales of crown lands was proving to be far greater than anything the British authorities had anticipated, the realization began to dawn that convicts were no longer the only human resource available for colonial development. Between 1831 and 1841, 96,606 free emigrants traveled from Britain to the Australian colonies, and this caused observers both in Britain and in Australia to question the continuance of convict transportation. Convict Australia's tainted bloodlines were already the cause of considerable concern, and even in Australia some exclusives like James Macarthur, to say nothing of Governor Richard Bourke himself, felt that free immigration provided a sounder basis for social growth and moral improvement of the population.

Meanwhile, agitation in Britain against the system of convict transportation and assignment had increased dramatically. Much of the opposition was mutually contradictory, but there was so much of it that change could no longer be avoided. Some believed that assignment and slavery were too similar and that it made a mockery of Britain's decision to abolish black slavery in 1834 if it still permitted white slavery to continue. Others felt that assignment failed to deter crime in Britain because life for convicts in Australia was a life of ease and comfort in a better climate in a land of opportunity. Another group of opponents were followers of Wakefield's, and they expressed concern that the continuation of assignment in New South Wales and Van Diemen's Land gave those colonies an unfair advantage in attracting migrants and capital over the nonconvict South Australia. They all shared an indignation at the continuation of a morally corrupt system of punishment and an ignorance of and unconcern with colonists' opinions on the question. The high moral ground became very crowded, and in 1837 opponents of transportation and assignment succeeded in securing the appointment of a Parliamentary Select Committee under the chairmanship of Wakefield's disciple Sir William Molesworth to inquire into the convict system. The committee was made up of known opponents of the status quo, and condemnation of existing penal institutions and practices was certain. In 1838, the Select Committee recommended that transportation to the settled districts of New South Wales and Van Diemen's Land should be abandoned as soon as possible and that the system of assignment be abolished forthwith.

In 1840, the British government abolished assignment throughout the Australian colonies, halted transportation to New South Wales altogether, and directed the entire stream of transported felons to Van Diemen's Land and its dependency Norfolk Island. A new probation system was introduced that was designed to ensure equality of punishment by gathering all convicts into a number of probation stations where they worked for the government in gangs. Treatment was to be uniform and harsh, but convicts could gain a steadily increasing degree of freedom by good behavior until they were released into the workforce as wage laborers.

GIPPS AND THE CONVERSION TO A FREE COLONY

The implementation of this new policy and the superintendence of New South Wales during its progress from penal settlement to free colony fell to the care of Sir George Gipps. Gipps arrived as governor of New South Wales in 1838 with an established reputation both as a soldier and as an administrator. His time in the colony coincided with a period of economic recession, pastoral expansion, the establishment of a partially elective Legislative Council, and a bout of political agitation that would have overwhelmed most men. He acted with courage and integrity in an impossible situation and returned to England eight years later with his health shattered and having been abandoned by the Colonial Office in his dispute with the squatters over land tenure. In fact, in the eight years Gipps spent in New South Wales, he found himself expected to play the role of referee between the landed gentry and the squatters, on the one hand, and a growing party of land-hungry urban radicals, on the other. The continuing dispute among colonists over landownership that had begun in Darling's time continued to bedevil Gipps's period in the colony, as did the town versus country tensions that can also be discerned here.

In 1842, Secretary of State for the Colonies Lord Stanley introduced a bill into the House of Commons for the better government of New South Wales. The bill expanded the Legislative Council to thirty-six members, two-thirds of whom were to be elected by the owners of property in the colony from among their own ranks. The new Legislative Council was empowered to make laws for the colony—subject to approval in Britain—but it was expressly forbidden from appropriating the land revenues or altering the Civil List from which official salaries were paid. The straight property qualifications for members of the Legislative Council and for voters heralded the end of open conflict between emancipists and exclusives, and it had become obvious that with the cessation of transportation the emancipists—in a comparatively short time—would be swamped under the flood of free immigrants.[8]

GIPPS AND THE LEGISLATIVE COUNCIL

The maintenance of British control over land policy infuriated the squatters who dominated the legislature. Conflict between Gipps and the Legislative Council became endemic as the pastoral interests openly attempted to force the executive officers of the crown into a position of financial dependence. The reserved Civil List rendered this impossible and therefore became an issue of contention when colonists claimed that it amounted to taxation without representation. It was over the land issue, however, that the dispute between Gipps and the Legislative Council came most sharply into focus.

When Sir George Gipps arrived in New South Wales in February 1838, the squatting boom was in full swing. Prices for Australian wool had begun to fall but were still buoyant, and the boom was fueled by a constant flow of investment capital from Britain to New South Wales. This marked the weak link in the pastoral economy, for the boom depended on a continuing inflow of new capital, and a series of events between 1838 and 1842 jeopardized this flow: there was a financial crisis in England, a drought in New South Wales, a slump in wool prices, and a labor shortage. As investment capital ceased to enter Australia in significant quantities, the precarious foundations of the preceding boom were fully exposed.

Squatters relied on the income earned from their sales of wool for the payment of debt to merchants and suppliers who extended credit to the pastoralists on the expectation of payment. Wool met the running costs, but the real profit came from the sale of the lambs. The increase in sheep, which were the capital of the enterprise, represented a capital accumulation. When sheep were sold, there was money to pay interest, dividends to investors in Britain, or returns on the original capital borrowed to buy the sheep and establish the station. The value of the entire enterprise was closely associated with the price of sheep, and while that stayed high, with would-be squatters arriving with capital to invest, thousands of sheep were required and profits were large. But when demand ceased fairly abruptly after 1841, the high price for sheep could no longer be sustained, and the bubble burst. Wool prices fell at the same time, and many squatters faced ruin. This economic situation gave an added stridency to the constitutional demands of the squatters in the Legislative Council during the 1840s, especially when Gipps attempted to rationalize crown land's administration.

GIPPS AND THE SQUATTERS

The license system instituted by Bourke was not working. It did force squatters to acknowledge the rights of the crown, but it also allowed a comparatively small number of men to control thousands of square kilometers of land for a comparatively trivial payment. The squatters claimed that these vast tracts of land had lain idle for centuries before they had arrived, and by hard work and risk taking they had rendered them productive. It was their effort and capital that had developed the colony, it was their vision that had opened up huge areas of inland Australia, and it was they who were denied any security of tenure by the crown's claim to ownership of the land. They argued that they were the economic mainstay of Australia, they provided the exports and the jobs for laborers, and they resented Gipps's proposals to levy financial burdens upon them at a time when their very survival was in question.

Gipps's attempts to rationalize and regulate the squatting industry caused him the greatest trouble of his turbulent years in New South Wales. In April 1844, he published two sets of regulations covering the occupation and the purchase of runs by the squatters. These were designed to force the pastoralists to contribute to the land fund of the colony and to make it possible for some security of tenure to be given to them. On the other hand, Gipps was attempting to ensure that the squatters did not lock up millions of hectares of land and deny it forever to future settlers. By combining a license system with a system of compulsory periodic purchase of a small portion of each station licensed, Gipps attempted to give squatters an incentive to improve their runs and to build homesteads on the freehold portion of the station. Unfortunately, Gipps was attempting to extract large sums of money from squatters who had become used to paying next to nothing, and he was trying to do this at a time when they had not recovered from a severe depression in which many pastoralists had been ruined. It is not surprising, therefore, to find that the proposed regulations aroused a storm of protest from the squatters and their supporters in the Legislative Council. After all, men like W.C. Wentworth and Benjamin Boyd would have faced payouts of several hundred pounds every year for licenses and many thousands of pounds every eight years for compulsory purchases where previously they had paid virtually nothing.

The squatters clamored that they faced bankruptcy and ruin, and many undoubtedly did. But Gipps had failed adequately to appreciate the centrality of the pastoralists to the colonial economy of New South Wales. Quite simply, the squatters were crucial to the survival of the urban merchants and financial interests who had extended them credit during the halcyon years of the boom. If the squatters went into wholesale bankruptcy, then these debts could not be recovered and the providers of credit would also be ruined. The linked indebtedness meant that if pastoralists went to the wall, then the urban merchants and bankers went with them. For these reasons the city interests opposed Gipps's regulations and fully supported the squatters in their campaign against the governor.

Moreover, Gipps's political naïveté was such that he was surprised to find that the laboring classes in the towns and in Sydney showed similar support for the pastoralists. The reasons for this strange and short-lived alliance between urban radicals and conservative pastoralists lay in one of the anomalies of the economic depression, whereby laborers in the city experienced widespread unemployment and hardship at the same time as the squatters faced an acute labor shortage. When Gipps announced that one of his aims with the new regulations was to produce a revenue with which to resume the shipment of assisted immigrants from the British Isles, he outraged working-class urban dwellers who had experienced such devastating unemployment. They refused to move into the pastoral districts because of the poor reputation of squatters as employers who mistreated and victimized their workforce and preferred to remain in familiar urban environments subsisting on charity. At the height of the depression, several hundred of them actually emigrated to Chile rather than take up positions offered by the squatters. Nevertheless, urban workers found themselves supporting the pastoralists against the governor because they regarded any intake of new migrants as a threat to their living standards and wage levels.

The final nail in the coffin for Gipps's regulations came from British wool manufacturers. They lobbied the British authorities and pointed out that Gipps's restructuring of the land system in New South Wales had more than just colonial significance. It could seriously disrupt the flow of wool exports to British industries that had become completely dependent on Australian supplies. One immediate consequence of any stoppage in supplies would be widespread unemployment throughout the industry. Gipps's tinkering with the land system in Australia therefore could produce embarrassing political fallout in Britain.

Given the torrent of opposition he aroused, Gipps soon found himself abandoned by the Colonial Office. Successive Secretaries of State distanced themselves from their loyal servant, until in 1847 the third Earl Grey passed an Order in Council that granted the squatters everything they had demanded in the form of fourteen-year leases in the pastoral districts plus preemptive rights of purchase, should the government decide to put the land up for sale. Gipps's regulations were never put into effect, and he left New South Wales in dishonor and disgrace.

THE DISCOVERY OF GOLD

Isolated finds of gold had been reported in New South Wales from the 1820s onward, but the colonial authorities suppressed the news. The unsettling effects of a gold rush in a convict colony were too awesome to contemplate. There was also the question of legal ownership of gold or any minerals found on crown land or even on freehold land. One of the great differences between the land systems of the United States of America and the Australian colonies lay in the fact that in America ownership of land automatically brought with it ownership of all minerals found on or under the surface of that land. British colonies, however, maintained the British system that held that minerals always remained the property of the crown even when found on private land. When Edward Hammond Hargraves set off a gold rush in 1851, to the Bathurst district of New South Wales where he claimed to have unearthed some small though promising nuggets of gold, the rush overwhelmed the crown. By the time the colonial authorities realized they faced a crisis, it was too late for them to do anything about it. Hundreds were already digging on the field named Ophir by Hargraves, after the field in California of the same name, and thousands more were on their way.

The new colony of Victoria formed from the Port Phillip district of New South Wales in 1850 faced the alarming prospect of losing the bulk of its population as men streamed north toward Bathurst. To counteract this population loss, the Victorian government resolved to offer rewards for the first payable goldfields discovered in the colony. Very soon, the fabulously wealthy alluvial fields at Ballarat and Bendigo had turned Victoria into a magnet for gold seekers, who came in the hundreds of thousands from all over the world. In 1851 the population of Victoria stood at approximately 80,000, and a decade later it numbered more than 500,000.

The authorities in both New South Wales and Victoria resolved to license the gold diggers. The possession of a miner's license permitted a digger to keep whatever gold he found on his own claim. In return for the license fee, the crown waived its rights of ownership over the gold. But failure to possess a license meant that the digger was effectively stealing crown property and was liable to suffer criminal proceedings at law. The license system caused great outrage among the miners. The problem was that the license had to be purchased in advance, it cost £1 10s. ($3) per month, and it had to be paid irrespective of the digger's success or failure in his search for gold. Miners who struck it rich experienced no difficulty in paying the license fee, but it became a definite cause of resentment among the majority who enjoyed only moderate or no success. Moreover, the license system on the Victorian diggings was rendered even more explosive by the excessively low caliber of the police employed to enforce the law. They became notorious for their brutality and corruption, and before long they were the most detested people on the diggings.

The huge influx of population caused enormous administrative difficulties for the fledgling Victorian government. Most of the police and civil servants decamped for the diggings. Those few who remained were unable to cope with the situation. Crews abandoned ship in Port Phillip Bay and headed inland to the goldfields, husbands and fathers deserted their families in favor of the diggings, employers found it virtually impossible to get workmen, and the squatters lost the bulk of their labor force. The effects on the wool industry did not produce the catastrophe squatters expected, as the sheep were shorn in the shearing season, and there were just enough men to look after the flocks between shearings. Moreover, the large goldfield populations proved eager purchasers of mutton and agricultural produce, so that many small farmers found that they could make a good living out of the gold diggings, if not by gold digging.

Life on the goldfields was very hard. Men worked up to ten meters (thirty-three feet) below ground, often up to their waists in water at the bottom of shafts that were poorly shored up and that occasionally collapsed, killing those below. Nationalities tended to congregate together, and certain areas became the unofficial territory of the Irish, the Americans, the French, and the Germans. Periodic brawls would break out as, for example, the men from different Irish counties fought one another, or the Irish turned in a group on the Van Diemonians. Corrupt law enforcement officers made regular license hunts, for the law insisted that a miner must carry his license at all times and produce it on demand for a duly authorized officer of the law. The licenses were made of paper, and carrying them at all times presented a difficulty to men who were working underground in water. Diggers were often called to the surface of their shafts many times a day to satisfy police demands. Again, men would sometimes accumulate a load of gravel on their claim, and then carry it quite long distances to wash for gold in the nearest creek or river; and the police took a special delight in stopping such heavily laden miners and demanding that they produce their licenses. Failure to produce the license—no matter what the excuse—led to miners, even those who owned a license, being hauled off, chained to a nearby log, and then fined by the resident commissioner.

RISING TENSIONS

By 1854, the days of alluvial mining by individuals or a small group of friends working in partnership were clearly numbered. There was an ominous switch to deep-lead mining with crushing plants and machinery requiring heavy capitalization. The miners' realization of this inevitable tide of change gave an added urgency to their efforts and helped produce a volatile situation. In November 1854, a series of public meetings took place, and the miners formed the Ballarat Reform League, to seek a change in the licensing system and the vote for every man. A local issue relating to the alleged corruption of a local magistrate who was suspected of accepting a bribe in a murder trial helped to fuel the diggers' anger.

On Friday, 1 December, the miners—under the leadership of Irish immigrant Peter Lalor—erected a rough palisade of logs and withdrew behind it to defy the police and the army. It was a symbolic action rather than a serious rebellion, and by Saturday night most of the diggers had quietly faded away and returned to their claims. Many were alienated by the increasingly Irish nature of the affair, and others were aware of the stockaders' great shortage of arms and ammunition. Early on the morning of Sunday, 3 December, more than 400 police and soldiers rushed the 120 or so miners still within the stockade, and after ten minutes of vicious hand-to-hand fighting it was all over. The stockade was destroyed and the rebel flag of the Southern Cross was hauled down and trampled into the dust by the soldiers. The affair was largely confined to immigrants and foreigners. Not one of the leaders or casualties was a native-born settler. The leaders in the days before the attack were Irish, American, German, Italian, and Canadian; and the casualties were overwhelmingly Irish. It appears that the Irish domination of the movement was so great that many diggers refused to become involved.[9]

In the trials that followed the Eureka Rebellion, as this little fracas became grandiloquently titled, juries refused to find any of the miners guilty, and the authorities wisely decided to let the matter drop. The Eureka Stockade did, however, bring to light one interesting facet of the developing national character, in that it showed clearly that native-born Australians would not take up arms for their political beliefs. The large exodus of men from the stockade before the events of Sunday morning indicates a propensity to sympathize with the demand for a fair go from the authorities but also a healthy regard for their own skins. Events in the next decades were to show that colonists would take up arms to enhance their own individual welfare, but they would not do so in significant numbers for any political or social cause.

RESPONSIBLE GOVERNMENT

Gold placed the financial viability of both Victoria and New South Wales beyond dispute and removed any remaining excuse for Britain to withhold self-government from its Australian colonies. In all the colonies with the exception of Western Australia, the general direction of political development followed a similar pattern. The colonial legislatures during the 1850s eventually produced constitutions calling for bicameral systems comprising lower houses of Assembly and upper chambers of review called Legislative Councils. The squatters sought to entrench themselves in power in the colonial Legislative Councils by a variety of devices. In New South Wales, W.C. Wentworth proposed the establishment of a hereditary aristocracy of pastoralists who would become a colonial House of Lords. This self-serving suggestion was scorned by a colonial populace from whom Wentworth had become increasingly estranged. Derided as a "Bunyip Aristocracy"—Bunyip is a mythical aboriginal creature—the proposal was ridiculed out of existence. Nevertheless, the squatters did succeed in securing a nominated Legislative Council in New South Wales, in which they hoped to withstand the attacks of the urban liberals and radical democrats in the Legislative Assembly. In Victoria, Tasmania (as Van Diemen's Land became known), and South Australia, the pastoral elites managed to entrench themselves in the Legislative Councils by means of restricted property franchises. By 1861, all the Australian colonies, except Western Australia, possessed bicameral legislatures with universal manhood suffrage for the Legislative Assemblies and various sorts of restriction based on possession of property making the Legislative Councils the exclusive preserve of the rich.

5

Gold and the Long Boom
(1856–1890)

In 1859 the new colony of Queensland was formally excised from New South Wales and established with its own bicameral legislature and Responsible Government. It was quite a concession, since the white population barely numbered 20,000.

Squatters and large landowners dominated the economy, and a shortage of labor resulted in 1863 in the importation of indentured Pacific Islanders to work on the sugar plantations of the colony. Europeans were believed unsuited for hard physical work in a tropical climate, and the trade in South Sea "Kanakas," as they were called, became a brisk one. During the next five years close to 2,000 Kanakas were introduced into Queensland. The trade was a brutal variant of slavery, and many Kanakas became the victims of kidnapping by unscrupulous ships' captains who found that they could turn a handsome profit by trafficking in human beings. Reliance on South Sea Islanders as a tropical workforce continued for the rest of the nineteenth century, eventually becoming one of the major hurdles to be surmounted on the road to federation.

LAND POLICY REVISITED

Meanwhile, in the other colonies, a new variation on an old theme had begun to cause considerable concern. From the 1830s, emigration propaganda in Britain had stressed the possibilities of laboring men possess-ing their own land in Australia, and the unwillingness of workers to travel out into the bush and work for squatters did not mean that they lacked the desire to own small farms and properties.

From 1856 onward, the new Legislative Assemblies found themselves repeatedly petitioned by requests that the crown lands be thrown open to settlement. Indeed, one of the great stimulants to electoral reform and the introduction of universal manhood suffrage in all the colonies stemmed from the realization by liberals and radicals that the pastoral-ists' grip on the lands of Australia could only be broken by reducing their political predominance. By 1859, political reform in New South Wales had ensured that Charles Cowper, Henry Parkes, and John Rob-ertson formed a liberal government with a majority in the Legislative Assembly. Robertson, as Secretary for Lands, pledged to supervise the establishment of an agricultural paradise of small yeoman farmers by unlocking the crown lands and making them available for selection by smallholders.

ROBERTSON'S LAND BILLS

Robertson was both a landowner and a squatter, and these were quite moderate enactments. He proposed to make the crown lands available for selection but not indiscriminately and not without safeguards. The amount of land an individual could select varied from a minimum of 40 acres (16.2 hectares) to a maximum of 320 acres (129.6 hectares), at a price of £1 an acre ($2 for 0.405 hectares). The selector was free to select land anywhere in the rural districts, irrespective of whether or not it was currently part of a squatter's run. But the land had to be paid for at the rate of 4s. ($.40) an acre on the day the selection was officially registered and the balance over the next three years. Land therefore was not freely available to every urban worker who wanted it but only to those who had accumulated a substantial capital investment. Only the "meritori-ous" were to be rewarded by an opportunity to become owners of land. There was no place for the impoverished in Robertson's paradise, and the plan reflected middle-class values like self-help and individualism.

Nevertheless, the squatter-dominated Legislative Council initially balked at Robertson's bills before reluctantly permitting them to pass. Cowper, the premier, threatened to swamp the upper house with addi-tional nominees if it proved unwilling to cooperate. More radical meas-ures might well follow if the pastoralists insisted on thwarting the lower chamber of the legislature. In Victoria, on the other hand, the Legislative

Council was elected and proved far more effective an opponent to liberal governments because its property-based franchise could not be altered without its consent.

In the event, Robertson managed to pilot his measures through the Legislative Council at the end of 1861, and the new act received an enthusiastic welcome from liberals in Sydney. The liberal newspaper the *Empire* maintained that New South Wales stood on the threshold of a bountiful new era for both pastoralists and small farmers. The increasing population would provide ever-growing markets for both groups, and the country seemed set to become a society of property owners.[1] It was this conservative stress on property and the rights of property owners that led the conservative *Sydney Morning Herald* to grant a measure of reluctant acquiescence to the legislation. Doubtless the poor and landless laborers of Sydney were anxious to obtain access to the land, but there would be no confiscatory attacks on wealth under the terms of this legislation.[2]

Robertson's free selection act provided something of a model for similar enactments in other colonies, but they all shared the principle of the right to select land held under lease by pastoralists. In 1862 the liberal government of Charles Duffy introduced selection after survey in Victoria with a maximum selection of 640 acres (259.2 hectares), later reduced to 320 acres (129.6 hectares) in 1869. In Queensland and South Australia similar legislation was passed at the end of the 1860s, defining agricultural areas where selection could occur and emphasizing occupation of the land selected.

FREE SELECTION

The acts in Queensland and South Australia stressed actual occupation of the land because of the speculation and dubious behavior indulged in by both squatters and selectors in New South Wales and Victoria. The legislation actually made it possible for squatters to select prime sections of their own runs. A squatter could select land in his own name, in the names of members of his family and friends, in the names of willing employees, and in the names of nonexistent people. Such subterfuges became known as "dummying," and Robertson's original legislation made it possible because the act had assumed that only genuine selectors would make use of its provisions and had therefore not insisted that the selector actually occupy his holding. By careful selection of waterholes and river and creek frontages, squatters could acquire the most valuable land, a process known as "peacocking." Pastoralists were not alone in misusing the legislation, and unscrupulous "land sharks" also indulged in peacocking, thereby forcing squatters to ransom their runs. As time went by, squatters also complained about the depredations on their flocks and herds inflicted by impoverished free selectors. Much of the rural poverty and misery so widespread in New South Wales and Victoria in the second half of the nineteenth century stemmed from selectors attempting to wrest a living from land manifestly unsuited to small-scale farming in a climate heavily influenced by the El Niño cycles of long periods without significant rain. The properties were too small to be viable in the long run and condemned the majority of selectors to inevitable ruin.

The traditional view is that free selection was not successful in human or in economic terms and that it meant indescribable hardship and drudgery for families that persisted. Children came to be regarded as cheap "hands," and great tensions existed between the heads of the families and their workforce of sons. The farms were too small to be divided among the sons and retain even marginal viability, so they were usually left to the oldest boy, and the other sons either left the land or eked out an existence as rural laborers.

Women and children, like their menfolk, lived lives of backbreaking labor to secure a precarious living from an unwilling soil. The women became breeders of cheap labor for their husbands, and large families were the norm. Many selectors' wives died in childbirth, and second and third marriages were not uncommon for the men. The only future for their daughters lay in following the same pattern as their mothers and incubating the next generation of hands. It was very difficult for selectors' families to break out of the poverty cycle while the family stayed on the farm, though occasionally some exceptional women like the suffragist Louisa Lawson would just walk off the property while their husbands were absent and take themselves and their children off to the city to start again.

Those smallholders whose dreams of independence were shattered often turned to petty crime in order to survive, and squatter complaints of stock theft were endemic in the vicinity of selectors. A few found themselves sucked into a life of more violent crime, and the widespread admiration and support found among the smallholders for bushrangers like Ned Kelly and his gang caused alarm and anger to those in authority. Kelly and his followers were the products of failed farms, and they turned to predation when local authorities attempted to harass and intimidate them into leaving their selections. Shared hardship produced an "us versus them" mentality that shrewd men like Kelly were able to manipulate to their advantage. In general, conditions of life for most smallholders were such as to produce what one writer has described as a race of "bush barbarians."[3]

There were parts of Australia, however, where the reality was not so bleak. In South Australia and in Queensland, free selection cannot be dismissed as producing human and economic failure. By the end of the 1860s, South Australia already grew half of Australia's wheat and exported grain to the other colonies as well as to Mauritius, South Africa, and Britain. In 1869 Surveyor General George W. Goyder named six agricultural areas describing the nature of the soil and the average annual rainfall for each one. Free selection began in those districts. A series of good rains in a wet El Niño cycle led Goyder's carefully calculated line of demarcation between agricultural districts with sufficient rain and pastoral districts with insufficient rain to be shifted northward until in 1874 the whole colony was thrown open for free selection. The wet cycle of El Niño continued for a few more years, and selectors moved far beyond Goyder's line into pastoral districts where farming had never before existed. Eventually, between 1881 and 1884, the run of wet seasons broke, and in the following dry cycle Goyder's judgment was thoroughly vindicated when the vast majority of farmers north of his line lost everything. Selection continued successfully to the south of Goyder's line.

In South Australia, free selection had ensured that almost 2 million additional acres (810,000 hectares) of land came into agricultural production. The colony reaped annual wheat harvests greater than those of New South Wales and Victoria combined, and a prosperous middle class of farmers had been successfully established by 1890. South Australia provides the success story in attempts to establish small-scale agriculture in Australia. In Queensland, the soil of the Darling Downs district was volcanic and so rich that it could be farmed for years without the need for fertilizer. Mixed farming of wheat, maize, and vegetables became the norm, and when a good wheat crop was reaped—every three years or so—the financial rewards were lucrative. But in social terms the price was high, and selectors' families worked like slaves to force the land into a payable proposition.

CONTINUING ABORIGINAL TROUBLES

With conditions of life so hard, it is no surprise to find that few Australians in the second half of the nineteenth century spared much time to consider the welfare of the Aborigines. In urban areas the blacks constituted a degraded remnant of the local tribes who lived by prostitution and begging. Destroyed by disease and alcohol, they eked out a precarious existence on the outskirts of the cities and by their condition and way of life went far toward reinforcing the prejudices of the whites who had begun to think of them as a race predestined for extinction.

In the inland districts, however, the situation was different. In parts of New South Wales and Victoria during the gold rushes Aborigines had replaced whites as shepherds and stockmen, and the further north one went, the more important the Aborigines became as cheap rural labor. The Queensland cattle industry came to rely heavily on Aboriginal stockmen who received rations or a mere pittance to the wages that would have been paid to them, had they been white.

Moreover, the warfare between blacks and whites over control of the land and access to women continued until well into the twentieth century in both Queensland and Western Australia. Blacks resisted the incoming whites in both colonies, and the result was a series of murders and massacres conducted by the settlers until the back of native resistance was broken. Early pioneers like the Jardines in northern Australia are reputed to have killed hundreds of Aborigines in establishing their stations. Once the men had been disposed of, the station owners and their employees took black women whenever they wanted them, precipitating a repetitive spiral of violence beginning with Aboriginal reprisals that were followed by a further round of murders.[4]

Aboriginal men and women were routinely kidnapped to work in the pearling industry in Western Australia, where attempts to escape resulted in floggings and branding to identify troublemakers. The unwillingness of traditional hunter-gatherers to work for the whites "proved" beyond doubt that Aborigines were lazy, incapable of improvement, and destined to die out as the inevitable result of contact between a superior civilization and a primitive race of nomads.

THE CHINESE

The alleged superiority of the Australian variant of British civilization was also expressed at the expense of the Chinese who came in large numbers to Australia during the gold rush years. By the middle of 1854 there were just over 4,000 Chinese diggers on the goldfields of Australia, most of them in Victoria. The trickle of Chinese grew into a torrent. In 1855 the Victorian legislature passed an act imposing a poll tax of £10 ($20) per head on every Chinese immigrant landed. Shipowners, however, soon discovered that they could avoid this imposition simply by landing their Chinese passengers at Robe in South Australia, from whence they could travel overland into Victoria and avoid the new tax. By 1857 there were 23,623 Chinese on the Victorian goldfields and a growing sentiment throughout the colony that something would have to be done. At Buckland River in July of that year, miners attacked the Chinese and drove them from the diggings, becoming in the process thieves and ruffians as they stole Chinese possessions and maltreated Chinese miners.

Discontent and rationalization now focused on the habits of the Chinese. The trappings and language of racial prejudice became increasingly common as opponents of Chinese immigration appealed to the emotions of their fellow colonists. The Chinese were said to be immoral because they came without women and therefore engaged in unnatural vice or else attempted to debauch white women. Furthermore, they were heathens who indulged in strange religious rites in their joss houses (Chinese temple or shrine) and even smoked opium, habits that had no place in a British colony. And finally, they sent their gold out of the colony back to China and purchased only the necessities of life and so contributed little to the colonial economy.

Pressure from Victoria finally led South Australia to impose a poll tax of £10 ($20) on all Chinese arriving in the colony, to permit only one Chinese immigrant for every ten tons burden on ships from Chinese ports, and to enforce a ratio of one Chinese passenger to every six European immigrants. This had the desired effect, and within a few months the port of Robe had become almost deserted. In New South Wales, miners and urban working men sent petition after petition to an unresponsive legislature requesting a curb on the flood of Chinese. Here, a major cause of the animus appears to have been economic, and many such petitions came from inner-city areas where there were few Chinese residents. It is noteworthy, that the language of the petitions became increasingly prejudiced and hysterical as proximity to large goldfields' communities of Chinese increased.

Eventually, the pot boiled over in New South Wales on the Lambing Flat goldfield in 1861, when over a thousand miners marched into the Chinese encampment behind a brass band and drove the Chinese out. They blamed the current insolvent condition of most alluvial miners on the fact that Chinese diggers swarmed like locusts and beat them to the prizes. The Chinese tents were burned and all their possessions stolen, though no Chinese lost their lives as a result of the violence. The government responded after the event by sending soldiers to the field to restore order, but when some of the diggers' leaders were brought to trial, juries consistently refused to find them guilty. Anti-Chinese sentiment was a widely shared phenomenon wherever itinerant miners traveled, and they traveled the length and breadth of the country.

By 1877 on the Palmer River goldfield in Queensland the same problem emerged once again, and here, as in the other colonies, it was the fear that European miners would be swamped under a sea of Chinese diggers that seemed to activate the hatred. At Palmer River there were 18,000 Chinese gold seekers and only 1,500 Europeans. To make matters worse, the Chinese encampment dissolved into communal conflict with more than fifty deaths involving pick handles, meat cleavers, axes, and shovels. Bloody fighting continued for about four days until the native police force intervened and disarmed the combatants. When they returned to their tents, the Chinese discovered that in their absence the Europeans had robbed them of all the gold they had won. No whites were ever charged with the theft of Chinese gold at Palmer River, and the concept of the fair go manifestly did not apply to peoples like the Chinese or Aborigines. Whether it applied to whites of a different gender was also questionable.

COLONIAL WOMEN

Women in nineteenth-century Australia were in many ways second-class citizens. The early years of settlement, with the great preponderance of males among the convicts and emancipists, had produced a society in which masculine values dominated. Power was exercised by men, and women were reduced to the level of moral influence and regeneration of their menfolk. Where equality between the sexes did exist, it was the equality of hardship on the smallholdings of the selectors. But in the eyes of the law of the various colonies, women were not equal to men. They could not vote or stand for Parliament; once married they could not possess property in their own right, but all they owned passed into the control of their husbands; they were discriminated against in the divorce courts where men could obtain a divorce far more easily than could women. In New South Wales, divorced women were not entitled to a license to sell intoxicating liquors, and females were not permitted to enter the professions or obtain university degrees until almost the end of the nineteenth century.

Work opportunities and consequent social mobility were less available to women, and their chances of employment were extremely limited. In polite circles, being a domestic companion and teaching or governessing were the only occupations open to females who did not want to risk losing their respectability. More menial possibilities included becoming maids and cooks, washerwomen, bar maids, sales assistants, dressmakers, nurses, waitresses, and of course prostitutes. There was a chronic shortage of domestic servants in the houses of the well-to-do during the second half of the nineteenth century caused by the preference of the native-born girls for the independence of factory employment despite its low wages in preference to the higher pay available to domestics working for the rich.

In the factories and in tailoring outwork, women received substantially less money than the men. For example, a male tailor earned 14s. ($1.40) for making a coat; a female making an identical coat earned 2s. (.20). Women generally received only a quarter of what men earned in the tailoring trade, although they made identical articles. The combination of low wages, long hours, and poor conditions in the sweatshops of Melbourne sparked the tailoresses' strike of 1883, which led to improved conditions and the growth of militant unionism among the women factory workers. Nevertheless, as the lives of female labor leaders like Louisa Lawson and Emma Miller make plain, women ran into a great deal of prejudice from the trade union movement, which tended to view working women in much the same way as it regarded Chinese workers—as threats to the jobs and living standards of men. It was to take nearly another century of struggle before the principle of equal pay for equal work was established as a right of all workers in the 1970s.

Women were also heavily involved in politics via the suffrage movement and the Women's Christian Temperance unions wherein they fought to obtain the vote and to affect legislation on a wide range of social issues, particularly temperance. Prominent members of these campaigns included Rose Scott and Louisa Lawson in New South Wales, Emma Miller in Queensland, Vida Goldstein in Victoria, and Catherine Spence in South Australia. Louisa Lawson founded a journal, the *Dawn*, in order to concentrate on women's issues. Despite all the agitation such activist women were capable of, however, the constitutional crises of this period were not about women's role in colonial society but were concerned with reducing the powers of the colonial upper houses.

CONSTITUTIONAL CRISES

The power of Legislative Councils to obstruct governments flared up on a number of occasions during the second half of the nineteenth century, especially in relation to free selection and tariffs. In 1877, another conflict between the two houses of the Victorian legislature broke out over the issue of payment for members of Parliament. The upper house opposed the whole idea of wages for service in Parliament, as it would encourage "ruffians"—it meant workers and unionists—and lower the tone of proceedings. Premier Graham Berry attached the measure to the budget bill, whereupon the Legislative Council refused to pass an appropriation bill with additional extraneous political proposals grafted onto it. Payment for members of Parliament eventually occurred in all colonies, but the power of Legislative Councils to hamstring policy implementation by popular governments remained a political problem in most parts of Australia until well into the twentieth century.

COLONISTS IN ARMS: THE SUDAN

One constant feature of nineteenth-century Australia was that colonists declined to take up arms to assert their political rights. At no time did a resort to force appear likely. Politics and politicians did not engage the emotions of colonists at that visceral level. But should Great Britain, the empire of which Australia formed such a small part, come under attack, colonists would then enlist to fight in a conflict thousands of kilometers away and of no relevance to them whatsoever.

Since 1883, British forces had been fighting in the Sudan against the followers of the Islamic leader known as the Mahdi. When Australians learned of the death of General Gordon in Khartoum at the hands of the Mahdi's supporters in February 1885, it caused an outbreak of imperial patriotism and indignant calls for revenge. New South Wales offered a contingent of troops to a surprised British government, which gratefully accepted. On 3 March, a public holiday was proclaimed in New South Wales to enable people to farewell the troops as they marched through Sydney and embarked for the Sudan. The New South Wales contingent consisted of 532 infantry, a battery of artillery numbering 250, and an ambulance group of 36. Two hundred horses also embarked with the force. Some recruits came from the New South Wales volunteer militia regiments, some from the police force, and some were colonists who had served in the British army. About half of the group were native-born Australians. Thousands of people lined the route of the march and gave the soldiers a riotously patriotic send-off. Victorian Premier James Service assured England that as long as Victoria possessed a man, a shop, or a shilling, the mother country would never lack assistance.[5]

THE STRENGTH OF BRITISH TIES

Britain enjoyed considerable support from Australians in the nineteenth and early twentieth centuries. Colonists saw no conflict in being both Australian and British simultaneously. They could attack imperial functionaries for being obstructive and unhelpful in times of constitutional crisis. They could deplore the lack of activity shown by British officials in supporting colonial attempts to annex territories to the British empire in the antipodes, and the lower levels of colonial Australia—especially those of Irish background—could delight in pricking and pillorying the pomposity of the English and their insufferable condescension toward things colonial. But these were superficialities and cannot be allowed to obscure the basic reality that Australians were inordinately proud of their British origins; that idolatry toward Queen Victoria and other British royals was embarrassingly profuse throughout all levels of colonial society; and that republicanism and the desire to make Australia free of all ties to England and the crown were persistently rejected by the majority of the colonial populace. The anti-British republicanism of the Reverend John Dunmore Lang and the nationalistic republicanism of the *Bulletin* late in the nineteenth century represented only a tiny segment of colonial sentiment.

Nor did the pride of the native-born in being Australian involve any thought of the development of a new ethnic group that had become distinct from the original English and Irish stock. Colonists seemed more than capable of identifying with the countries from which their parents came in preference to the country of their birth. For example, William Charles Wentworth retired to live out his final days in England; and Ned Kelly gloried in the fact that he was an Irishman and swore to raise the green flag of Ireland in Australia once he had swept the police and troopers out of his path. Both men were Australian born, yet their loyalties were to the wider Anglo-Saxon or Celtic cultures from which their forebears came. There appeared to be no conflict in colonists proclaiming themselves to be patriots to their own local Australian territory and nationalists enjoying their place in the widespread British empire. At the dinner for the Federation Conference in Melbourne in 1890, Henry Parkes used the phrase "the crimson thread of kinship" to describe the ambivalences embodied in a people who prided themselves on being Australian Britons and perceived no contradictions in such an assertion.

In cultural terms, however, there was a growing movement of artists, writers, and musicians away from a rigid adherence to European forms and appearances and toward an acceptance that Australia was so different from the parent culture that it demanded a new artistic expression of its own. The Heidelberg group of impressionist artists became the first to give tangible form to native-born sentiment that Australian landscapes were noble and breathtaking and that they were worthy of depiction in their own right without the filter of European romanticism that had hitherto corrupted the work of most artists in the colonies. Previously, where a romantic gloss had been eschewed, most colonial artists had followed the tradition of the illustrators who accompanied the scientific voyages of Cook and others and had recorded anglicized depictions of colonial life and landscapes for an English audience. The Heidelberg group was led by Tom Roberts and included Frederick McCubbin, Arthur Streeton, and Charles Conder. They established bush camps in the countryside around Melbourne after Roberts returned to Australia in 1885, one of which was at Heidelberg, where they painted landscapes as they appeared to the artists and according to the light that encompassed them. They abandoned the romantic filter of seeing the bush through European eyes and instead portrayed the unique light, color, and untidiness of the Australian bush and scenes of rural life.

Native-born writing also took on a somewhat nationalist hue in the final decades of the nineteenth century when the magazine the *Bulletin* was founded in 1880 and produced its own stable of writers who reflected an increasing national awareness and wrote about Australia for an audience of native-born Australians. Poetry and prose found a place in the new magazine, and it quickly became known as the "bushman's bible" as much for the aggressive Australian tone of its writing as for its concentration on rural issues. Writers in the magazine included well-known nationalists like Henry Lawson, A.B. "Banjo" Patterson, Joseph Furphy, Victor Daley, Miles Franklin, and Shaw Neilson. The *Bulletin* took a republican political stance and cautioned against too enthusiastic a support for British causes. Australian self-interest was not necessarily identical with British advantage, and the *Bulletin* sounded a warning note of caution to those in the majority like Henry Parkes who espoused the "crimson thread of kinship."

Such overt racial pride in being part of an empire on which the sun never set did not imply that colonists applauded everything that Britain did or failed to do. There were times when Britain's failure to act infuriated colonists, especially when dilatory behavior by the mother country was believed to compromise Australian security. In 1883, the government of Queensland preemptively annexed New Guinea on behalf of the British empire in response to German interest in the area. Unfortunately Sir Thomas McIlwraith, the Queensland premier, had not obtained British permission, and the annexation was repudiated by Britain. When Germany then colonized northeast New Guinea the following year, Australia found itself with a powerful European imperial rival as a near neighbor. Colonists were nervous that Britain showed such evident unwillingness to confront Germany on an issue of colonial security, and these feelings became even more pronounced over a similar reluctance to confront France concerning French attempts to colonize the New Hebrides. When the French landed 400 marines on the New Hebrides and Britain did not regard the issue as worth a war, colonial governments were reminded of their powerlessness and inability to affect British policy.

EDUCATION, RELIGION, AND THE IRISH

Reliance upon Britain for the defense of the continent did not unduly concern most Australians, but there was a group within colonial society that felt less enamored of their status as Britons, and that exception was the Irish and in particular the Irish Roman Catholics. In matters of religion and education, Roman Catholics of Irish background were highly suspicious of the Anglican and Presbyterian churches. Since the time of Governor Richard Bourke, the education system had persisted as a hybrid whereby colonial governments made grants to all religious denominations in support of their schools. This proved to be both expensive and inefficient, and a time had to come when some form of rationalization became essential. That time arrived during the 1870s and the 1880s.

In 1879, the need for a secular system of education had become overwhelming, and the government of New South Wales cut financial assistance to religious schools altogether. It was a process mirrored in all the Australian colonies and roused considerable sectarian bitterness whenever the topics of religion or education came up for discussion. The non-Catholic denominations reluctantly acquiesced in the new scheme, but the Roman Catholics, under the leadership of Archbishop John Bede Polding, decided to follow their own path. Polding regarded an entirely secular system of education as a surefire method of eradicating Christianity altogether and likened it to the administration of poison in small doses over a prolonged period sufficient to prove fatal. He stoked sectarian fires when he announced that Roman Catholics could not in good conscience make use of the education system financed and administered by the state and called on them to build their own schools, train and equip their own teachers, and prescribe their own textbooks.

The ideal of a free nondenominational education system had been that it would unite the colonists by providing equal access to a basic education for all children irrespective of religion or location. It was part of the fair go ethos that all children should be treated equally, but the effect of the legislation was paradoxically the opposite. Many Roman Catholics retreated into an educational and religious ghetto that separated them from the general life of the community. Roman Catholic schools were staffed with unqualified nuns, brothers, and priests from Ireland who taught huge classes without payment and who inculcated all the prejudices and divisions of the old world in their pupils. Irish separatism had existed in the Australian colonies since the time of the first Irish convicts and was aggravated in 1867 by community outrage when a deranged Irish migrant attempted to assassinate the touring duke of Edinburgh at Clontarf in Sydney; but the educational division gave it a structural substance and a new lease on life that carried it well into the twentieth century.[6]

AN URBANIZED COUNTRY

Urbanization marks the very origins of European occupation of Australia, which began with the formation of the town of Sydney. It was a process that continued throughout the nineteenth century, so that by the 1890s almost two-thirds of the population of Australia already lived in cities and towns, and the proportion of urban dwellers was constantly increasing.[7] The use of towns as administrative centers and ports meant that they inevitably became the centers of commercial life as well. The later development of road, rail, and telegraph links only strengthened this early trend, as did the preferences of countless immigrants who came from urban environments in the old world and sought them out in Australia. Service industries and manufacturing came behind this population growth and took advantage of it. A multiplier effect operated here, as industries developed to cater to the needs of this large and expanding population, and they in turn attracted more expansion and a further inflow of investment capital.

PROTECTION

Manufacturing industries developed in both New South Wales and Victoria at about an equal rate during the years before 1890, even though New South Wales had nominally embraced free trade, whereas Victoria had gone in for tariff protection for its infant industries. New South Wales justified its tariffs by claiming that they were not designed to protect local industries but to raise revenue for the government. A revenue tariff was acceptable to the free trade ideology, while a protective tariff was not. In fact, no colonial government was about to risk causing widespread unemployment in its cities by allowing local industry to compete openly with mass-produced goods from Britain, and the levels of tariff protection were not very different in either colony. Local governments also tried to ensure that at least some contracts were granted to Australian manufacturers when railway construction or other large infrastructure projects were undertaken; and on the private market, industrial goods and machinery like ploughs, harvesters, and threshing machines, which were made to local designs and suited to Australian conditions, were usually preferred by most colonists.

HOUSING THE POPULATION

One of the major growth areas after the gold rushes was the housing industry. Melbourne set the pace and became the fastest-growing city in Australia. It earned the soubriquet of "Marvellous Melbourne" during the 1870s and 1880s, when a housing and land boom caused it to become Australia's foremost city.

In both Melbourne and Sydney the population grew in spectacular fashion, as unsuccessful gold diggers flooded back from the goldfields and a rising tide of immigration ensured a continuous supply of people in need of housing. This was in addition to a high rate of natural increase stimulated by a tendency to early marriage common to new settlers and the native-born. But Melbourne proved to be the phenomenon of the age, increasing its population between 1881 and 1891 by just under 100 percent to 497,000. They had to be housed somewhere, and the building industry boomed. By the end of that decade, nearly half of the city's houses were less than ten years old. Sydney developed in similar fashion, and by 1891, its population stood at 383,333. In both cities new suburbs developed in tandem with the spread of rail and tramway systems.

The cost of this building program was enormous and funded largely, though indirectly, from overseas borrowings. British investors poured money into railway construction, banks, and pastoral companies. Some small British investors, attracted by high interest rates, placed their savings with the English branches of Victorian Land Banks and Building Societies. In Australia, colonists also ploughed their savings into the Land Banks and Building Societies, but the vast bulk of the money to fuel the boom came from the continued inflow of capital from Britain. Most of this investment went into suburban development, land speculation, and public works. Comparatively little was invested in productive industries or new production. Land values soared in Melbourne during the 1880s, as they did also to a lesser extent in Sydney, but in Melbourne some allotments increased in value from five to twenty times over in the space of just a few years. One writer has summed up the situation and the tenuous connection it had with reality in the words: "The big speculators were selling to the medium speculators, the medium speculators were selling to the small speculators, and madness was in the air."[8] This dangerous exposure was exacerbated by the extent to which bribery and corruption had become common among the officials and politicians who were supposed to be supervising the situation but who consistently turned a blind eye to flagrant breaches of the law. For many Melbournians at this time, the old hope of making a quick killing on the goldfields had been replaced by the new hope of making a quick killing on the real estate market.

SILVERADO

The focus of the speculative hysteria was not restricted to Victoria, and a second mineral provided the impulse for a further period of financial effervescence in New South Wales. A foretaste of what was to come occurred in 1882–1883, when rich deposits of silver were discovered at Silverton. Thousands of miners flooded in and smelters were built before the find petered out in 1885. That same year a syndicate of seven men was formed to develop a promising show of silver on George McCullough's station. The shares started at a nominal amount of £19 each ($38), and when rich silver in soft clay was uncovered, the share value soared to £409 each ($818) by February 1888. New smelters were built, miners flocked to the area, and the Broken Hill Proprietary Company hit the big time. By 1891, the town of Broken Hill had become the third largest city in the colony, with a population of 20,000 and rising. Speculation in mining shares matched the speculation in Melbourne real estate for its failure to provide any reality check for its participants, and men seemed prepared to gamble on any piece of share scrip as fly-by-night operators and bogus companies made the most of the public mania for gambling and the desire to become rich without working. This boom was also founded on false expectations, for the price of lead and silver declined continuously during these years, and by 1894 silver brought just a little over half the return it had earned ten years earlier.

REGIONALISM: A STUMBLING BLOCK FOR FEDERATION

By 1891, the native-born percentage in the total population of Australia had risen to just under three-quarters, and a new generation was coming into its own. This did not mean, however, that a widespread national sentiment also existed. Although locals rejoiced in the defeat of English cricket teams and individual sportsmen by native-born competitors, it did not presage the emergence of any sort of continental patriotism or sense of identity. In fact, colonial particularism, or regional loyalty, was to prove a major stumbling block in the next decade to attempts by Australian nationalists to federate the colonies into a single Australian nation. This intense regional rivalry is best illustrated by the folly of different railway gauges in the various colonies. Instead of all using the same gauge, which would have facilitated trade and communications, Queensland adopted one gauge; Victoria chose another; South Australia experimented with several gauge sizes; and they all did this so as not to be seen falling into line with the mother colony of New South Wales, which had a gauge size different from all of them. Nor were the rivalries between the colonies restricted to practical things like the size of the railway gauges. Melbourne resented Sydney's claim to greater wisdom and experience, and Melbournians smoldered with anger when they were patronized by the press and politicians of Sydney. South Australians regarded all other Australian colonies as possessing undesirable bloodlines because of their association with convictism, while Tasmanians struggled to throw off the shadow of Van Diemen's Land. Western Australia stood finally on the threshold of Responsible Government, having at last been able to pay its way. The years of isolation and stagnation in the west had produced an inward-looking population quite distrustful of the aims and ambitions of the other Australian colonies and determined to go its own way, whatever the other colonies did. In Queensland, the sugar plantations, with their thousands of Kanaka laborers, brought the charge of slavery from Britain and from the other colonies, a stigma destined to prove a major bone of contention when federation became a subject for serious debate.

One thing the colonies did share was fear. They feared German and French activities in the region and their obvious inability to defend themselves or to affect the decisions of the great powers in Europe regarding the regional balance of power. They feared being swamped under an avalanche of Asian immigrants if restrictive immigration legislation was ever removed. They had become totally reliant on importing capital from Britain to fuel the boom of the second half of the nineteenth century; and as indications began to appear that the source of the capital was about to dry up, they feared the day of retribution when the entire edifice of Marvellous Melbourne and the lesser speculative booms in the other colonies would come to an end, and ruin and bankruptcy would stare them in the face. How would Australian workers, who had become used to a higher standard of living than almost anywhere else in the world, react to the ending of the long boom? Was Australia on the eve of one of those great confrontations between capital and labor that periodically convulsed the old world, or would the concept of the fair go be sufficient for colonists to muddle through by relying on sensible men to avoid conflict and work their way to a compromise? Was a time dawning when the traditional refusal of Australians to take up arms in pursuit of domestic political or economic aims might be subject to revision?

6

The Bubble Bursts and the Road to Federation (1891–1900)

As Australia entered the 1890s, the economies of the various colonies were characterized by dangerous structural weaknesses, and the roots of the coming collapse can clearly be seen in the years of the long boom. Capital had appeared to be unlimited, and massive indebtedness resulted as colonial governments and private individuals borrowed heavily. Long-term infrastructure projects did not produce short-term returns; nevertheless, much of the money that underwrote these projects came from the short-term money market and from overseas and local investors who wanted quick returns. The flood of capital into the colonies concealed these structural weaknesses for a time, enabling private and governmental borrowers to meet their interest payments on past loans from current borrowings, but the economies of Victoria and New South Wales were in a dangerous state of imbalance. A combination of international and local events between 1890 and 1893 ensured that the inevitable readjustment would be an extremely painful one.

THE DECLINE OF THE ECONOMY

During the 1880s, the terms of international trade moved inexorably against the Australian colonies. The decade marked a period of slow but steady decline in the price of wool on overseas markets. Pastoralists, who were heavily in debt and needed to maintain their incomes to meet interest payments, responded to the situation by increasing the size of their flocks and raising the level of production. This flooded an already glutted market with more wool and accelerated the fall in prices. Australian wool producers had temporarily outstripped world demand for their product, and excess production could no longer readily be absorbed. Silver prices suffered a similar decline throughout the decade, and the price of wheat also tumbled.

The deterioration in the terms of trade resulted in a contraction of credit and investment finance. An unexpected collapse of the Premier Building Society of Victoria in 1898, followed by a slump in the Argentine and the collapse of Baring's investment house in 1890 frightened British investors; and the loans that hitherto had been floated so regularly by Australian colonial governments in London failed. British investors had grown wary of the continued borrowing of the Australian colonies. As the unease grew, smaller investors began to withdraw their money from the London offices of Australian banks, land banks, and building societies.

By the early 1890s, there were already about £275 million ($550 million) worth of overseas investment in Australia. The interest payments on these loans were met by additional loans as government revenues were insufficient and export prices declining. When the loans stopped, the public works projects also ceased, producing serious unemployment in the cities and towns. In the rural districts, pastoralists and farmers had already begun a retrenchment policy as their export earnings dried up, and they battled the continuing influence of El Niño through a period of prolonged drought. As if this was not enough, a plague of rabbits converted many previously viable properties into dust bowls of sand and erosion. The trend toward growing unemployment affected both town and country.

It was not long before the shaky foundations of the 1880s financial institutions were exposed for all to see. Corrupt government officials and financial regulators had turned a blind eye to infractions of the legislation that was designed to protect society from the effects of financial mismanagement. The banks and building societies had effectively escaped regulation in the era of economic free-for-all, and many of the financial institutions were dangerously exposed with a very low level of immediate capital in relation to the total amount of deposits they had accepted. They freely loaned money for land purchases during the boom years when land values rose continuously. They had never envisaged a situation occurring in which the assets they held in land titles would be valueless due to tumbling prices and a lack of purchasers. They had behaved as though the boom would never end. When it did come to a crisis, they were unable to liquidate enough of their assets to cover the significant proportion of their depositors who lined up to remove their money while they still could.

As rising unemployment began to bite, more and more small investors found themselves forced to withdraw their savings in order to live. Others, fearing that the institutions were unstable, also began to withdraw their money, and a run on the banks and societies developed to the point that they began to default, unable to meet their depositors' demands and unable to realize the assets in which their capital was tied up. The first collapses triggered a chain reaction and provoked a run on those banks and societies still operating. As they collapsed in their turn, a panic broke out among depositors who saw their life's savings disappearing without trace. The casualty rate among institutions and depositors proved to be high.

COLLAPSE OF THE BANKS

On 3 August 1891, the doors of the Bank of Van Diemen's Land in Hobart remained closed. In Melbourne during 1891–1892, twenty-one building societies, banks, and loan companies failed, and in Sydney a further twenty suffered the same fate. In March 1892, the large Mercantile Bank of Victoria collapsed, to be followed the next year by the Federal Bank. A further eleven banks closed their doors, and their depositors lost most, if not all, of their money. The Bank of South Australia saved itself by merging with the Union Bank, but the Bank of Van Diemen's Land proved to be beyond resuscitation. Many of these institutions ended by paying their depositors only a fraction of their original savings, and thousands of individuals and businesses were bankrupted. In Victoria, where the problem was most acute, the law permitted bankrupts to make secret accommodations with their creditors—there were seventy-eight of these agreements made in 1892 alone—and for amounts in excess of £5 million ($10 million). Nobody could tell which businesses or individuals were sound and which were on the point of collapse. The upshot of such a lack of transparency was that rumors and gossip weakened confidence still further.

The colonial governments reacted to the crisis in different ways. In New South Wales, budgets had been extensively underwritten by the revenue stream flowing from the sale of crown lands, but that major source of income temporarily dried up. The Dibbs government rushed emergency legislation through the legislature in the form of the Bank Issue Act, which empowered the government to declare bank notes legal tender for one year. This halted the damaging and destabilizing run on the banks where customers were demanding that the banks' notes be replaced with gold coinage. Some of the banks that had gone to the wall had been banks of issue, that is, they had printed their own bank notes, and the firm action taken by the Dibbs ministry reassured colonists of the soundness of the bank notes, and the developing run on the banks soon halted. In Victoria, on the other hand, the Patterson government's policy only exacerbated the crisis. As an emergency measure following the collapse of the federal and the commercial banks, the government sought a cooling-off period and proclaimed a five-day bank holiday. Far from dampening down the crisis, this action cast doubt on the viability of the entire banking system in the colony and precipitated a panic and a further run of collapses.

By 1893 most of the banks were back in business, though substantially restructured. The favored method of reconstruction involved the compulsory conversion of a proportion of each deposit into shares in the bank, with the balance of the deposit to be available for withdrawal after five years. The moratorium on withdrawals gave the banks time to rationalize and realize their holdings of land and other assets, though it was no help at all to the thousands of small depositors who needed their money for survival. In order to help such people, both the New South Wales and Queensland governments passed legislation authorizing the colonial treasuries to advance up to half the value of their frozen deposits to them.

TRADE AND INDUSTRY FALTER

The whole fabric of society lay in ruins during these years, and the slump in the terms of international trade continued, ensuring that primary industry remained at a low ebb and the building trades with all their associated industries such as quarries, brickyards, and timber yards persisted in the doldrums. Factories continued to close, and unemployment to rise. Industrial action by trade unionists to protect their livelihoods only made matters worse. Eventual recovery may well have been certain, but this was no consolation to the thousands of unemployed who suffered severely during the depression. Even skilled tradesmen, especially those in the building industry, experienced high levels of unemployment, and the level for unskilled workers was even higher. Conditions were desperate because colonial governments hopelessly short of funds refused pleas from the unemployed for a public works program to create jobs and begin the recovery. In an era of laissez-faire, the colonial governments refused to accept responsibility for looking after the unemployed and their families. Once the wage earners' savings had been spent or frozen, the only recourse was to private charity and the soup kitchens and refuges run by the religious organizations and the benevolent societies.

GOLD IN WESTERN AUSTRALIA

To men in such grim conditions, the discovery of vast alluvial and reef-based gold deposits in Western Australia proved a godsend. As the depression in the eastern colonies deepened, many men eked out a precarious existence searching for gold on the old goldfields of the 1850s or traveled to the Kimberley goldfield—newly proclaimed in 1886—in the far north of Western Australia. But in 1892, two prospectors, Arthur Bayley from Queensland and William Ford from Victoria, discovered what was to become the Coolgardie goldfield. They found alluvial gold and surface reef gold in abundance: Nuggets were lying on the surface of the earth, waiting to be picked up, and the reefs were so rich that a man could collect hundreds of ounces in a single afternoon. The following year, another prospector named Paddy Hannan and his partner discovered the vast Kalgoorlie field, and further discoveries came thick and fast. Many unemployed men from the other colonies flocked to the diggings in Western Australia and sent substantial sums of money back to their families and dependents. They joined thousands more from all around the globe, drawn to the lure of the last big gold rush of the nineteenth century. Gold production went from £226,000 ($452,000) in 1892 to £787,000 ($1,574,000) in 1894; and by the end of the decade, annual gold production in Western Australia had passed the £6. million ($12. million) mark.

Conditions in the difficult waterless region were tough, but most prospectors could make a living, and some could strike a fortune. Later on in the decade, when the alluvial gold had been largely worked out, mining companies set up on the fields and provided secure and well-paid jobs for men willing to undertake the hazards and discomfort of deep-lode mining or of work in the huge crushing plants. The population of Western Australia doubled and then doubled again during the 1890s, and the desert goldfields boomed. Coolgardie had two stock exchanges, twenty-five registered stockbrokers, twenty-six hotels, three breweries, four clubs including a Japanese Club, and three daily newspapers plus another four weekly papers. Kalgoorlie, Southern Cross, and Boulder also competed with Coolgardie for the title of premier goldfield town, and overseas investment poured in, in ever-increasing torrents into Western Australia at a time when the other Australian colonies found it impossible to raise money in London. In addition to importing people, Western Australia also increased by 700 percent its imports of food and machinery from the other colonies and thereby helped their industries to trade their way out of the depression. It was a rather grim irony that the newest self-governing colony in Australia should experience an unprecedented and utterly unexpected boom at a time when the older colonies found it difficult merely to survive.

TRADE UNIONISM

As if the economic and commercial crisis was not bad enough, conditions in the eastern Australian colonies were rendered immeasurably worse by a major industrial upheaval as the decade began. Trade unions had existed in Australia since 1840, when the Australian Society of Compositors was founded in Sydney, but the early unions tended to be combinations of skilled craftsmen who were as much interested in keeping unskilled labor from poaching their jobs as in improving working conditions and obtaining shorter hours. These small unions were largely friendly societies that concentrated on aiding indigent members and the widows and families of members who had died. There were a number of strikes in favor of higher wages and the eight-hour day, and some headway had been made in achieving these aims during the years of the long boom. By 1860, a Trades Hall Council was formed in Melbourne, and the Sydney Trades and Labour Council was established in 1871. The first intercolonial trade union congress met in Sydney in 1879. The years of prosperity encouraged the extension of the union movement into the ranks of the semiskilled and unskilled workers in mining and the bush. The bush unions came last and were the hardest to organize, but the job was tackled successfully by William Lane and W.G. Spence during the 1880s.

The prosperity of the long boom had engendered a false sense of security in the trade unions. Many members felt that there was no essential conflict between the aims of capital and the aspirations of labor and that both could work cooperatively to produce favorable outcomes for workers and capitalists together. Employers, anxious not to jeopardize high profits, would often cave in to union demands for wage increases and improvements in conditions. Prosperity masked the basic differences of position and produced a veneer of cooperative harmony, but it could not last. Union successes during the boom years led them to believe that organization and solidarity would always be sufficient to win them the gains they desired. Between 1890 and 1894 a series of major strikes occurred during which the blinders fell from their eyes as they all ended in disaster for the unions.

THE GREAT STRIKES

The outbreak began with a seemingly insignificant dispute between shipowners and the Maritime Officers' Association. The employers had refused to negotiate with the small union of marine officers, and in desperation, it sought affiliation with the Trades Hall Council. Shipowners were horrified that professional men would throw in their lot with the workers. They believed that such a thing would subvert all discipline at sea. The officers walked off their ships in every Australian port, and within a few days the strike had spread to include wharf laborers, seamen, stewards, and cooks. The miners and shearers quickly came out in sympathy, and the scene was set for a very bruising confrontation.

The economic collapse had already produced a growing pool of unemployed and desperate workers, so a successful outcome of what was close to being a national strike seemed unlikely. Pastoralists were able to obtain nonunion shearers and to transport their wool to the wharves, where shipowners and their supporters loaded it onto ships under the protection of armed special constables. At Circular Quay in Sydney, the riot act was read, and in Melbourne, troops of the Victorian Mounted Rifles received a warning from their commanding officer Lieutenant Colonel Tom Price that if necessary he would order them to fire directly into the crowds of demonstrating strikers, and in such an event he wanted his troops to "fire low and lay them out."[1] Public opinion was clearly divided on the issue. Victorian Chief Justice George Higginbotham and Queensland Chief Justice Sir Charles Lilley both agreed that the strikers had a strong case. In New South Wales, Roman Catholic Cardinal Moran also supported the strikers, but in Western Australia, a year or so later, Roman Catholic Archbishop Clune took the side of the employers, whereas his Anglican opposite number supported the workers. By and large, the governments of all the colonies opposed the strikers and used police and troops against them. There was no fair go to be found here, and it exploded once and for all the comfortable idea that there was any compatibility between the interests of workers and employers. It would be an experience unionists did not forget.

The strike continued from August to October 1890, until the unions collapsed and the marine officers returned to work on the shipowners' terms. In 1891 the Queensland shearers struck again when the graziers repudiated their agreements with the shearers' union and brought in nonunion labor to break the strike, while the unionist shearers gathered in large camps of armed men near the larger shearing sheds. Armed conflict appeared ominously close. The conflict was articulated around a division of freedoms. The pastoralists demanded freedom of contract, the right to offer employment to whomsoever they liked, on whatever terms they liked. The unions demanded freedom of association, the right of workers to associate together and to bargain collectively. The union was determined to enforce the closed shop where only union members could work in the industry, and the employers were just as determined to break the closed shop by offering employment to nonunionists.

Clashes occurred between strikers and scabs (strikebreakers) who were afforded police protection, and police and troops raided several of the miners' camps. The Queensland government sent over 2,000 troops armed with artillery and machine guns. It dismissed any railway workers who made donations to the strike funds of the shearers' union, and it secured the appointment of judges and magistrates who would use the antiunion laws of early-nineteenth-century Britain against the strikers. Such laws had long since been repealed in Britain but were still enforceable in Australia, because they had never been specifically repealed here. The best-known incident occurred at Barcaldine in Queensland where almost 1,000 armed men had established a camp under the Eureka flag. For a moment it appeared that Australians were about to take up arms for a domestic political cause, but when the Queensland police and troops arrived, the movement collapsed like a pricked balloon. Eighty-two men were jailed on trumped-up charges of conspiracy, intimidation, and riot. Here, as at Eureka earlier in the century, radical and revolutionary rhetoric fell far short of action in an Australian political and social confrontation. In 1894, the shearers went out again, and some unionists set fire to a river steamer named the *Rodney* as it carried scabs up the Darling River. The culprits were never arrested, but a further fifty union leaders were imprisoned in the crackdown that followed. Other unionists were jailed at Broken Hill and during further unsuccessful strikes that took place in the coal mining industry in 1893 and 1896 in New South Wales and Queensland.

By the middle and second half of the 1890s, the combination of unsuccessful strikes, widespread unemployment, the collapse of the financial institutions, the imprisonment of union leaders, and the disappearance of trade unions that could not survive in such difficult circumstances had left the union movement in total disarray. The failure of the great strikes generally worked to the advantage of those within organized labor who recognized that the opportunity for realizing labor's goals lay through politics and not through direct and militant industrial action. It also helped to increase interest among both unionists and liberal politicians in the development of an arbitration system whereby those injurious and bruising confrontations between capital and labor could be managed or avoided altogether. Furthermore, the fact that colonial governments had not hesitated to use military force and the law to repress strikes was not lost on the labor movement. If the state possessed the power to break strikes in such a way, then it was obvious that workers would have to find some means of capturing the state and gaining control over the apparatus of power. The ballot box would provide the road forward for a workers' political movement that had met with such calamitous defeat when it tried direct action.

THE BEGINNINGS OF THE LABOR PARTY

It is important to realize that the idea of a parliamentary labor party did not follow as an effect from the failures of militant trade unionism, though there is no doubt that industrial failure gave the movement toward political representation an urgency and a focus that it had not hitherto possessed. But the movement toward organized political representation can be traced back to 1890, when union leader Robert Harris presented the Trades and Labour Council with a proposal that it establish labor electoral leagues in every electorate and that a structure be prepared for the organization and management of these leagues. The council accepted the proposal, and the following year the leagues came into existence with an annual membership subscription of 2s. (20¢), half of which went to the central body to form an electoral fighting fund.

The development was made all the easier by the acceptance of the New South Wales legislature in 1889 of an act introducing the payment of members of Parliament. A salary made it possible for any member of the labor movement to run for office. Hitherto, there had been individuals whose trade unions had paid their salaries while they were members of the Legislative Assembly, but such arrangements were individualistic and ad hoc. Certainly, a political party could not be organized on such a basis, particularly one that would be so narrowly sectional as would the new Labor Party. On the other hand, however, there had been payment of Members of Parliament (MPs) in Victoria since the 1870s, and a Labor Party had not emerged there. The experiences of the 1890s can be seen as an important stimulus to the formation of a new political movement, but as an accelerator rather than as a generator of its formation.

After 1894, the new Labor Party held the balance of power between free traders and protectionists in New South Wales and maintained the free traders in office in return for concessions and the partial implementation of Labor policies. Similar developments took place in the other colonies, and Labor appeared in the Victorian legislature from 1892 onward, where it supported the liberal protectionists. In Queensland the first Labor men appeared in 1891, and the party became the largest opposition grouping with sixteen members in 1893. In 1899 the first Labor government anywhere in the world held office in Queensland under Anderson Dawson for a single week before losing a confidence vote to its combined liberal and conservative opponents. In South Australia, political Labor appeared in 1891 and supported the Liberals, and in Western Australia and Tasmania, the first Labor members were not elected until the early years of the twentieth century.

ACHIEVEMENT AND REFORM

Labor's achievements of reform in return for concessions proved impressive. Plural voting was one of the first targets and was abolished in New South Wales in 1898 and soon after in all the other colonies, as were property qualifications for members of the Legislative Assemblies. There were significant advances in social legislation. Between 1894 and 1900 all the mainland colonies legislated for the regulation of factory working conditions, and minimum standards were enacted controlling wages, employment of juveniles, hours of work for women, and the conditions of apprenticeship. Maximum working hours for shop assistants were specified, and in Victoria the Liberal government with Labor support established wages boards empowered to fix minimum wage rates and to ensure that employers passed on to their hands a portion of the financial benefits they enjoyed under tariff protection. By the end of the decade more than twenty industries came under this legislation. New South Wales went further than this in 1901 when it founded an Arbitration Court consisting of a judge, an employers' representative, and an employees' representative, which possessed the power to make awards and settle disputes in resolutions that would have the force of law and be binding on an entire industry.

In the fiscal field, most colonies introduced land and income taxes during this decade, and in 1900 both New South Wales and Victoria brought in old age pensions. The concept of land tax held a natural appeal to Labor, which found the argument that those who owned the land should pay some contribution to offset that made by the worker with his labor inherently attractive. Naturally landowners rejected this view and found *Progress and Poverty* (1879), by Henry George, a San Francisco printer who developed important economic ideas, and the single tax program that sprang up to implement his ideas verging on the revolutionary. Finally, all colonies accepted the necessity of excluding the Chinese and developing a full white Australia policy. Queensland hesitated because of its reliance on Kanakas in the sugar industry, but the other colonies all passed acts prohibiting the immigration of all Asians, Africans, and Polynesians. These enactments violated international agreements and treaties between Britain and China and Japan and insulted the inhabitants of both Asian nations: consequently Britain disallowed them. Eventually a compromise was found in the mechanism developed by the government of Natal in southern Africa whereby an immigrant could be compelled to take a dictation test in any European language. Failure in the test resulted in exclusion without any reference to color or race. It was a mechanism that appealed to the new federal government after 1901.

The Labor parties during these years established a reputation for being pragmatic nondoctrinaire organizations. They were certainly not socialist parties and seemed more than happy to follow a policy of supporting either free traders or protectionists in return for piecemeal social and industrial reforms. They were not out to overthrow existing society but to improve it; they did not aim to confiscate and redistribute wealth but merely to improve the opportunities for their own members to accumulate wealth for themselves. Australian society was to be reformed, not fundamentally restructured.

TOWARD FEDERATION

The late 1890s was more than just an era of small gains and improvements in the aftermath of the depression, and the decision to convert the independent and isolated colonies into a single nation made the decade an indisputable watershed. In retrospect, the case for federation seems to be overwhelming, but contemporaries did not find it so, and it is worth remembering that substantial minorities in all colonies voted against federation in 1898 and 1899 and that if the opposition vote is added to the number of electors who did not bother to cast a vote at all, it could well be argued that federation never enjoyed true majority support.

Basically, there were two cases against federation, the first amounting to an argument for a different type of union, an imperial federation, in which the colonies would become provinces in a Greater Britain and elect members to the Parliament at Westminster; and the second and more popular being in favor of colonial particularism and the status quo. After all, the colonies had been settled at different times and for different reasons and were in dissimilar stages of economic development. The capital cities were thousands of kilometers apart, and until the recent gold rush Western Australia had been as much *terra incognita* for most of the inhabitants of the eastern colonies as was China or Tibet. The smaller colonies feared that in any political association they would be swamped by the more populous colonies of New South Wales and Victoria, while the moral pretentiousness of the South Australians led them to look down upon the inhabitants and suspect bloodlines of the former convict colonies. Added to this was the difficulty of conflicting economic systems and values, with Victoria staunchly protectionist in opposition to New South Wales' enthusiastic embrace of free trade. To top it all off, there had been decades of rancor generated by the rivalry between Victoria and New South Wales, and all the colonies were heavily involved in their own schemes of development and desired to go their own way.

On the other hand, arguments in favor of federation grew stronger as the 1890s progressed. The electric telegraph and the advent of railways had helped to break down the psychological isolation of the various colonies, bringing them to a realization that they shared the continent with sister colonies that were experiencing similar problems. Trade and labor, especially rural labor, tended to move freely about irrespective of colonial boundaries, and the irritations of colonial customs barriers on the Murray River annoyed businessmen and the larger banks that wanted intercolonial commerce to be free of all restrictions. In 1888, the first intercolonial conference of the Chambers of Commerce issued strong demands for uniform legislation in areas like insurance, debt recovery, partnerships, patents, and trademarks. The large trade unions were already national in coverage and operated in all the colonies. Intercolonial union congresses and the shared fear of cheap Kanaka and Asian labor made many trade unionists favor federation, but the labor movement was split on the fiscal question, and many labor men were suspicious of a movement that drew such wide support from their political enemies.

DEFENSE

As the decade of the 1890s unfolded, the twin issues of defense and nonwhite immigration ensured that the topic of federation did not slip entirely off the agenda. Defense became a real issue after Japan's success against China in 1895 and the later Anglo-Japanese Treaty and naval agreements. It was one thing to fear being swamped under a tide of Asian labor, but it was quite another to be confronted by an Asian military power where hitherto the only threat had been discerned from Britain's European rivals. Once again fear was to prove a major stimulus in forcing the pace of Australian political development.

At an intercolonial conference in 1880 on the vexed question of tariffs, Henry Parkes of New South Wales had proposed the establishment of a federal council to deal with matters of common interest to the colonies. Although such an organization did eventually come into existence in 1885 by an Act of the Imperial Parliament, it was virtually a powerless debating society that was unelected and restricted to offering advice. In 1889, Parkes tried again, and in a famous speech at Tenterfield in northern New South Wales, he stressed the burning issue of defense and proclaimed his belief that all the colonial military forces should be combined into one great federal army. It was necessary for the colonies to produce an effective system of federal government to achieve this aim:

The great question which they had to consider was, whether the time had not now come for the creation on this Australian continent of an Australian Government, as distinct from the local Governments now in existence. (Applause.) In other words, to make himself as plain as possible, Australia had now a population of three and a half millions, and the American people numbered only between three and four millions when they formed the great commonwealth of the United States. The numbers were about the same, and surely what the Americans had done by war, the Australians could bring about in peace without breaking the ties that held them to the mother country. (Cheers.) Believing as he did that it was essential to preserve the security and integrity of these colonies that the whole of their forces should be amalgamated into one great federal army, whenever necessary,—feeling this, and seeing no other means of attaining the end, it seemed to him that the time was close at hand when they ought to set about creating this great national government for all Australia.[2]

As a result of Parkes's passionate advocacy, a conference of colonial premiers met in Melbourne in 1890 to discuss the issue, and although nothing was decided on the federation question, it was agreed to hold a national Australasian convention in Sydney the following year to take the matter further and to come up with definite proposals.

PRODUCING A CONSTITUTION

In due course the convention met, and Queensland Attorney General and Premier Sir Samuel Griffith drafted a proposed constitution that was the main work of the convention. Griffith's bill called for the colonies to cede certain specific powers to a new central government, the chief of these being defense. There should be free trade between the colonies, though the question of a national tariff was not raised, leaving the debate over whether the new nation would embrace free trade or protection still to be fought out. The bill also attempted to calm the fears of the smaller colonies by calling for a bicameral legislature with a House of Representatives elected on the basis of population and a Senate in which each colony would be equally represented. Though this draft subsequently was altered extensively at the conventions of 1897–1898, the fact remains that its basic framework did not change, and Griffith is in a very real sense the founding father of Australian federation.

In the meantime the elderly Parkes lost office and faded from the scene, and the leadership of the profederation forces passed to two native-born politicians. In New South Wales Edmund Barton, a protectionist politician and lawyer, became the focal point; and in Victoria, Alfred Deakin, lawyer, former deputy premier, and leader of the protectionist liberals in the Victorian Parliament, emerged as the chief protagonist. Both men shared a consuming vision of a single Australian nation, and both worked tirelessly to realize this vision by addressing public meetings and mobilizing public opinion. In July 1893, interested groups from both colonies met at a private conference in the border town of Corowa, where they passed a resolution that the Parliament of each colony should be requested to pass an enabling act to set up another conference to be composed of elected representatives chosen by the people. This convention would then draw up a constitution that would be put to the people in a referendum. This proposal took the federation issue out of the hands of colonial politicans and involved the people, and the democratic nature of it helped to reconcile labor to the federation movement.

The convention of delegates met for the first time in Adelaide in March

1897. The voters had supported the general direction by sending powerful advocates of federation like Barton, Deakin, and Kingston, the premier of South Australia, all well-known proponents of the cause. They used Griffith's draft bill as the starting point for their deliberations and held additional meetings in Sydney and Melbourne to take further advice from the colonial legislatures. Discussions centered on the role of the Senate and its function of protecting the rights of the smaller states, as the constituent colonies would be known after federation. It was finally agreed that the powers of the Senate would be the same as those of the lower house, except that while it could reject financial measures outright, it had no powers of amendment over such money bills. Governments would be made and unmade in the House of Representatives, but the Senate could not be ignored.

The constitution bill also vested the powers of defense, immigration, external affairs, posts and telegraphs, conciliation and arbitration involving disputes extending beyond a single state, and payment of invalid and old age pensions in the federal government. Powers not specified in the constitution were to remain with the states, and it is clear that the federalists had no intention of centralizing power and administration except in certain limited areas. Unification under a single central government was not at all what they had in mind.

THE REFERENDUMS

The bill was put to referendum in all colonies except Western Australia, which was not interested at this stage, but in New South Wales the premier George Reid insisted that the vote not only had to win, but the majority had to number at least 80,000 votes in total. Reid earned the soubriquet of "Yes-No Reid" during this referendum by advising the voters that while he personally intended to support the bill by voting yes, the people of New South Wales should realize that the bill as it stood did not entirely safeguard their interests. Many labor men actively opposed the referendum and complained that it had so many concessions to the smaller states that it was no longer really democratic. They also believed that they had been excluded from having any real input into the process, and the result was a constitution that favored elites. Other vested interest groups in the colonies opposed federation for their own reasons. Small manufacturers were concerned that they would have to compete with the powerful and well-established industries of Victoria without the protection of a local tariff. They tended to vote no and seem to have persuaded their employees to vote along with them. Similarly with Victorian sugar beet farmers, who knew that they would be unable to compete with Queensland sugar on the open market and voted no in protest.

In the event, colonists obviously recognized that they had more in common with one another than differences from one another. A common language, a common ancestry, and a growing sense of a shared Australian nationality helped to buttress the fears they also shared. Majorities were recorded in favor of federation in the four participating colonies (Queensland and Western Australia did not participate), but the majority did not reach the necessary figure in New South Wales.

Reid immediately invited the other premiers to a meeting to discuss ways of making the bill more palatable to New South Wales electors, and a series of compromises was hammered out to cover his difficulties and to entice Queensland into participation. Aside from financial rearrangements, perhaps the main concession gained by Reid was that the new federal capital would be sited in New South Wales, although it was stipulated that it had to be at least 100 miles (160 kilometers) from Sydney. Until an acceptable venue was found, the Federal Parliament would meet in Melbourne.

Reid now declared himself well satisfied, and in a second referendum in 1899 the vote in favor of federation passed in all the eastern colonies. Western Australia proved to be a reluctant bride, but Premier John Forrest found that the other colonies would make no concessions at all to accommodate the colony and that he faced a secession movement on the goldfields of Coolgardie and Kalgoorlie. The miners were determined to be in federation and petitioned the British government to form a new colony to be known as Auralia from the goldfields districts, which would then vote to join the federation. Under heavy pressure from the Colonial Office and the miners, John Forrest changed his mind, and at the eleventh hour in 1900, Western Australia voted on a referendum to federate on the same terms as the other colonies.

7

Advance Australia Fair
(1901–1919)

FEDERATION ACHIEVED

The Commonwealth of Australia Constitution Act received Queen Victoria's assent after it had passed through the British Parliament in July 1900, and in September, the queen proclaimed that on the first day of the new century the people of the Australian colonies would be united as the Commonwealth of Australia. It was to be the first continental nation in the world.

Accordingly, on a sweltering New Year's Day, in all the Australian colonies, elaborate ceremonies were conducted to celebrate the birth of the new nation. Grand military parades helped to remind the onlookers that the new Commonwealth was at war in South Africa and in China. When the Boer War broke out in 1899, all Australian colonies had sent volunteers. Australians fought throughout the South African campaign as colonial volunteers even though they became a federal responsibility after federation. The lure of adventure and a sense of shared British nationalism may help to explain why colonists volunteered to fight in a war so far away. Nor was anything more tangible offered as an inducement to volunteers to aid Britain by participating in the international expedition to repress the Boxer Rebellion in China. Both New South Wales and Victoria sent men from their naval brigades, Queensland offered its unseaworthy gunboat, and South Australia's gunboat was actually co-opted into the Royal Navy for the duration of the emergency and steamed north to China. The men in China did not see much action, but the 16,000 Australian soldiers in South Africa confronted a brave and determined enemy defending their homeland against a British invasion. So the new nation began its life with its citizens serving in two foreign locations where they sought to crush resistance to British control from nationalist patriots. It was an irony that did not seem to strike most of the thousands of Australians who crowded the capital cities of the new states to watch the festivities, though in 1899 the *Bulletin* had published a cartoon titled "An Ominous Start" commenting on the fact.[1]

THE FIRST COMMONWEALTH GOVERNMENT

The initial business of the new government led by Edmund Barton was the organization of the first federal elections, to be held at the end of March. There were seventy-five members to be elected to the House of Representatives in addition to thirty-six senators, and the elections were conducted under the electoral laws then in force in the different states. This meant that women could only vote in Western Australia and South Australia, though in the interests of uniformity, this was extended to all states in 1902 when most white residents over the age of twenty-one received the vote.

The newly elected members were an experienced and talented group. Out of the seventy-five members of the House of Representatives, there were ten former premiers and twelve others who had ministerial experience. The party system was in its infancy with the exception of the Labor Party, and there were loose divisions of free traders and protectionists rather than formal political parties. Consequently, it took some time to discern which faction had won the election, but eventually Barton was able to form a broadly protectionist government, and George Reid became the leader of the free trade opposition. Labor, which had won twenty-four seats, joined neither group, but continued its tried and true policy of support in return for concessions. This meant in practice that the party usually supported the protectionists, but it would keep any government in office that was willing to bring forward progressive social legislation. Protectionists and free traders were united into cohesive groups only on the fiscal question, and the members were reasonably eclectic on other issues. Labor, on the other hand, quickly introduced the discipline of caucus, pledge, and annual conference and on 8 May 1901 formed itself into the Federal Parliamentary Labor Party under the leadership of John Christian Watson from New South Wales.

The new federal politicians represented a combined Australian population of 3,765,894; because some states did not include Aborigines in their census figures, only about a quarter of the estimated 67,000 Aborigines then resident in Australia were counted in this figure. When the Commonwealth conducted its first population census ten years later, it excluded all full-blood Aborigines as a matter of course. The federal constitution left Aboriginal affairs to the states, and Aborigines were excluded from the federal franchise unless they already possessed the vote for their state legislatures: Very few of them did. Finally, Section 127 of the Commonwealth Constitution held that in estimating the population of the continent at times of national census "Aboriginal natives shall not be counted," which neatly maintained the exclusion of Australian blacks from any say in the government of a country in which they had lived for more than 60,000 years.

EARLY LEGISLATION AND WHITE AUSTRALIA

Parliament enacted legislation in two crucial areas that enjoyed a virtual consensus from all members of the new legislature. The first of these was ensuring a white Australia and protecting the population from contamination by supposedly inferior races and the workers of the country from the threat of cheap labor. It was not that a current threat actually existed from the millions of Asians in Australia's region of the world but rather to ensure that such a threat never arose. The Chinese population of the country had fallen to below 30,000 by 1901, and there were fewer than 10,000 Kanakas working in the Queensland cane fields. Nevertheless, Australians had become acutely conscious of themselves as a small white enclave that could be swamped by Asians in a very short space of time, unless steps were taken to keep them out. The rising military power of Japan also caused concern, and a desire to avoid allowing a large number of Japanese nationals who might become a future security risk helps to explain the uniform support the Immigration Restriction Act received. The Natal system was introduced, which demanded the passing of a literacy test in any European language selected by the civil servant administering the test, before non-European migrants would be permitted to enter the country. The test was not to be applied to whites, and the officer was expected to select a language with which the colored migrants were unfamiliar.

TARIFFS

The next piece of crucial legislation passed by the Barton government proved far more contentious, because it related to the vexed question of tariffs. All parties recognized the need for a revenue tariff, but even the modest degree of protection Barton aimed for became the cause of deep divisions and a prolonged debate. Eventually, a tariff ranging from 5 to 25 percent ad valorum (according to the value of the item) duty was accepted by the Senate, where the free traders had a majority, and with the Customs Tariff Act of September 1902, a policy of protection became the law of the land.

SUPPORTING THE BRITISH NAVY

At a colonial conference in London during 1902, the subject of defense was discussed, and Barton agreed to subscribe £240,000 ($480,000) a year as Australia's contribution to the costs borne by the Royal Navy in defending Australia. The money was to help maintain a British naval squadron of one armored cruiser, six light cruisers, four sloops, and a naval reserve of twenty-five officers and 700 men in Australian waters. The officers and men would be trained by the British and form eventually the nucleus of the Royal Australian Navy, though that development was not one favored by the British in 1902. The arrangement was cheap but left Australia with little say in its own defense and was obviously a stopgap measure. Both Barton and Deakin believed that an Australian navy would ultimately have to be formed, for it did not require the gift of prophecy to foresee that Britain's strategic requirements might not always coincide with Australia's needs. But moves in that direction as early as 1902 would have been premature. The scanty colonial naval forces that passed into Commonwealth control in 1901 were anything but impressive and consisted of a few colonial gunboats and torpedo boats.

THE COURTS

In September 1903, the High Court of Australia came into existence with Sir Samuel Griffith, the early draftsman of the constitution, appointed as the first chief justice. Prime Minister Edmund Barton and Leader of the Senate R.E. O'Connor both resigned from Parliament to take up the two positions on the bench of the High Court. All three of the new justices had been actively involved in the federation movement and were expected to apply their extensive knowledge and experience to the judicial interpretation of the new constitution. Deakin succeeded Barton as the leader of the protectionist liberals and as prime minister.

In the years between 1903 and 1909, substantial strides were made in the area of progressive social legislation. The Labor Party usually supported Alfred Deakin during these years and even ruled as a minority government in 1904 and 1908. The combination of Deakin and Labor produced legislation that had a profound effect on Australian society. In 1904, a temporary alliance of free traders and some protectionists under George Reid brought forward an Industrial Arbitration Bill that was heavily influenced by proposals introduced by the first Labor government. A Federal Arbitration Court was established to exercise the powers granted by the constitution to the Commonwealth in disputes covering more than one state.

NEW PROTECTION

The Court of Arbitration and Conciliation was constituted in 1905, and under the leadership of Justice Henry Bournes Higgins, it was destined to play a major role in the years 1905–1908 in establishing an approach to industrial issues and wages that became known as "new protection." What was new about this system of protection was that it became a court-centered attempt to ensure that a manufacturer who benefited from the imposition of protective tariffs against overseas competition should charge a fair price for his products and pay reasonable wages to his employees. Employers learned that protection from competition carried social responsibilities, and that protection would be reduced or eliminated altogether from employers who did not pay adequate wages to their workers.

In his Harvester Judgment in 1907, Justice Higgins thought in terms of minimum needs of the workforce rather than in economic values, and he proclaimed a "fair" wage to be one that permitted an employee to keep himself and his family in modest comfort. His average worker had a wife and three children to support, and Higgins took into account the amount of money such a family would need for food, clothing, rent, and day-to-day living expenses. Largely by this measure, the Harvester Judgment arrived at a figure of 7s. ($.70) per day as a fair and reasonable wage to pay an unskilled laborer. Skilled workers received additional amounts under a system of margins for skill. This basic wage was established on sustaining a decent, if modest, standard of living, not on the capacity of the employer to pay. The ethos of the fair go underlay the system of arbitration and conciliation and was about to be enshrined in legislation.

In order to secure a viable foundation for a needs-based wage system, Deakin, with Labor support, extended protection in 1908 via a new tariff that gave a 5 percent margin of preference to British-made imports over those from countries outside the empire. Moreover, although the High Court later struck down most of the new protection legislation, the concept had been established and accepted throughout the Australian community that the needs of the worker had to be taken into account when state or federal courts handed down rulings on wages. Furthermore, because the industrial courts would only deal with representatives of organized associations, there was a rapid growth in the number of trade unions, and overall union membership tripled in the years between 1906 and 1914.

New protection undermined the basic creed of the free traders in the preeminence accorded to market forces, and the growing power of the Labor Party had begun to alarm its political opponents on both sides of the fiscal divide. When George Reid resigned as leader of the free traders and was replaced by the more moderate Joseph Cook, the ground was prepared for an anti-Labor alliance. In 1909, Labor withdrew its support from Deakin, and to a chorus of Labor denouncements Deakin responded by negotiating a fusion between the free traders and his own followers into the Liberal Party. Labor and its opponents had established the basis for two-party politics in Australia, a pattern that has continued with minor variations ever since. The new party under Deakin's leadership lost the elections of 1910, and the Labor Party found itself voted into power with majorities in both the House of Representatives and the Senate for the first time in its brief history.

AN AUSTRALIAN DEFENSE FORCE

Defense is another important theme of the first ten years of the Commonwealth. Deakin soon recognized that the subsidy scheme was not popular and did little to encourage the growth of Australian patriotism. In 1905 he suggested to the Admiralty a scheme for a flotilla of Australian destroyers, only to have it torpedoed by the British, who preferred a navy over which they exercised total control. Australian fears of Japan had been enhanced when the Japanese navy crushed the Russian fleet in the Straits of Tsushima that same year, and Japanese naval strength continued to grow.

The Japanese army had also scored landmark victories against China (1895 and 1900) and Russia (1905), and the weakness of Australia's land defenses similarly began to cause concern. From 1904 onward, with all-party support, a system of school cadet corps was established in which children learned the rudiments of drill and rifle shooting; and in 1909 the Deakin fusion ministry brought in a system of compulsory training for junior cadets aged twelve to fourteen, senior cadets aged fourteen to eighteen, and citizen forces aged eighteen to twenty.

In 1908, to the great displeasure of the British, Deakin had also secured for Australia a visit from the Great White Fleet of the U.S. Navy, then on a goodwill tour around the world. The name of the fleet reflected the color of the ships and not the racial complexion of the American navy, but the general public welcomed the fleet with great exuberance. If a comparatively new nation like the Americans could have such a powerful fleet, why not Australia? At the same time, Britain had become engaged in a race with Germany to build dreadnought battleships. Dreadnoughts marked a technological advance that rendered obsolete most existing warships and thereby undermined Britain's numerical position of naval supremacy. A genuine arms race was now under way, and because dreadnoughts were extremely expensive to build, Britain began to look more kindly upon Australia's ambitions to possess a fleet of its own.

In 1909, the Admiralty reversed its previous views and recommended that the dominions be permitted to create local fleets and that these should be to a certain extent under local control. At an imperial defense conference that year, the Admiralty proposed the creation of a Pacific fleet to which Britain, Australia, New Zealand, and Canada could contribute units. The Australian contribution paid for by the Commonwealth and crewed as far as possible by Australians was to consist of one armored cruiser, three light cruisers, six destroyers, and three submarines. The ships were ordered from English shipyards, and in 1911, the king granted the title of Royal Australian Navy to the new fleet. In Australian waters the fleet would be exclusively controlled by the Australian government, in foreign ports the ships would take orders from the British government, and in time of war they would automatically become part of the Royal Navy under the control of the Admiralty.

Early in 1910, the army received its equivalent of the visit of the Great White Fleet, when Lord Kitchener toured Australia and inspected its military establishment for the Commonwealth government. Kitchener recommended the formation of an army of 80,000 men, half to defend the cities and ports and the rest to constitute a mobile strike force that could be deployed anywhere in Australia. In order to facilitate the rapid deployment of this force, Kitchener advised the construction of a network of railways and roads connecting the entire country. He also recommended the establishment of an officer training school modeled on America's West Point, and in 1911 the Royal Military College of Australia officially opened at Duntroon.

As the first full term of Labor government began after the 1910 elections, all these earlier strands of development became interwoven. The fears that had underlain the urge to federate the Australian colonies had blossomed into an Australian naval squadron and compulsory military training for all Australian males between the ages of twelve and twenty. These institutions came into being as part of an Australian recognition that Japan constituted the main threat in any strategic assessment of this region; but at the same time, British strategic assessments identified Germany as Britain's most formidable opponent. The military forces being brought into existence by Australian fears of the waking Asian giant were ironically destined once more to be used to support another of Britain's wars in far-off parts of the globe. Nationalistic pride in the British empire felt by most Australians meant that they failed to perceive the contradictions in this state of affairs. It was purely a matter of good fortune that conflict with Britain over the use of Australian troops was avoided until the 1940s. The seeds of the disagreement were always there—they just took a long while to germinate.

LABOR LEGISLATION

In 1910, the Fisher Labor government brought in the first fully Labor pieces of legislation, when it introduced a land tax to be levied on unimproved properties over £5,000 ($10,000) in value. Conservatives and some Liberals were horrified at such blatant class legislation, but it produced a useful revenue, and subsequent governments found ways of rationalizing their refusal to rescind it.

The second distinctive enactment of the Fisher government was the establishment in 1911 of the Commonwealth Bank. It was to compete with the private banks in both savings and trading areas and was designed to guarantee that workers would never again lose their savings through banks collapsing as they had during the 1890s depression. The bank was not given central banking functions, though it did become the main bank of issue. The Commonwealth Bank used post offices as its early savings bank branches and became deservedly popular with the lower levels of Australian society, which appreciated a bank guaranteed not to fail.

EXPANSION AND GROWTH

The years prior to the Great War constituted a period of rapid development. Natural increase and a rapidly expanding British immigration boosted the population to just under 5 million by 1914. Cities grew quickly in these years, as a majority of the immigrants sought work in the rapidly expanding factories growing up under the umbrella of new protection.

In rural districts, the wider use of refrigeration opened up overseas markets for Australian frozen meat and dairy produce and gave a great boost to rural settlement. The area under wheat acreage doubled between 1901 and 1914, largely because of the increasing use of superphosphates to force Australia's fossil soils into artificial fertility. William Farrar contributed by developing disease-resistant strains of wheat better suited to Australian climate and dry-land farming. In the pastoral sector, wool production continued to rise steadily, and the 1905–1906 season produced a record 1 million bales of wool, with prices continuing to climb in subsequent years.

By 1914, Australia seemed to be poised on the brink of another one of those waves of pioneering and development that had been characteristic of the nineteenth century. Capital flowed into the country to finance the public works programs such developments required, and the growing population allowed the burden of annual loan interest payments to be disguised in such a way that it was hardly noticed. The federal system of government was obviously here to stay, and the rate of Commonwealth expansion could be seen in the increasing number of public servants, which had reached 35,000 by 1913, and by the federal government's annual expenditure, which had grown from £3.5 million ($7 million) in 1901 to £9 million ($18 million) by 1913.

But Australia was no longer quarantined by distance from the rest of the world, and if Australians failed to see any relevance for them in the assassination of Austrian Archduke Franz Ferdinand at Sarajevo in 1914, they soon discovered that even seemingly minor events far across the world could impinge in a most compelling and brutal fashion on their antipodean idyll.

AUSTRALIA AND WORLD WAR I

On 5 August 1914, Prime Minister Joseph Cook (Deakin had retired from politics two years earlier, and Labor had lost the 1913 election) called together representatives of the press and informed them that Britain and Germany were at war. Another election campaign was currently under way, and both parties pledged England their full support, though the laurels for coining the unforgettable phrase rested with Labor leader Andrew Fisher—who, while campaigning at Colac in Victoria on 31 July 1914—had promised that Australia would stand behind Britain to help defend and protect her "to our last man and our last shilling." Australia had no right to declare war or even to choose neutrality. As an automatic result of Britain's declaration of war with Germany and Austria/Hungary, Australia was also at war. The Liberal government offered Britain an expeditionary force of 20,000 men and placed the ships of the Royal Australian Navy at the disposal of the Admiralty. When Labor won a handsome victory in the elections a month later, Fisher moved quickly to honor the pledges made by the Liberals.

There was great initial enthusiasm for the war among Australians, and something very close to a national consensus existed on the necessity for Australia to be involved. Only the radical fringe of the industrial labor movement stood out against the tide of tribal atavism. The International Workers of the World, a small group of radical trade union syndicalists, called on the workers to resist calls to enlist in the armed services and urged them not to become murderers of their fellow workers from foreign countries. Between 1914 and 1917, when the leadership was jailed and the organization proscribed, the Wobblies, as they were known, campaigned consistently against the war. Why should workers sacrifice themselves in a conflict from which they stood to gain nothing? In 1915, Tom Barker encapsulated this outlook in a poster that caused him to receive jail terms totaling fifteen months and fines of £125 ($250). Barker's poster contained the words: "To Arms! Capitalists, parsons, politicians, newspaper editors and other stay-at-home patriots, your country needs you in the trenches! Workers, follow Your Masters!"[2]

In 1914, however, opposition to the war was minuscule, and men flocked into the recruiting offices of the Australian Imperial Forces. By year's end, more than 50,000 volunteers had enlisted, and a second contingent was added to the one already promised. Few of the men enlisted to protect the world from German militarism or even out of motives of imperial patriotism. That was the language of recruiting agents, clergymen, politicians, and the very group of stay-at-home patriots so clearly identified by Tom Barker; it was the language of those who did not expect to have to fight themselves. The vast bulk of the young men appear to have enlisted out of a thirst for adventure and the excitement of overseas travel. The pay was good, and their mates were joining up.

Nobody foresaw the awful carnage of trench warfare, and many feared that the war would be over before the end of the year.

By the quirks of circumstance, Japan had become an ally of Australia's in the war, and Japanese war ships helped protect troop convoys conveying Australian soldiers to the fighting on the other side of the world. There were thirty-eight troop transports in the first convoy to leave Australia in November 1914, and they were protected by four cruisers, one British, one Japanese, and two Australian. One of the Australian cruisers, HMAS *Sydney*, temporarily left the convoy to engage the German light cruiser *Emden* on 9 November and drove it ashore on the Cocos Islands, a battered and sinking wreck. It was Australia's second victory of the war and caused enormous celebration and jubilation. Earlier in the war, a hastily raised expeditionary force of three battalions had been sent to capture German New Guinea, and it was here that Australia's first casualties of the war were suffered in subduing the German garrison at Rabaul.

GALLIPOLI

Those activities were mere curtain raisers, however, and the first major campaign for Australians was against the Turks at Gallipoli in the Dardanelles. British strategy was imaginatively conceived but foundered on mismanagement and was to involve Australia in one of the worst defeats suffered by British forces during the war. The Australians and New Zealanders (ANZACs) were landed on an impossible beach by the British navy and found themselves confronted by a series of ridges and steep cliffs. Turks were entrenched in the hills overlooking the beach where the landings took place, and casualties were heavy. After eight months of extraordinary heroism and hand-to-hand fighting, the British High Command recognized that the Gallipoli campaign had been a total disaster and resolved to withdraw. The retreat was carried out with great cunning between 18 and 20 December 1915, and the ANZACs withdrew with only two casualties for the operation. But the toll had been considerably higher in the long months between April and December.

When the British evacuated Gallipoli, the ANZACs left behind some 10,000 comrades killed during the campaign. Furthermore, another 20,000 had been wounded, and the lengthening casualty lists published in Australia caused many to rethink their attitudes toward the war. On the other hand, the bravery, courage, and endurance of the ANZACs had occasioned considerable pride in Australia, and newspapers carried detailed accounts of the exploits of Australian troops. In one month during the fighting at Lone Pine, seven Victoria Crosses were awarded to Australian soldiers, six in one day, and the people back home gloried in the bravery. In 1916, the day of 25 April was proclaimed as ANZAC Day, and the speeches made at that first celebration demonstrated that Australia was celebrating more than just the soldierly abilities and manly courage of its army. The new prime minister, William Morris Hughes—Fisher had retired to be Australian High Commissioner in London—announced that the defeat at Gallipoli was a feat of arms almost unparalleled in the annals of war. When such bravery, nobility, and self-sacrifice could emerge, he asked, how could it be said that the war was wholly an evil? Frequent allusions were also made to the belief that Gallipoli somehow marked a baptism of blood that raised Australia to nationhood. It quickly became accepted as a rite of passage to maturity as a nation, purchased with the blood sacrifice of all those thousands of dead and wounded Australians. The troops had marched off to war in 1914 singing "Australia will be there," and Gallipoli proved that Australia had been there and had not been found wanting in the hour of trial.

INCREASING DISENCHANTMENT

Despite the eulogies, however, by 1916 things were not going well for Hughes and his government. The casualty lists from Gallipoli appalled many people. When the ANZACs were transported from the Middle East to Europe, where the British High Command seemed to use them as shock troops, the casualty lists grew longer and disenchantment increased. For example, in one nine-day period at Bullecourt, the Australians suffered almost 10,000 casualties. Volunteers no longer appeared in sufficient numbers, and recruitment levels steadily declined. Labor resistance to the war grew as the industrial movement swung more and more toward the views so consistently propounded by Tom Barker and the Wobblies.

The burden of the war fell most unevenly on the Australian populace, and from the end of 1914, living standards fell and wages were frozen, while prices soared out of control. Unemployment doubled during the war years, and rents rose alarmingly. The truth of Tom Barker's poster seemed self-evident to many workers who believed that profiteering was rife and that the increasingly conservative government was doing little or nothing to control it. The rising sense of grievance and disaffection erupted in 1916, when the prime minister attempted to introduce conscription for service overseas in the army.

CONSCRIPTION

In 1916, Prime Minister Hughes returned from a visit to Britain where the High Command had convinced him that conscription was the only way in which the Australian forces could replace the heavy losses they were suffering in France. Australia had about 100,000 men under arms in France, but if the high casualty rate was maintained, the declining monthly recruitments in Australia would be insufficient to sustain it. Enlistment figures had dropped during 1916 from just under 19,000 a month to less than 7,000 a month by the middle of the year.

Hughes could not just legislate for conscription, although legally he had the power to do so. He knew he would split the Australian Labor Party if he tried, and while he might get a conscription bill through the House of Representatives with support from the Opposition, he also knew it would fail to pass the Senate. The situation came to a head on 24 August when the War Office called Hughes requesting urgent reinforcements for Australia's five divisions in France. They demanded 32,500 men during September and 16,500 in each of the next three months. Volunteer enlistment figures showed such targets to be unattainable, so Hughes persuaded his government to put the question of conscription to the Australian people in a plebiscite. If he received the overwhelming majority he hoped, it might be possible to bully his opponents within the ALP into agreement. On 4 September, the New South Wales Labor League expelled Hughes, and the Australian Labor Party began to fall apart. By October, when the referendum was put to the vote, four of the ministers in Hughes's government had resigned over the issue.

The campaigns in the conscription referendums—a second one was held in 1917—were waged with an enthusiasm, a partisanship, and a virulence that Australia had not hitherto experienced. The community split reflected political divisions that ran along the class, racial, and religious fault lines of the society. Although the main outlines can be delineated fairly quickly, the divisions were often masked and far from clear-cut. Archbishop Daniel Mannix from Melbourne, for example, became a leading campaigner for a vote against conscription, compounding Irish hatred for English policies toward the country of his birth with the view that Australians ought not to be compelled to die in England's war. There is no doubt that Mannix represented the majority of Australian Roman Catholics in putting these views, but the Roman Catholic archbishops of Sydney, Perth, and Hobart supported the war and advocated a vote in favor of conscription.

The referendum campaigns revealed just how deeply divided Australia was over the issue. Arguments for a vote in favor stressed the ethnic Britishness of Australia and highlighted sentiments of loyalty and the need to defend Australian democracy by fighting German tyranny in Europe. Accusations of treason and disloyalty and of pro-German sympathies were freely flung at opponents of conscription, and old communal divisions of race and religion reappeared. Opponents of conscription concentrated on the argument that Australia had done enough already to help Britain and that no government had the moral right to compel its citizens to fight in a war outside their own country. The morality of the proconscriptionists was attacked, and they were described as people prepared to sentence innocent men to death. In 1916 the answer was no by a majority of 72,476. Victoria, the home state of Archbishop Mannix, Tasmania, and Western Australia voted yes, but New South Wales, the home state of the prime minister, Queensland, and South Australia voted no. Farmers may well have decided the outcome of the referendum by voting in the negative for fear of losing their labor force.

THE NATIONALIST PARTY

On 14 November, Hughes and his supporters in the federal Australian Labor Party walked out of an angry caucus meeting that was about to put a vote of no confidence in the prime minister. Hughes went into coalition with the Liberals and formed the Nationalist Party under his leadership to continue the war. Only twenty-five Labor parliamentarians went with Hughes out of a total of sixty-five, and the remainder formally expelled Hughes and his supporters from the ALP and elected Frank Tudor as their new leader. Similar splits occurred in all states except Queensland, and the split in the party was now nationwide. A deep and abiding bitterness accompanied the split: In the Western Australian branch of the party all files dealing with expelled members and their subsequent political activities were brought together under the simple filing classification "RATS." The conscription split was the first of three major disruptions of the Australian Labor Party on a federal level, and the party took many years to rebuild after each one.

In May 1917, a federal election was held, and the Nationalist government under Hughes was returned to office. The electorate clearly distinguished between a referendum and an election, and the majority vote against conscription did not translate into a majority against the war. The Nationalists won forty-six seats in the House of Representatives, leaving the ALP with only nineteen, and the Nationalists won all eighteen of the Senate vacancies. Rural districts that had voted against conscription voted to return Nationalist members as the country quickly reverted to its characteristic conservatism once the labor supply had been protected. This swing back to the government did not protect Hughes from another crushing defeat when in November 1917 he attempted a second referendum to introduce conscription. This time the negative majority reached 165,588, and Victoria also produced a "no" majority.

TOWARD PEACE

As the casualty lists continued to lengthen, workers' weariness with the war produced the biggest industrial upheaval Australia had seen to that date. By July 1917 workers had become thoroughly disenchanted with the war and the privations and hardships they had to endure under wartime restrictions. The strike eventually involved 95,000 workers in the crucial transport, maritime, and mining areas. The Nationalist government in New South Wales, in partnership with the Hughes government, determined to break the strike and called for "loyalist" workers to keep the industries running. *Loyalists* was a fancy name for scabs or strikebreakers, and they received preference in employment. The result was a total defeat for trade unionists who were forced to return to work having gained nothing. Friction between unionists and loyalists remained a problem in the workplace for years to come. What the general strike and the conscription referendums did demonstrate, however, was that the earlier consensus on the war had irretrievably broken down on class lines, with the middle class fervently pro war and the working class vehemently opposed. Enlistments continued to decline despite the best efforts of official recruitment campaigns.

As the war moved slowly toward German surrender, the cost justified the feelings of weariness. Australia's combined casualties were higher on a per capita basis than any other Western country. Sixty-five percent of its total expeditionary force became casualties during the war, compared to 51 percent for Britain, 50 percent for Canada, and 59 percent for New Zealand. With a population of less than 5 million, Australia lost just under 60,000 dead and returned over 152,000 wounded. In money terms the war cost Australia just under £377 million ($654 million) and saddled the country with a level of indebtedness that dwarfed prewar figures. In 1918 alone, the war cost Australia nearly £81 million ($162 million), and this was £3.25 million ($6.5 million) more than Britain spent in the same period. The money to meet these expenses had been borrowed largely from Britain, which effectively charged Australia for the sacrifices it made on behalf of the mother country.

Aside from the dubious honor of participating in the final victory, these sacrifices gained Hughes separate representation at the Peace Conference, which met in Paris on 18 January 1919. American President Woodrow Wilson's fourteen-point proposal formed the basis for discussions. Some of Wilson's points struck directly at Australia's interests, for they were theoretical maxims of behavior based on humanitarian idealism. Three in particular—relating to "freedom of the seas," "no indemnities," and "no annexations"—were lost by the president, and he clashed many times with Hughes's unashamed assertion of Australia's aspirations to annex New Guinea. The prime minister's reminders that Australia's casualty rate gave him a privileged position over the commander in chief of the late-arriving Americans wounded Wilson's sense of importance, and Hughes himself was singularly unimpressed by Wilson or his ideals.[3]

Perhaps Wilson did not understand that in Hughes he was facing a man attempting to demonstrate that Australian losses had not been entirely in vain. Moreover, in addition to his determination to secure New Guinea for Australia and to ensure that no Japanese-sponsored statements of racial equality impinged on Australia's sovereign right to implement an immigration policy of its choosing, Hughes viewed Australia's participation in the Peace Conference as a symbolic and formal recognition by Britain and other foreign powers that the nation was entitled to enjoy equality of status with all other countries in the world.[4]

Hughes secured a "C" class mandate (the territory would be administered by Australia and Australia's laws would be in force) over New Guinea for Australia, and he needled and provoked Wilson unmercifully to the great amusement of the other delegates. The prime minister enjoyed less success with his argument that the entire cost of the war should be levied against Germany, and Australia's war debts could not be written off against German reparations. The debt owed to English bondholders as a result of Hughes's failure on this point would come back to haunt Australian governments during the next depression. And this amounted to the sum total of benefits Australia received from four years of war and a 65 percent casualty rate. No wonder Hughes commented to the House of Representatives that the true gains were national safety and liberty—they, at least, could not be quantified—but the spectacle of the prime minister taking refuge in such vague generalities to justify four years of sacrifice was not a comforting one.

And what of the returned soldiers? What sort of a country did they find when they got home? Many of them seemed to be confused by the divisions in society brought about by the war. They returned to strife between unionists and loyalists in the labor force. The year 1919 was a year that continuous industrial conflict made the costliest period—in terms of days lost—since statistics had been kept. Returned soldiers found themselves in opposition to "Bolsheviks" and "shirkers" who allegedly had stirred up trouble at home while they were away fighting. Returned soldiers occasionally fought pitched battles against "reds" in Queensland and New South Wales, and in alliance with waterfront strikers against the loyalist National Workers Union in Western Australia. Employers and the middle classes tended to label this activism as evidence of Bolshevik sympathies and a willingness to engage in bloody revolution. Friction between returned soldiers and the police sometimes boiled over in riots and violence, to the horror of many well-to-do Australians who could not understand how yesterday's heroes could sink to such depths. The men were already tasting the "ashes in the mouth" that their victory had secured, and more and more would question, as the next two decades unfolded, whether all their sacrifices had been for nothing. The appeal of fascism and communism to such men as these in Europe was not without its parallels in Australia.

8

A Land Fit for Heroes and the Great Bust (1920–1939)

During the 1920s, the Commonwealth government made repeated attempts to honor its promises to the returning soldiers, while simultaneously confronting a rising tide of industrial militancy from a deeply disillusioned trade union movement. One of the most intractable difficulties involved the reintegration of thousands of returned servicemen into society and the workforce.

THE SOLDIERS RETURN

By the end of 1919, most soldiers had returned to Australia, but postwar reconstruction and resettlement proved difficult. How could employment be provided for more than 100,000 extra men in a twelve-month period? How could soldiers be reabsorbed into the community without disruption? And what of the soldiers themselves? They had been through up to four years of hell on earth; many of the younger ones had gone straight from school into the army and knew nothing but childhood and war. How did a grateful government equip such men for useful lives in the community? Many diggers, as the soldiers were called, who had held clerical positions found that women now occupied their jobs.

SOLDIER SETTLERS

Probably the most popular choice of the returned men was to become farmers on a piece of land of their own. Most of the soldiers who settled on the land were not farmers or the sons of farmers, yet the myth of the superiority of rural occupations in bringing happiness and security to a man and his family refused to die out in Australia. The Commonwealth and the various state governments cooperated, with the states providing the crown land and the federal authorities subsidizing the soldiers with loans, fertilizer, roads, and water bores. Almost 40,000 men elected to become soldier settlers in this way, but by and large, they met with the same lack of success as had all previous attempts to ignore the El Niño phenomenon and place a yeomanry on the land.

In Western Australia, the soldiers worked in groups clearing the land before each man received an allotment for his own farm. This "Group Settlement Scheme" was designed to produce a viable dairy industry in the southern areas of the state. Overenthusiastic support earned the premier the nickname of "Moo-Cow Mitchell." The men worked extraordinarily hard, and the dairy produce from the area did improve supplies, but at great cost. Consumers paid more, and the farms remained marginal. In New South Wales the situation was so bad that by 1929 the Commonwealth had lost £24 million ($48 million).[1] By then, thousands of the soldier settlers had already walked off their farms. Some areas like Griffith in the Murrumbidgee irrigation zone proved more successful, and 700 soldier settlers made a go of their properties there; but overall, the schemes revisited earlier free selection outcomes.

All the schemes for soldier settlement recapitulated the ancient and deluded assumption that this vast continent possessed an almost unlimited capacity to absorb farmers. Moreover, they relied upon the application of vast quantities of borrowed capital to unproductive land and involved an enormous outlay in public works like railways, water supplies, roads, and so on, to bring the produce of the new districts into existing market structures. The end result was soaring rural indebtedness as surviving farmers struggled along on credit, relying on the maintenance of stable, high prices for their produce. Many farmers and their creditors came to grief when tumbling export prices for primary produce heralded the start of the Great Depression.

NEW POLITICAL PARTIES

Two new political parties appeared during these years at opposite ends of the political spectrum. In September 1920 small groups of socialists, former Wobblies and admirers of the revolution in Russia, came together to form the Communist Party of Australia. Branches were established in Sydney, Melbourne, and Perth, and the program of action outlined in the party manifesto was put into effect, especially the educational work of raising the social consciousness of Australian workers. The organization was beset with factionalism and did not become a significant political force in the land until the rapid gains during the 1940s in the trade union movement.

The second party that enjoyed considerably more success was the Country Party under the leadership of Dr. Earle Page. The party came into formal existence in 1919 from a loose collection of conservative farmers' associations, all of which felt that the Nationalists led by Hughes no longer adequately represented rural interests. The Country Party initially favored removing tariff protection for manufactured goods on the grounds that tariffs increased costs to the farmers, especially on agricultural equipment and fertilizer. The elections of 1919 were the first in which preferential voting was used rather than the first past the post system (where the winning candidate is simply the individual who wins most of the votes). The preferential method permitted an exchange of preferences between conservative groups like the Country Party and the Nationalists, which did not split the anti-Labor vote as a second conservative candidate would have done under the old system. The Country Party might well be described as the child of the preferential voting system.

Prior to the elections of 1922, Hughes accepted a gift of £25,000 ($50,000) from anonymous sources, which scandalized the nation. At the polls, Hughes led the Nationalists to victory but lost enough seats to necessitate a coalition with the Country Party, which had increased its representation to fourteen seats. In these circumstances, Page announced that his party was quite willing to enter into a coalition, but it would have no truck with any government led by Hughes or in which Hughes held a ministry. Eventually the prime minister resigned and retired to the back benches. Stanley Melbourne Bruce, a Victorian businessman and Hughes's treasurer, became the leader of the National Party and prime minister of a Bruce-Page government that lasted until 1929.

TRADE UNION MILITANCY

The years of the Bruce-Page government marked a time when many middle-class Australians believed that the trade unions were intent on pulling the country down around their ears. Although this was a period of great industrial tension and militancy, the formation of the Communist Party had very little to do with fomenting the problem, despite the conservative discovery that there were electoral benefits in promoting the "red" scare.

What was notable was the apparent willingness of industrial labor to attempt to change society from below by union muscle rather than through the medium of electoral politics. The reasons for this disenchantment with political Labor were a legacy of the war years, when the ALP and then the Nationalists led by the renegade ALP leader Hughes systematically alienated the trade union movement by the conscription campaigns and the employment of scabs during the general strike of 1917. Moreover, wages had been frozen by former Labor politicians like Hughes and New South Wales premier William Holman, whereas prices and rents had been permitted to skyrocket. By the end of the war real wages had fallen by almost £1 ($2) per week, and unionists felt betrayed. Preference to returned soldiers also cut at the very basis of trade unionism and in New South Wales and Victoria, in particular, turned unionists into enemies of the ex-diggers. Finally, Bruce was an English-educated gentleman who drove a Rolls Royce, wore spats in the cold weather, and spoke with a carefully modulated English accent. The gulf between industrial labor and the federal government had never seemed so wide.

Industrial unrest became endemic during these years, in the Seamen's Union, on the waterfront, and in the coal mining industry. The Bruce-Page government swung like a weather vane in the strengthening industrial breeze, initially strengthening the system of Commonwealth arbitration and passing legislation allowing it to deport foreign-born industrial agitators. When this attempt failed, the government then attempted to pass back nearly all the Commonwealth powers in the area of industrial arbitration to the states. Eventually this inconsistency over the arbitration issue brought the government to electoral defeat at the hands of an exasperated populace on the eve of the Great Depression.

FINANCIAL RATIONALIZATION

The story of the Bruce-Page years is not entirely a negative one, however, and it did reconstruct the country's finances and clear the way for the Commonwealth government to take a position of financial leadership that had never been envisaged by the founding fathers in 1901.

Since federation, the Commonwealth and states had competed for overseas loans. Such competition raised interest rates and increased development costs. In 1924, Bruce persuaded the state premiers to establish a Loan Council to coordinate approaches to overseas money markets and to apportion the spoils. In 1927, he cajoled the states into formalizing the position of the Loan Council. The Financial Agreement of 1927 gave the Loan Council control over all government borrowing. Commonwealth power dramatically increased at the expense of the states, for the prime minister needed the support of only two of the premiers in order to impose his policies on all the states.

COMMONWEALTH BANK MADE INDEPENDENT

In 1924, Bruce's government also passed important legislation to render the Commonwealth Bank independent of political control. Previously, the single governor of the Commonwealth Bank had been directly responsible to the secretary of the treasury, but under the new legislation the governor became answerable to a board of directors of whom the secretary to the treasury was only one. The other six directors comprised men connected with manufacturing, agriculture, commerce, and banking. This change horrified the ALP because it removed at a stroke the ability of any government to control the policy of the central bank. It was an enactment that would haunt the incoming Scullin government and hamstring its attempts to deal with the depression.

THE PRICE OF PROTECTION

At federation, Australia had embraced a policy of protection of secondary industry. It did not come cheaply, and the extension of protection to primary industry—which was a significant focus of the Country Party—increased Australia's vulnerability during the Great Depression of the early 1930s. The burden of protection added to the costs of goods, and the general public paid higher prices. Since Arbitration Courts took prices into account when they set wage levels, one outcome of protection was a higher cost of living.

For as long as Australia's exports of primary produce and minerals continued to earn well overseas, the community could afford the social costs of protection and absorb them. During the 1920s, however, the power of the Country Party and the anxiety of the government to provide markets for the produce of the soldier settler farmers led the government to extend protection by way of subsidies to many primary industries like sugar, butter, dried fruits, and timber. By 1928, it was calculated that protection to industry cost £26 million ($52 million) per year, and protection to primary producers £22 million ($44 million) per year; yet without protection the standard of living could not be sustained.[2]

SOCIALISM AND THE ALP

At the annual conference of the ALP in Brisbane in 1921, a motion was carried to the effect: "That the socialisation of industry, production, distribution, and exchange be the objective of the Australian Labor Party." This objective was carefully modified by the rider: "That the party does not seek to abolish private ownership even of any of the instruments of production where such instrument is utilised by its owner in a socially useful manner and without exploitation." But this precaution did not stop Labor's opponents from seizing upon the objective as proof that the party was dangerously revolutionary. The new objective saddled the ALP for the next fifty years with a form of words that antagonized electors and gave a weapon to its opponents. Moreover, although it was an objective that encapsulated the ideal of the fair go, the party never seriously attempted either to implement or to explain it.

AN ERA OF DOMESTIC CHANGE

As the age of jazz and flappers, the Charleston, and short dresses became established, and drinking, smoking, and having a good time became the prevailing sentiments of the generation that had survived World War I, the older generations clucked with disapproval. The foundations of life seemed to be under attack, with conventional morality overthrown, religion mocked, and women like the Western Australian Edith Cowan winning a place in the state's Legislative Assembly in 1921. When Federal Parliament moved to its new home in Canberra in 1927, one of the many worries concerned the effect of unsupervised hostel living on the young, particularly the single young women who followed their jobs to the new capital.

Nor was it just the moral conventions that were being subverted. The airplane also played its part in making the 1920s a decade of accelerated change. Australians had been flying in the Middle East and Europe during the war, and the application of the plane to breaking down the isolation of distance in Australia moved apace. In 1919, the first transcontinental flight from Point Cook to Darwin took place, and Bass Strait was crossed the same year. Ross and Keith Smith made the first flight from England to Australia. In 1920, the first regular passenger service was inaugurated between Charleville and Cloncurry by the Queensland and Northern Territory Aerial Service (QANTAS). In Western Australia the following year, Charles Kingsford-Smith and Norman Brearley began regular flights between Geraldton and ports on the northwest coast as far as Broome. By 1928, Kingsford-Smith had crossed the Pacific from the United States to Australia in the famous *Southern Cross* airplane, and the historical isolation of Australia from the rest of the European world, which had begun to break down with the electric telegraph in the 1870s, was finally over. The sense of being isolated was a distinctly Australian psychological phenomenon, and it remained ingrained as part of the national ethos until World War II when Japan demonstrated very clearly that the continent was much closer to Asia than felt comfortable, whatever Australians might feel about their distance from Europe or America.

INTERNATIONAL RELATIONS

The 1920s also marked a rapid change in Australia's formal relationships with the wider world. When Bruce became prime minister, he secured the appointment of Richard Casey as a liaison officer in London who would be attached to the British Foreign Office and keep the Australian government apprised of changes in British policy and the state of affairs in Europe. Casey was appointed to a position as Australian Liaison Officer in the secretariat of the British Cabinet, the Foreign Office and the Colonial Office, and Bruce had an inside account from then on of the international situation and of the state of British politics.

The appointment of Casey marks the beginning of the Australian diplomatic service. In 1926, the Balfour Declaration heralded a major alteration in the relationship between England and her dominions that were henceforth to be regarded as fully independent sovereign nations. This was formalized in 1931 when the British Parliament passed the Statute of Westminster and gave legislative force to Balfour's declaration of intent. The Statute of Westminster, however, was not ratified by the Australian government until 1942, when the ALP under John Curtin formally accepted for Australia a place among the independent nation–states of the world. Australian governments of whatever political persuasion during the 1930s were in no hurry to cut the ties that bound Australia and Britain together.

DEPRESSION LOOMS

Issues such as the embryonic diplomatic service or Australia's legal status as a dominion in a British empire composed of autonomous states were far from the Scullin government's mind when it assumed office after the 1929 elections. To be sure, Scullin insisted successfully on the government's right to recommend the appointment of the first Australian-born governor general in 1930, despite the king's obvious disapproval for the chief justice of the High Court Sir Isaac Isaacs. But the state of the economy preoccupied the government, as the country plunged deeper into depression with every passing day.

It was the old story all over again. Australia had borrowed approximately £225 million ($450 million) between 1919 and 1929, and nearly three-quarters of it had been used on long-term development projects. Originally Australia's overseas debts in London stood at £400 million ($800 million). The money required an annual interest payment of £27 million ($54 million), and there were no returns from such development investment in the short term to help pay this. Moreover, interest still had to be paid on the large loans raised during the war. These structural economic weaknesses were exposed when Australia's export earnings fell dramatically between 1928 and 1931, and the country slumped rapidly into depression.

Wool and wheat accounted for three-quarters of Australia's exports, and prices tumbled to only a quarter of the predepression price by 1931. Overseas loan funds were unavailable, and this increased the impact of the depression and made the recovery a slow, painful, and drawn-out affair. Australia was hit harder than most countries and the gap between conditions of life before and during the depression was more marked than for most other peoples. Australia fared only marginally better than Germany in terms of unemployment, and in Germany the hardship produced Adolf Hitler and Nazism. Unemployment in Australia rose from about 8 percent to 30 percent during the winter of 1932, and the annual unemployment average during the depression period was 23.4 percent.

Despite the misery and the hardship, interest on overseas loans still had to be paid. The Loans Council and the establishment of the federal government's statutory control over the borrowings of the states had come too late to help in averting the debacle. How to pay the overseas interest bills from a declining revenue base became one of the major problems confronting the Scullin administration, but there were others that rendered the job well-nigh impossible.

THE EFFECT ON GOVERNMENT

It had taken the ALP more than ten years to return to government following the split over conscription. Bruce left two legacies that caused immeasurable concern and helped, only two years later, to destroy the government. The first of these poisoned wells was a hostile Senate controlled by a large Nationalist majority. The ALP found itself in office but not in power. Bruce had recognized that an economic depression was inevitable and that its intensity would be so great that the voters would blame whoever happened to be in office. The astute Bruce correctly foretold the fate of every government, state and federal, in Australia. They all fell from office at the next elections.

The Senate proved crucial because Labor could not alter Bruce's second legacy, the Commonwealth Bank Act, without a majority in both Houses. Senior ALP figures recognized that regaining control of the Commonwealth Bank was essential if the government hoped to exercise any significant leverage over the Australian economy. The newly elected members, however, displayed a great reluctance to risk their seats and shied away from the prospect of forcing a double-dissolution election while the party still retained the goodwill of the electorate. To the despair of more radical members like Frank Anstey, the cabinet decided not to call the Senate's bluff, although by Christmas 1929, Robert Gibson, the governor of the Commonwealth Bank, was already proving difficult.

YEARS OF HARDSHIP

Ruin was a specter that stalked the land during these years, and although the lower levels of society bore the brunt, its severity affected even those higher up the social scale. Many small businesses went bankrupt during this time, and more genteel members of society who relied on interest payments and investments for their income found themselves badly hit. Similar hardships were experienced by landlords, who were by no means always the black-hearted villains of society they appeared to the members of the Unemployed Workers Union and to all workers and their families who lived in daily dread of the descent of the bailiffs and eviction.

There is no doubt, however, that the social hardships of the depression fell most unevenly upon Australian society, and as always, those at the bottom of the heap fared worse. The general necessities of life like food and lodgings could no longer be guaranteed. Social relief, sustenance payments, and charitable handouts may have been sufficient to ensure that nobody actually starved to death, but this does not mean that people did not go hungry or that women and children did not suffer from malnutrition and the want of clothing and shelter. Evicted men and their families lived wherever they could, and shantytowns grew up in Sydney's southern suburbs on vacant crown land. Some camped in old cars while the breadwinners searched for work, while closer to the city others squatted in caves in the Domain around the local site overlooking the harbor known as Mrs. Macquarie's Chair. Police were instructed to move the cave dwellers on so that they did not offend more respectable members of society.[3] The use of newspapers as bedding and blankets became distressingly common. No one could afford medicine for sick children or adults, and many men were forced into pilfering and burglary in order to feed and clothe their dependents. Camps like these existed on the outskirts of all the capital cities and some of the larger rural towns. In Western Australia, the camp at Blackboy Hill at the foot of the Darling Range behind Perth housed well over 1,000 men by the end of 1930.

Anxiety over jobs increased the stresses in society, as those fortunate enough to retain enployment worried about its continuity, and those out of work applied more and more desperately for the few positions advertised. Families often separated as the men left their families behind looking for casual work in the rural districts and seasonal jobs during the fruit picking, wheat harvesting, and shearing seasons. It was policy to keep such men moving, and local police would refuse to issue ration certificates once men had been in the district for a couple of weeks. Many men went rabbiting or prospected for gold on the old alluvial diggings. It kept them busy, and some made pocket money, but it was no substitute for regular work.

Bitterness among the sufferers was increased by reminders of the propaganda that had lured them off to war in 1914–1918. Labor newspapers contrasted the current situation with that during the war when the soldiers had been told they were fighting to make the world a better place:

> Patriots, who howled for conscription and the fight to a finish with the last man and the last shilling, are silent nowadays at this dreadful aftermath of the war. The Bugle no longer sounds. . . . The profiteer has filled his coffers, and is now hatching fresh schemes of exploitation by which he can accumulate more wealth at the expense of Mugwumps.[4]

FEAR OF VIOLENCE

Resentments often erupted into riots during this period, particularly over the matter of evictions, and members of the radical Unemployed Workers Union occasionally fought pitched battles against police and bailiffs to keep workers and their families from being evicted. Shelter, even in a house devoid of furniture, was infinitely preferable to being dumped onto the streets with nowhere to go. Riots also occurred, sometimes under communist leadership, as men protested against the dole system (known as "susso"), the foods that were permitted or restricted under the food voucher system, the mindless silliness of some of the work they had to do to qualify for sustenance payments (those on susso were not permitted to do work that might be done by someone already in employment), and the lack of action or the incompetence of the various state governments in ameliorating the effects of the depression.

Apprehensions about violence and rioting in the streets aroused a fear of revolution. One reaction by some middle-class returned servicemen bore certain superficial similarities to the reactions of other conservatively minded ex-servicemen in Europe, as Australia experienced the formation of quasi-fascist secret armies. Perhaps the best known of these were the New Guard in New South Wales and the White Army in Victoria, but there were others. The members of these clandestine organizations dedicated themselves to upholding the established political system and to resist any radical or communist government that might threaten a capitalist status quo. The ethic of the fair go did not extend to governments, even elected governments, if they flirted with redistributing wealth from the people at the top of the social pyramid to those more needy souls at the bottom. The rise of the New Guard and its eventual decline paralleled almost exactly the rise and fall of the second ALP government in New South Wales under Premier Jack Lang.

THE LANG PHENOMENON

Jack Lang dominated the depression years in New South Wales. He roused passionate hatred in his opponents and equally passionate support in his followers, who were to campaign in 1932 under the slogan "Lang is greater than Lenin." In October 1929, the ALP returned to office in New South Wales. Lang had promised brighter times and had his own plan for recovery. Basically this involved refusing to pay the interest due on overseas loans and using the money thus saved for the employment of Australians.

In April 1931 and February 1932, the Lang government defaulted on the interest due on its overseas loans. Under the terms of the 1927 Financial Agreement, the Commonwealth government had to pay the overseas bondholders itself and took legal action to recover the costs of the payments. Lang directed that all state revenues should be deposited with the state treasury and not with the banks where the Commonwealth could seize it. Eventually in May 1932 Lang was tricked into issuing an illegal instruction to state civil servants, and the governor, Sir Philip Game, dismissed him from office and called an election. Lang lost badly, but in his wild and reckless career he had not only brought about his own defeat but had participated in destroying the Scullin government in Canberra and in splitting the Labor Party into three irreconcilable factions. Lang must also bear part of the responsibility for the eruption of the New Guard's right-wing thugs onto the streets of New South Wales.

FEDERAL APPROACHES TO THE DEPRESSION

The government did what it could to reduce its expenditure. The immigration agreement with Britain was suspended, compulsory military training for all adult males was abolished, and heavy cuts were made in defense spending. In an effort to discourage imports, Scullin raised tariffs, but this had the unlooked-for side effect of reducing federal revenues at the same time. Income tax steeply increased, and a sales tax was introduced that alarmed business. All private gold exports were suspended, the currency was devalued, Australia came off the gold standard, and bullion was shipped overseas to help pay the country's debts. This, and rising gold prices, gave a new lease of life to the gold industry, especially the Western Australian goldfields like Kalgoorlie and Coolgardie, and some men found work there as a result of the expansion.

In 1930, on Scullin's invitation, Sir Otto Niemeyer was sent out from the Bank of England to confer with the prime minister and the state premiers. Niemeyer had no sympathy with concepts like the fair go or a wages system based on the needs of workers and took the view that Australians had been living above their means for some time and must accept reduced standards of living. It was harsh medicine, but the premiers agreed unanimously to make strenuous attempts to balance their budgets for the financial year 1930–1931 and to maintain balanced budgets thereafter. They also agreed that the Loan Council raise no overseas loans until the existing debts had been paid off and that any internal loans would be spent on projects that would realize quick financial returns. This exercise in belt tightening became known as the Premiers' Plan, and its stress on deliberately lowering living standards caused enormous resentment among those already on the razor's edge of survival. Undisguised disillusionment characterized the reaction of most working people to the Premiers' Plan and helps explain the support for the more radical solutions offered by Jack Lang. The political Labor movement was seen to have betrayed its supporters:

> We have recently had the ignominious spectacle of the Premiers of the great Australian nation sitting like a class of schoolboys to be lectured to by an emissary of British moneylenders, and told how they should govern their own land. It made one hang ones head in shame. . . . We owe a lot of money to England's money lords, and they are going to screw it out of us remorselessly . . . rapacious hands are reaching across the seas and stripping us bare.[5]

There was another plan put forward in opposition to Niemeyer's orthodox restraint and Lang's repudiation, and it bore the name of its proposer, the federal treasurer Edward "Red Ted" Theodore. Briefly, Theodore's proposition involved stimulating the economy with careful injections of capital to revive it and get it moving again. It was radical thinking for the times, though in later decades much of what Theodore suggested became accepted financial orthodoxy. Theodore proposed that the Commonwealth Bank expand credit and that the volume of money circulating in the community should be increased by additional printing of currency that was to be backed by the Commonwealth Bank to preserve public confidence. Two things militated against the adoption of Theodore's plan, these being the Senate and the board of the Commonwealth Bank. Theodore pushed legislation through the House of Representatives, only to have it defeated in the Senate; and Robert Gibson and the board regarded suggestions of expanding credit in a time of depression as quite irresponsible. To add to Theodore's troubles, in the midst of the depression he had to stand down from Federal Parliament to face criminal charges.

The ALP government limped into 1931 on the verge of another split. This time it was a three-way division with the majority continuing to support Scullin and Theodore, but a substantial minority throwing in their lot with the demagogue from New South Wales and becoming a Lang Labor faction. A third group, including some ministers who regarded Theodore as dangerously left-wing, coalesced around the former premier of Tasmania, the postmaster general in Scullin's cabinet, the disloyal and ambitious Joseph Aloysius Lyons. The Scullin government began to fragment.

In June 1931, the implementation of the Premiers' Plan began: A 10 percent cut to all wages fixed by awards including state and federal public servants, a reduction of 20 percent in all government expenditure, a reduction in interest paid on government bonds to Australian investors by 22.5 percent, increased taxation, a moratorium on private mortgages where repayments caused hardship, and devaluation of the currency, marked the practical impact of the plan. The Premiers' Plan was justified to sceptics on the grounds that it ensured equality of sacrifice since all sectors of society would be affected by its provisions.

THE UNITED AUSTRALIA PARTY

The Labor Party, however, had already begun to split. In January 1931 the federal parliamentary caucus recalled Theodore to the ministry. This caused the resignation of Joe Lyons and James Fenton, two of Scullin's ministers, and with three other ALP members they formed an alliance with the Nationalists and ultimately a new party, the United Australia Party (UAP) led by Lyons. Meanwhile, Lang's followers in the federal party undermined Scullin's government. Despite expulsion from the party, Lang's power over the federal Labor members from New South Wales remained significant, and seven of Lang's followers in the ALP federal caucus formed a breakaway group, though initially they continued to support Scullin.

Robert Gibson obstructed Scullin throughout 1931, announcing that he would cut credit to any state or federal government that did not reduce its deficit and even refusing to provide £5 million ($10 million) credit to the Commonwealth for relief works for the unemployed. In November, the Lang group in Federal Parliament moved to deliver the coup de grâce. Lyons and the UAP supported this move, and the government was defeated by a combination of its opponents led by former members of the ALP. In the ensuing election, the ALP won only thirteen seats, the Country Party held sixteen, Lang Labor five, and the UAP found itself in the happy position of being able to govern in its own right. Lyons's new party had swept to a remarkable success.

The UAP owed much of its achievement to the national inclination of voters to turn all governments out of office during the depression years; but there was no doubting the appeal of Joseph Lyons himself. Unlike the former Nationalist leader Bruce, Lyons came across as a man of warmth and humanity with a large family and humble origins. He was a man of the people, and he did not wear spats or drive a Rolls Royce. Bruce returned briefly to Parliament at this election and summed up the conservatives' attitude of admiration and lofty disdain for Lyons:

> He was a delightful person. He couldn't run a government but he could win elections. His resemblance to a cheerful koala, his eleven

children, his family-man appeal and his essential humanity were irresistible to the voters. He did, however, need someone to hold his hand in the early days and I did it, although I had to be careful to be discreet about it.[6]

RELIEF IN SIGHT

When Lyons came to office in January 1932, the slow haul out of depression had already begun. Unemployment figures continued to show almost 500,000 men out of work, and an armed insurrection by the New Guard to topple the Lang government in New South Wales remained a distinct possibility until Sir Philip Game dismissed the unruly premier later in the year, but there were distinct signs of improvement. Prices for wool and wheat at last began to rise, and a rapid increase in the price of gold added to the value of the output from Western Australia. As a result of the Ottawa Economic Conference and the general acceptance of imperial preference in tariffs, a wide range of Australian primary produce, especially meat, wine, dairy products, and canned fruit, began to find overseas markets. The high tariffs established by the ALP were lowered, stimulating efficiency in secondary industry, which pleased the Country Party. Furthermore, as a result of an initiative from the U.S. president, the former Western Australian gold mining engineer Herbert Hoover, an international moratorium was declared on interest payments on war loans until the depression was over, and this helped Australia stabilize the economy and freed up funds for domestic use that had hitherto been earmarked for overseas interest payments.

Such improvements were quickly reflected in the budget figures. Within its first year of office the Lyons government managed to complete the 1931–1932 financial year with a surplus in excess of £1 million ($2 million), and Australia's overseas trade position recovered from a £33 million ($66 million) deficit the preceding year to a £31 million ($62 million) surplus. Despite the lowering of tariffs, receipts from customs duties remained a growth area in the budgets for the years 1933 and 1934 and indicated that a sustained pickup in economic activity had begun. Slowly reductions in the high depression levels of taxation occurred, and income tax, land tax, and company tax were progressively reduced. Pensions and public service salaries were slowly increased, and in 1934 the Federal Arbitration Court rescinded the 10 percent emergency reduction in the basic wage and restored the margins above the wage for possession of a trade qualification or a skill.

Meanwhile, former prime minister S.M. Bruce had been sent to London as resident minister and then High Commissioner for Australia to negotiate a conversion of the interest rate on Australia's overseas debts. Throughout 1933 and 1934, Bruce badgered and harassed the London money market and the governor of the Bank of England and succeeded in converting most of the high interest loans to rates between 3.5 and 4 percent. It was a significant accomplishment and a great saving to Australia.

THE SMALLER STATES

Prime Minister Lyons had formerly been premier of Tasmania, and this background undoubtedly made him more sympathetic toward the problems experienced by the states with smaller populations. The recognition that that population provided an unsatisfactory base upon which to allocate federal monies emerged quite early in Lyons's first term of office. Since 1925, the Bruce-Page government and its successors had made additional grants to states like South Australia and Western Australia with large territories and low populations, to encourage development. A system of grants based solely on population amounted to a permanent and self-perpetuating advantage for New South Wales and Victoria. Consequently, in 1933, Lyons established a Grants Commission that was to comprise three commissioners empowered to advise the Commonwealth government on the merits of special cases for additional grants to the small states. The objective was to allocate money on the basis of need rather than population. The establishment of the Grants Commission owed much to Lyons's background as a premier from one of the mendicant states.

LYONS UNDER CHALLENGE

In 1934, the UAP was returned to office, though this time Lyons needed Country Party support and went into coalition. The coalition won all the Senate seats and entered the new three-year term in a strong position. At this election, a rising young Victorian politician named Robert Gordon Menzies arrived in Canberra and became attorney general. Menzies came from a poor background and had made his way in the world by winning scholarships for school and university. He had developed into a brilliant trial barrister and a highly respected constitutional lawyer before he embarked on a career in politics in 1928. The party elders and he himself expected that he would go far.

RENEWED INTEREST IN WORLD AFFAIRS

During the depression Australia perforce had become an introverted country. The rigors of economic collapse and recovery concentrated people's attention on domestic affairs, and Japan's aggrandisement in China or the rise to power of Mussolini and Hitler in Europe had failed to capture public attention. As the pace of recovery quickened, the focus of Australians broadened to include affairs in the wider world.

In 1935 the Department of External Affairs was formed as a separate department with its own minister in cabinet. Bruce's negotiations on loan conversions had shown that Australia's best interests were not necessarily served by subservience to the mother country. This being said, there is absolutely no doubt that Australia cravenly followed the English policy through every shift and turn of the discreditable appeasement period and happily echoed Britain's views as its own.

The rising power of Japan and Japanese atrocities in China, together with the activities of Hitler and Mussolini, led Australia into a new policy of rearmament. As part of a reassessment of potential threats to northern Australia, the government began negotiating with prominent Jewish spokesmen for the establishment of a Jewish home state in the Kimberley region of Western Australia. Both federal and state governments pursued these negotiations, and considerable progress was made before the outbreak of World War II rendered the discussions academic. A Jewish state in northern Australia would provide population, produce a buffer between Japan and the remainder of the continent, and become a useful strategic shock absorber in the event of an invasion.[7]

In 1937, the defense vote dramatically expanded when a decision was taken to begin development and construction of military aircraft. The new defense program also involved an upgrading of the navy. This increased expenditure was a step in the right direction, but nowhere near enough to satisfy the new federal leader of the ALP, John Curtin, who had campaigned during the 1937 federal election for a rapid buildup of the air force to at least parity with the number of planes capable of being carried as part of any Japanese carrier-borne strike force. The new plane, the Wirraway, was to prove tragically inferior to the Japanese Zero in combat during the early 1940s.

EUROPEAN REFUGEES

Refugees from Europe began arriving in Australia throughout 1938 and 1939 to a sympathetic welcome. In 1938, the Australian government decided to take 15,000 refugees over a three-year period, a policy that won bilateral support from the ALP. Their coming served to heighten feelings of apprehension within the community about the turn of events in Europe and the possibility of war. Meanwhile in 1939, Japanese militarism in China provoked the wharf laborers at Port Kembla in New South Wales to strike and refuse to load pig iron for shipment to Japan. They argued that the pig iron would be used to make armaments for use against the hapless Chinese and perhaps at no distant date against Australians as well. Menzies, as attorney general in the Lyons government, attempted to force the wharfies to load the pig iron by threatening them with punitive legal action. From this, Menzies gained two things— first a reputation for being pro-fascist, and second, a lifelong nickname that he abhorred: "Pig-iron Bob." In the end a compromise was reached where wharf laborers loaded only 23,000 tons of pig iron rather than the 300,000 tons for which the Japanese had contracted.

PRIME MINISTER MENZIES

In April 1939, Prime Minister Lyons died in office. Menzies had been the obvious heir, but his impatience to replace Lyons had lured him into an indiscreet though veiled attack on the prime minister's abilities, and he had subsequently resigned from cabinet and, amid charges of disloyalty, had departed to the back bench. Approaches were made to Bruce in London to return as leader, but Bruce wavered. Finally, Menzies was elected and took office as prime minister on 26 April 1939.

Soon after becoming prime minister, Menzies spelled out the essence of the relationship between Britain and Australia as he understood it. He made no reference to Australia as a mature, independent, and autonomous nation but wrote in terms of an Australian obligation to defend Britain's interests and Britain's peace, which he regarded as identical to Australia's. "If she is at war we are at war—defending our own shores." Despite this, however, he went on to point out that what was the Far East to Britain was the near north to Australia, who needed to establish and maintain its own lines of communication and intelligence gathering in the region and to inaugurate its own diplomatic contacts with foreign powers.[8] In the Menzean vision such developments were to take place within a framework in which Australia was a minor province in a global British empire. Given the overall primacy of Britain in the Menzies possessive view of the world, it came as no surprise to most Australians when, on 3 September 1939, Britain and France declared war on Germany, and the prime minister sonorously announced: "It is my melancholy duty to inform you officially that, in consequence of a persistence by Germany in her invasion of Poland, Great Britain has declared war upon her and that, as a result, Australia is also at war."[9]

9

War, Reconstruction, and the Cold War (1940–1966)

Robert Menzies as a war leader seemed problematic to many Australians. In 1938 and 1939, he had unashamedly favored appeasement and had managed to discern "a really spiritual quality in the willingness of young Germans to devote themselves to the service and well-being of the State."[1] Nor did he believe that Australia should support Czechoslovakia or Poland against Hitler's territorial demands.[2] These sentiments, together with his obvious desire to appease Japan and the ill feeling within his own party arising from his attacks on Joseph Lyons, caused serious uncertainty and weakened his ability to unify the country.

AUSTRALIA IN ANOTHER WORLD WAR

Public enthusiasm for the war did not approach the excitation level achieved in 1914. Perhaps there were too many who remembered the horrors of World War I. Many workers were still unemployed, and some of these at least felt they owed nothing to a country that had treated them so badly. Lack of worker enthusiasm for the war was a problem destined to bedevil the future Curtin administration even when a Japanese invasion appeared imminent.

On the other hand, the army offered the unemployed their first regular job since the depression, and there was no shortage of volunteers to join the Second AIF, which began recruitment following the declaration of war. The original plan had been to send the expeditionary force for advanced training to the Middle East and then to use it on the battlefields of Europe. The speed of the German blitzkrieg and the rapid fall of Europe made it plain that land battles there were years away. The declaration of war by Italy, and the advance of Italian armies in the Middle East and Greece, ensured that the Australian troops had plenty to do before they contemplated fighting Germans in Europe. Australian forces were sent to the Middle East to fight Italians. They won great success, but when Erwin Rommel and the German Africa Korps became involved, the early successes were reversed and followed by several years of heavy fighting. In the event, Australian troops did not participate in the great European land battles of World War II.

CONSCRIPTION INTRODUCED

The government faced massive problems in preparing for war in 1939. The tide of volunteers was obviously sufficient to recruit successive divisions of the AIF, but this did not address the problem of home defense. The AIF was expected to fight overseas, and volunteers naturally flowed into that organization. Accordingly, in October 1939 the government reintroduced military conscription for the local militia for domestic defense. All single men who were due to reach twenty-one years of age before 1 July 1940 were called up for three months of military training. The objective was to bring the militia up to a strength of 75,000 men who would be available in the event of an invasion.

Prime Minister Menzies reassured the electorate that training for the militia imposed no obligation for service abroad, and the scheme was for Australian defense only. Despite such reassurances, many trade unionists were thoroughly sceptical and regarded the plan—correctly as it turned out—as the "thin edge of the wedge" for the introduction of conscription for overseas military service.[3]

MENZIES OFFERS A UAP/ALP COALITION

In Britain, the emergency of the war had resulted in the formation of a national government composed of Tories and Labor. Winston Churchill became the leader of this composite government, and the Leader of the Opposition became deputy prime minister. Menzies repeatedly requested the ALP under John Curtin to join him in a similar venture, even offering to relinquish the leadership in favor of Curtin for the duration of the war.

The ALP believed that Australia would be better served both in war and in the subsequent peace by a fully committed Labor government, though Curtin and a number of his front benchers did agree to serve on an Advisory War Council to which they contributed support and advice. The government was under no obligation to accept the views of this Advisory War Council, but it provided a mechanism whereby the opposition could be kept informed. There was bilateral support in June 1940 for amendments to the National Security Act, which gave the government complete control over the country's resources, production, manpower, and people for the duration of the war. The amendments conferred full executive authority to do whatever was necessary to prosecute the war. The revised act authorized civilian conscription of services, and many tradesmen found themselves directed to far distant regions of Australia where their skills were needed to buttress the war effort and for necessary defense works.

In September 1940, elections produced a hung Parliament, with the ALP and the UAP/Country Party coalition holding thirty-six seats apiece, and the balance of power resting with two independents. The government lost the support of the two independents early in October 1941 and the governor general commissioned John Curtin as prime minister. The new government held office on the support of the independents until the elections of 1943 gave Curtin a comfortable majority in both houses.

AUSTRALIANS IN BATTLE

When Curtin came to office in 1941, the Australian forces were extended. The Sixth, Seventh, and Ninth Divisions of the AIF were serving in the Middle East, and the bulk of naval and air force personnel were also deployed on the other side of the world. On 7 December 1941, when the Japanese launched their surprise attack on the American naval base at Pearl Harbor, Australia suddenly had the war in her own backyard.

Three days after the disaster at Pearl Harbor, the Japanese sank two British battleships—the HMS *Prince of Wales* and the HMS *Repulse*—and reduced the allied naval forces in Asian waters to ineffective impotence. Within two months the Japanese army had flung back the British, Dutch, Indian, and Australian troops opposing them and had occupied Guam, Wake Island, Hong Kong, British North Borneo, Rabaul in New Britain, the Netherlands East Indies, Burma, and the entire Malay Peninsula. The so-called impregnable fortress of Singapore surrendered on 15 February 1942, and within a week Japanese planes had bombed Darwin, and before the month was out, HMAS *Perth* had gone to the bottom in the Battle of the Java Sea. The Japanese onslaught seemed irresistible, and the new Australian government faced a national nightmare come to life; the yellow peril seemed likely to submerge the country, just as the rascist propaganda from the 1850s onward had always foretold.

Labor reacted to the news of Pearl Harbor by declaring war on Japan without waiting for a British declaration. It was clear that Australia could not expect significant help from the British who were fully engaged against Germany. Indeed, Churchill regarded the war in the Pacific as a side issue and took the view that the most important task was to defeat Hitler. After that had been achieved, the Japanese could then be dealt with. If this strategy resulted in the loss of Australia, that was regrettable, but Australia could always be recaptured. Naturally this view did not recommend itself to the Australian government, and in December 1941 the prime minister made a historic declaration in which he refused to accept that the struggle in the Pacific was of secondary importance or that Australia was dispensable:

> Without any inhibitions of any kind, I make it quite clear that Australia looks to America, free of any pangs as to our traditional links or kinship with the United Kingdom. . . . We are, therefore, determined that Australia shall not go, and we shall exert all our energies towards the shaping of a plan, with the United States as its keystone, which will give to our country some confidence of being able to hold out until the tide of battle swings against the enemy.[4]

The call to America aroused resentment in Churchill and in Curtin's political opponents in Australia. Ironically, unbeknown to Curtin, President Roosevelt of the United States had already agreed to Churchill's "beat Hitler first" strategy, but Australia did have attractions as a base from which the reconquest of the Pacific could be launched. For that reason, U.S. General Douglas MacArthur was ordered to leave the besieged American forces on Corregidor and proceed to Australia where he would take command of the new army that would gather to hurl back the Japanese and punish them for their aggression. MacArthur arrived in Australia in March 1942 and was accepted by all the Allied governments as Supreme Commander in the South West Pacific area. Because the only soldiers available at that time were Australian troops, the Australian General Thomas Blamey was to command all land forces.

In the same month as MacArthur's arrival, Japanese forces invaded New Guinea and began to advance on Port Moresby. They were not destined, however, to get much farther.

AN INCREASINGLY INDEPENDENT SPIRIT

When Singapore fell, the greatest strength of Australia's armed forces was still in the Middle East. To meet the oncoming Japanese, Australia possessed the militia of about 200,000 men and some 50,000 AIF volunteers who were better trained but without battle experience. The Australian General Staff demanded that the three battle-hardened veteran divisions be brought home from the Middle East to help defend Australia. Curtin's cabinet agreed unanimously and cabled Churchill. Churchill had other ideas. He suggested sending the Seventh Division to Burma and had even ordered the fleet carrying the men to head for that country when to his astonishment Curtin insisted on their return to Australia. British statesmen expected deference, and both Churchill and Roosevelt exerted enormous pressure on Curtin. In Australia, the opposition, led by Menzies and Fadden, supported Churchill in this confrontation, but Curtin would not be moved. With very bad grace, the order was sent to the fleet to change course again for Australia, and to the great delight of both government and people, the transports arrived without mishap.

These AIF veterans made a major difference to the action in New Guinea and played an important role in defeating the Japanese threat to Port Moresby. Indeed, they were responsible for inflicting the first major defeat on Japanese land forces of the war. Had Churchill and Menzies had their way, a further two divisions of the AIF would have joined the Eighth Division as prisoners of the Japanese when Burma fell soon afterward, and the consequences for Australia could well have been disastrous. In February 1943, the Ninth Division arrived home and further bolstered Australia's military capacity.

CIVILIANS PLAY THEIR PART

Early in 1942, new regulations were issued under the National Security Act that declared some industries to be "essential industries" and certain occupations to be "reserved" occupations. Men working in these areas were not permitted to enlist in the AIF, as their labor was deemed essential to the war effort. Iron founding and heavy industry were two such areas, and others were added to the list as required. Every employable man and woman came under the new manpower plan and had to work wherever they were directed. Some were maintained in munitions industries, some were released for military training, and some were directed to essential civilian occupations.

As men were progressively called up for military training, more and more women flooded into the workforce. They took jobs in all sectors that had hitherto been the province of men and performed extremely well. For example, the Women's Land Army provided agricultural labor and thereby freed men for service in the armed forces. As the war continued, Australians found themselves unable to escape its effects. Income taxes rose drastically, and so-called luxury items like petrol, imported wine and spirits, or tobacco felt the weight of restrictions. Day-to-day items like butter, eggs, clothing, and eventually even meat were rationed. Of course enormous quantities of these goods were produced in Australia, but the war effort had first call on everything, and wool cloth for uniforms, foodstuffs for feeding two armies (American and Australian), plus the need to supply Britain left precious little to distribute among the civilian population.

Paradoxically, wages also rose during the war years—in contrast with the collapse of real wages during World War I—not because of salary increases but because of the amount of overtime worked in all the essential industries. War workers labored around the clock in some industries like munitions, and public transport operated twenty-four hours a day to take them to and from their jobs. In 1942, the Commonwealth government took over sole income taxing rights from the states and raised the levels across the board to help finance the war. Nevertheless, one of the effects of war on the civilian population was an increase in prosperity. There was full employment and overtime for nearly all workers. In the rural sector, farmers were similarly well off: They had a guaranteed market for everything they could produce as the government bought up all the wool, wheat, meat, and dairy produce at agreed prices. People certainly complained about the high taxation levels, but the complaints were muffled when returning AIF soldiers waiting for transport to take them to New Guinea pointed out that they received the same rate of pay as the First AIF soldiers in World War 1, and they got no overtime.[5]

Some of the extra money undoubtedly went on the black market. As rationing affected most aspects of everyday life, a thriving black market built up to supply the demand. Cigarettes and alcohol were the main items available, but clothing and food could also be obtained. Even a little petrol was occasionally available for those who knew where to look for it. Many Australians attempted to beat the cutback in beer production by making their own home brew, and illicit stills proliferated in a way that had not been seen since the very early days of the convict colony. The American servicemen received a substantially higher rate of pay than did the Australians, and they could obtain American cigarettes very cheaply at their military PX stores. Australian servicemen resented the differential in pay and the success that Americans seemed to enjoy with Australian girls. Occasionally such frictions led to fighting and riots, the best known being the Battle of Brisbane, which involved hundreds of soldiers from both armies. During this fracas one Australian private was killed and another seven wounded as a result of American military police using shotguns; and about forty soldiers from both armies required medical attention for their injuries. Fighting between the armies was not the norm, however, and hundreds of marriages occurred between American servicemen and Australian girls during the years of World War II.

THE TIDE TURNS

Hostilities against the Japanese during 1942 presaged that turning of the tide of battle for which Curtin had hoped when he had called on America for assistance. Australian troops vanquished the Japanese in New Guinea, while at sea American and Australian ships inflicted two heavy defeats on the Japanese in the Battles of the Coral Sea and Midway. In fact, Allied losses had been heavier than Japanese in the Battle of the Coral Sea, but they could be replenished, whereas the Japanese fleet was being slowly extinguished by attrition. In the Battle of Midway, the Japanese lost four aircraft carriers that were irreplaceable, and their ability to supply their far-flung armies and to protect convoys of supplies was seriously undermined.

American conscripts were involved in this fighting, and pressure to make Australian militiamen share the risks with their Ally proved impossible for Curtin to resist. The Australian militia had been used in New Guinea without breaking the guarantee not to use conscripts overseas on the technicality that New Guinea was actually Australian territory since the mandate won by Hughes in 1919. The militia had fought with distinction alongside the AIF in New Guinea, and in 1943 Curtin introduced legislation that authorized the use of conscripts against the Japanese as far north as the equator.

Curtin found it impossible to support the contention that it was acceptable for American conscripts to die fighting the Japanese north of New Guinea but not for Australian conscripts. The irony was that Curtin had been one of the foremost agitators against conscription for overseas service during World War I, and fate had placed him in a position where he had to introduce it during World War II. The threat from Japan was so immediate, however, that conscription did not prove particularly divisive.

THE LIBERAL PARTY

In 1944, at a conference of anti-Labor forces in Canberra, Menzies proposed the formation of a completely new party that would mirror the successful organizational structure of the ALP, with party branches and a mass membership of rank and file who would all have an input into policy formulation. Menzies also recognized that to attract members to his new party, it would have to offer more than just opposition to the ALP, and he carefully spelled out the ideology of the Liberal Party. The new movement aimed to secure for Australia an environment in which all who had risked their lives in its service could enjoy honor and security and which looked primarily to the encouragement of individual initiative and enterprise as the dynamic force of reconstruction and progress.[6]

It was the stress on individual initiative rather than the state as the motive force for reconstruction and change that clearly distinguished the Liberal Party from the ALP in ideological terms, though the record was to show that in practical affairs the Liberal Party could be quite as committed to state welfarism as was the ALP.

CURTIN GIVES WAY TO CHIFLEY

As the war ground to its conclusion, an ailing prime minister became Australia's most senior war casualty when he died of a heart attack in July 1945. Curtin had been an unashamed nationalist who put the welfare of his own country above all other considerations. In the process he had incurred the hostility of Churchill and Roosevelt and established the basis of an undying legend within the Australian Labor Party. At the same time, his sincerity and wholehearted devotion to Australia had won him the respect of his political opponents despite their ideological differences, and his loss was deeply felt.

The next meeting of the caucus of the Federal Parliamentary Labor Party elected Joseph Benedict (Ben) Chifley, former treasurer in the Curtin government, as the new prime minister. It fell to Chifley to see out the final months of the war and to handle the vast task of postwar reconstruction. When the war in Europe ended in May 1945 and in the

Pacific three months later in August, Australia had lost just under 34,000 dead. This was only half the total of military dead from World War I, and the population had risen to just over 7 million, so in terms of service deaths, World War II had less impact on the community than had the first. Nevertheless, it would also be fair to say that the population had been conscripted, rationed, and controlled during World War II in a way that it had never before experienced. By war's end more than 500,000 Australians were in uniform, and large numbers of civilians had been conscripted under manpower regulations. These had all to be reabsorbed into the general community. The Chifley government faced a daunting task.

Ben Chifley was the product of two depressions. He had experienced the depression of the 1890s as a small boy living on his grandfather's farm, and he had been a member of the Scullin government during the 1930s depression. In both cases, he had witnessed ordinary people suffering as a result of banks collapsing and of bank policies. He had seen the Scullin government hamstrung by the opposition of the Commonwealth Bank, and he had come to regard the private banks and their relentless pursuit of profit as parasites. Control over the economy was a necessary part of Chifley's plans for reconstruction, and controlling the banks became a core component of government policy for the postwar era.

FINANCIAL RECONSTRUCTION

Even before the war ended, Chifley had introduced two banking bills into Federal Parliament that were designed to lay the financial groundwork for reconstruction. The Commonwealth Bank Board was abolished, and the bank was placed under a single governor directly responsible to the secretary of the treasury. In addition, the Commonwealth Bank was to function as a Reserve Bank and superintend and control the activities of all private banks; and all state and local government instrumentalities were to bank with the Commonwealth or with one of the government-run state banks. This final provision was ultimately ruled unconstitutional by the High Court in 1947, but the basic provisions establishing firm governmental control over the banks, and the monetary system remained unaltered. Despite subsequent tinkering with the system by Liberal/Country Party governments, the basis established by Chifley's legislation remained unaltered until 1984.

The private banks were appalled at what they described as Chifley's policy of "creeping socialism," and for the rest of its period in office, the government faced the combined and powerful opposition of vested financial interests anxious to bring it down. It took time to undermine a government, and despite Menzies's best efforts, the Chifley administration won the general election of 1946. Clearly, at that stage, the electorate preferred the dry humor and folksy style of the prime minister, which stood in marked contrast to the flashing wit and urbanity of the leader of the opposition.

DEMOBILIZATION

In contrast to the dislocation and unemployment returning servicemen experienced after World War I, the cessation of hostilities in World War II coincided with an economic boom. Moreover, the government offered a wide range of possibilities to the ex-servicemen whereby they could equip themselves for a return to civilian life. Free training was available to all with entry qualifications to universities and colleges, and living allowances were paid as low interest loans to those who undertook full-time education. Free training was also on offer for those who opted for skilled trades and semiskilled occupations. Although the attractions of the land were not as great as they had been after World War I, thousands of ex-servicemen opted to take up the rural life, and they were assisted with loans, land grants, and free training and assistance until they managed to establish themselves. The El Niño phenomenon was still unknown, but the land had been chosen with greater care, and the size of the allotments was adjusted to take into account local conditions, the nature of the soil, and the rainfall patterns. In the long run, however, most of these ventures failed, and after years of hardship, the survivors often walked off their properties with nothing but the clothes they stood up in.

THE POSTWAR BOOM

All that lay in the future in 1946 as the country experienced booming economic conditions in both primary and secondary industries. The war had led to a massive increase in Australia's industrial capacity, and these plants changed over rapidly to peacetime production. The building industry took off with an insatiable demand for private housing and for the household goods that had been unavailable during the war. Items like radios and motor cars were snapped up as soon as they came onto the market. Economic conditions ensured that there were very few problems absorbing the demobilized servicemen into civilian life, and the public works programs the ALP had on standby were largely unused.

In primary industry, the profitable times continued after the war. Much of Europe was devastated, and many countries were unable to feed or clothe themselves. Australia's exports of wool and wheat remained buoyant, and much additional land was brought into production to cater for the increased demand. British consumption of meat and dairy produce remained high, and exports of canned fruits and dry fruit also increased.

IMMIGRATION

By 1947, the economy was performing so well that the government decided to embark upon a major program of assisted immigration. The conflict with Japan and the rising power of the communists in China evoked fears of Asian hordes. Both sides of politics agreed that Australia's population needed to be increased substantially. Minister for Immigration Arthur Calwell attacked the problem with great energy. The most favored migrants were British, and Calwell made strenuous efforts to attract them. Calwell also looked to the refugee camps of Europe containing almost 1 million people made homeless by the war, many of whom included professionals and skilled tradesmen. Such people were needed in Australia and could make a real contribution to the country. In return for a free voyage out, the immigrants agreed to work for two years, at regulation wages, wherever the Commonwealth government directed them. The program served the dual purposes of populating Australia and providing a workforce for large projects of national importance. Preference was still given to whites, however, and blacks and Asians were rigorously excluded.

Between 1946 and 1949, approximately 700,000 immigrants landed in Australia. Subsequent Liberal/Country Party governments continued the program so that by 1959 the national population had reached the 10 million mark; and by 1970 more than 2.5 million immigrants had arrived in Australia. Many of these postwar migrants experienced some level of hostility and prejudice from the Australian populace, but words of abuse like "Dago," "Reffo," and "Balt" were quickly replaced by the more acceptable "New Australian," and the feeling that even migrants were entitled to receive a fair go in Australia eventually prevailed.

MEDICINE AND BANKING

Chifley's nationalism and sense of fair play brought him into conflict with powerful vested interests in his attempts to nationalize medicine and banking. During the war years, the medical profession had resolutely opposed attempts to establish a system of free medical attention and free pharmaceutical benefits paid from the tax revenues. They regarded such developments as dangerously socialistic and used the teething problems of the new British public health system to claim that it would produce a bureaucratic nightmare if anything similar were to be attempted in Australia. The British Medical Association (Australian Branch), soon to become the Australian Medical Association, set a standard for selfish and irresponsible behavior when its members made plain their resolution to defend their privileges, whatever the cost to their patients. Nationalized medicine would permit governments to limit and control doctors' incomes, and such socialistic meddling would not be tolerated.

It was with his plans to nationalize banking, however, that Chifley experienced his most vitriolic and ferocious opposition. His 1945 legislation had escaped almost unscathed from the High Court appeal against it, and although his attorney general Dr. Hebert Vere Evatt strongly advised that there was no need to proceed further because the banks were already subject to the overall control of the government, Chifley was determined to press ahead and crush them altogether. A conservative government might always reverse the controls and once again make the Commonwealth Bank independent. Chifley proceeded to attempt full nationalization. It was a fatal mistake.

The banks and financial interests responded with one of the most bitter and sustained attacks on a government ever seen in Australia. Their customers were deluged with propaganda in which Chifley was portrayed as a crazed socialist, and to ram home the point, cartoons were published of a pipe-smoking Ben Chifley alongside a pipe-smoking Joseph Stalin. As the 1949 elections approached, the banks gave extended paid leave to many of their managers and executives so that they could work for the election of the Menzies Liberal Party. It was a thoroughly professional and overwhelming campaign, and it did much to unseat the government.

AUSTRALIA IN A WIDER WORLD

The campaign against socialism and the attempt to connect socialism and communism in the public mind did not take place in a neutral environment but in a world already fearful that it trembled on the brink of another war. The cooperation between the victorious Allies that had carried them through to victory against the Axis Powers and Japan did not survive the peace. Increasing hostility between Soviet Russia and the

West from 1947 onward heralded the beginning of the Cold War, and in the Far East the communists under Mao Tse Tung continued to win impressive victories. In Europe, the Soviet-sponsored communist regimes in Hungary, Poland, Estonia, Latvia, and East Germany quickly showed themselves to be as repressive and brutal as anything the Nazis had organized.

The world increasingly came to resemble two armed camps as smaller nations aligned themselves with one or other of the superpowers. American policy was dominated by the need to contain communism, and Australia as a loyal Ally soon fell into line with this worldview. Indeed, it was one that proved to be wholly congenial to Menzies and the more conservative politicians in the Liberal and Country Parties, but it posed real problems for a party like the ALP, which paid lip service at least to its socialist objective. As the international situation deteriorated, anything that smacked of socialism or communism became progressively easier to depict as treasonable. The Communist Party in Australia had ended the war with more than 20,000 members and with communists in control of many of the country's largest and most important trade unions. Membership of the party fell rapidly as international tensions escalated, but communists proved harder to dislodge from the trade unions, and from the Australian Council of Trade Unions (ACTU).

Public discourse was further poisoned by startling revelations from former Soviet agents in Canada, the United States of America, and even Victoria, which indicated that a far-flung and sinister network of communist infiltration masterminded by the Soviet Union existed throughout the "free world." These agents were working from within to undermine the capacity of the West to defend itself via a network of secret cells in government departments and key industrial trade unions. Committed socialists were described as "fellow travellers" with the communists, and their beliefs were felt by many Australians to be dangerous to national security. Thus, when trades unions in the public utilities went out on strike after 1945, they met with little sympathy and increasing hostility as the decade progressed. The conservatives hammered the theme that the ALP was a socialist party and therefore must be sympathetic toward communism. In the growing Cold War climate, to be soft on communism would prove to be the electoral kiss of death.

This was the context in which Chifley's attempts to nationalize the banks and the doctors were fought out after 1947, and the longer the issues dragged on, the less sympathy the government enjoyed. Events culminated in the industrial arena with the great coal strike of 1949, when miners under communist leadership in New South Wales went on strike, and miners in other states quickly joined in. This last great strike of the 1940s brought almost the entire industrial life of the country to a stop, for without coal there was no gas or electricity. Eventually, the Chifley government froze the bank accounts of the striking unions so that strike pay could no longer be supplied to their members, and it sent in the army to work the coal mines and get industry started. It was firm and resolute action, and the strike was broken, but Menzies and the rabid anticommunists were the long-term winners.

On the eve of the election in October 1949 the final touch of anticommunist publicity was generated by Lawrence Sharkey, chairman of the Communist Party of Australia, who was found guilty of uttering seditious words with a seditious intention earlier in the year when he had informed a startled public that if Soviet forces in pursuit of aggressors entered Australia, then Australian workers would welcome them. It was a stupid, thoughtless, and inflammatory thing to say, and he received a sentence of three years in jail. Sharkey had been prosecuted by Dr. Evatt, Chifley's attorney general, yet even this did not help the ALP shake off the taint of being procommunist.

There were other lesser irritants that helped to swell the feeling that the government was well past its prime. Chifley believed that it was necessary to continue wartime rationing and restrictions in order to assist in the process of reconstruction, but these were only marginally useful and not worth the ill will they caused in a community that had grown heartily sick of government controls. Menzies promised to remove the restrictions and restore value to the currency, which had eroded due to inflation during the postwar economic boom. At the end of the election, the Liberal/Country Party coalition had secured seventy-four seats in the House of Representatives to Labor's forty-seven, though the ALP still retained control of the Senate. Robert Gordon Menzies became prime minister of Australia for the second time, and the Australian Labor Party began—though it did not know it then—twenty-three years in the political wilderness.

THE MENZIES ERA

For the next sixteen years, Menzies presided over Australia. By the time he retired in 1966 there were young adults who could not recall any other prime minister. The period became known as the Menzies Era and had some notable distinguishing characteristics. It was a time dominated both domestically and internationally by fear of communism. Menzies proved to be the supreme political opportunist in appealing to the Australian electorate time after time on a rabidly anticommunist platform. Election campaigns throughout these years became exercises in "red-baiting" or "kicking the communist can," as they were colloquially described. Anticommunism had been a political weapon in Australia since the time of Billy Hughes, but it combined with traditional fears of Asia once China went communist in 1949 into an extremely potent electoral asset for Menzies and the conservatives. The ALP routinely and regularly could be attacked for its socialist objective, for trade union links with communist agitators, and for the allegedly procommunist foreign policies such links produced in the ALP platform.

To this must be added a recognition of the utter inadequacy of ALP leaders after Chifley—who died of a heart attack in 1951—to match Menzies in any field of political endeavor. Neither Dr. Evatt nor his successor Arthur Calwell were up to the job of confronting the prime minister in Parliament or on the hustings, and the ALP split yet again in 1955, following further hair-raising allegations of the communist conspiracy that emerged during the Royal Commission into Soviet espionage in Australia. The split was on sectarian religious lines, and a small but fanatical group of mainly Roman Catholic zealots formed the Democratic Labor Party (DLP) with the express purpose of denying office to the ALP by the distribution of electoral preferences. In this they proved eminently successful. Moreover, their virulent attacks on the ALP and its leaders for softness on communism played right into the hands of the prime minister, and there is evidence that the Liberal/Country Party coalition assisted such a useful electoral asset with financial donations.[7]

PROSPERITY AND STABILITY

Part of the secret of Menzies's continued success lay in the fact that he was fortunate enough to be in office at a time when prosperity and stability became the norm for much of Australia. There were periodic fluctuations of employment, but overall the Menzies Era was characterized by full employment and rising prosperity domestically, amid turmoil and misery abroad. The large migrant population from war-ravaged Europe wanted stability and to live in a country free from terror and persecution. Such people tended to become avid supporters of the prime minister, and his anticommunist rhetoric appealed to their well-founded prejudices. But to Australians in general, the Menzies appeal—even the virulent anticommunism—was entirely pragmatic. Export prices for primary produce and industrialization of the domestic economy delivered a way of life and a standard of living that were equal or superior to those of almost any other country in the world. There was a great, if ad hoc, expansion in state welfarism, with contributory medical insurance, subsidized pharmaceutical benefits, increased child endowment and other measures, and a vast increase in federal government spending on education from primary to tertiary level. Menzies broke the mold of entrenched anti-Catholicism in the conservative side of politics, and his administration marked the beginning of substantial resources being shifted to support the Catholic school system. His government seemed to accept that it was the proper role of government in Australia to ensure a fair go for all members of society, or at least those parts of society that were electorally significant. Poverty and prejudice continued to affect the lives of some Australians, particularly the Aborigines, but since most were not citizens, they could not vote and continued to suffer the trauma of forced assimilation and the state-sponsored kidnapping of their children. Whatever may be said about the Menzies Era, it must be kept in mind that the prime minister remained in office because he gave a majority of the Australian people what they wanted.

COLD WAR FOREIGN POLICY

As the Liberal/Country Party coalition took over the running of the country in 1950, one of the hallmarks of the new administration was its handling of foreign policy. Menzies endorsed the American approach of attempting to contain and isolate communism like an infectious disease. The initial step in this policy was withholding recognition from Communist China, and the second was the arrangement of a series of treaties and diplomatic agreements that were designed to strengthen and support anticommunist regimes to Australia's north.

The first brick in this defensive structure was laid as early as January 1950 when the new minister for external affairs, Percy Spender, proposed to a joint meeting of foreign ministers from the British Commonwealth that concerted action be taken to raise the living standards of people in South and Southeast Asia. The idea was to improve conditions of life for the people of the region and thereby make them less susceptible to the allurements of communism. In essence it was an attempt to do internationally what Menzies was to do domestically and to give the residents of the region a vested interest in maintaining and protecting the status quo. The scheme became known as the Colombo Plan, and the originating members agreed to offer finance for capital equipment and technical assistance to the governments of undeveloped nations. Australia contributed over £30 million in the following six years in education and infrastructure development. The plan was not restricted to Commonwealth countries and included a large number of non-Commonwealth undeveloped countries.

The following year, in return for Australia's acceptance of a peace with Japan that was a great deal less punitive than Australia had wanted, the cornerstone of postwar Australian security was laid with the signing of the ANZUS Treaty between Australia, New Zealand, and the United States. Although the wording of the treaty is deliberately vague, Australia has always interpreted it to be a guarantee of American assistance, should Australia be attacked. The ANZUS Treaty marked Australia's recognition of its strategically precarious position in a Cold War world. The search for security became more significant in June 1950 when Communist North Korea invaded South Korea, and the United States assumed leadership of UN forces opposing the invasion. The Australian government pledged "the closest possible collaboration" with the United States, and Australian military forces joined in the war. By the time an armistice was signed in 1953, Australia had lost forty-two pilots and 1,538 soldiers either killed, wounded, or missing in action.

The preoccupation with erecting a defensive firewall of allies and friends between China and Australia received further impetus on 8 September 1954, with the signing of the Southeast Asia Collective Defence Treaty (SEATO). The signatories were Australia, France, New Zealand, Pakistan, the Philippines, Thailand, Britain, and the United States, and the treaty bound them together in a defensive alliance against communist governments in the region.

Under an agreement between Australia, Britain, and New Zealand, Australian troops were also committed to fighting communist insurgents in the Commonwealth country of Malaya during the early 1950s and later on in defending the borders of the new Commonwealth state of Malaysia against Indonesian attacks. China's invasion of Tibet and India, and the stunning defeat suffered by the French in Vietnam at Dien Bien Phu, helped to produce a siege mentality in many Australians who feared losing a comfortable and affluent way of life, by a combination of outside invasion from Asia aided and assisted by a shadowy fifth column of communist agents and sympathizers within Australia itself. This combination of greed and fear lay at the heart of Menzies's success.

KICKING THE COMMUNIST CAN

One of the first bills brought forward by the Menzies government in 1950 was an act to outlaw the Communist Party. The law was immediately challenged in the High Court by the Communist Party and a number of trade unions, one of which—the Waterside Workers Federation—briefed Dr. Evatt to appear as counsel on its behalf. Evatt had a long history of concerned interest in civil rights issues and had been a renowned barrister. On the other hand, he was a former ALP attorney general and Chifley's heir. His acceptance of the brief made it very easy for Menzies to label Evatt and through him the ALP as procommunist. How could the deputy leader of the ALP appear before the High Court without the appearance of involving his party?

Within ten days of a High Court verdict that the act was unconstitutional, Menzies had secured a double dissolution from the governor general. Menzies promised that if returned he would ask the people of Australia in a referendum to give him the power to outlaw the Communist Party. Earlier in the month he had declared that another world war would occur within three years.[8] These tactics proved eminently successful, and the Liberal/Country Party government was returned to office with a majority in both houses.

The referendum on communism was fixed for 22 September 1951, and Evatt flung himself into the "no" campaign with all the vigor at his command. The "no" case eventually crept over the line by a small majority, but in political terms, Menzies won the victory. The leader of the opposition had totally identified himself in the public eye with a defense of the civil rights of communists, and being sympathetic toward communism was an accusation that haunted Evatt and his party for decades to come. Menzies had crafted a weapon against the ALP that he and his successors would use thereafter with telling effect. It made no difference when in 1960 the ALP replaced the unstable and erratic Evatt with his Roman Catholic deputy Arthur Calwell. The "reds under the beds" attack on the ALP continued to be the first weapon in the coalition's political armory.

MENZIES'S LAST YEARS

In 1962, Prime Minister Menzies authorized the dispatch of a small number of military advisers to South Vietnam and three years later sent an entire infantry battalion. The decision to commit Australia's armed forces to fight communists alongside American troops in Vietnam followed logically from the treaty relationships with America and the underlying purpose of those treaties to obtain a U.S. commitment to the defense of Australia. It seemed only reasonable that this would demand a reciprocal response from Australia when American soldiers were fighting in Asia, and the government accepted the proposition that American protection had to be purchased by Australian participation. The issue, which in 1966 became further complicated by the question of conscription for service in Vietnam, split the Australian community. The Americans were delighted to receive support in such an unpopular war, and a Melbourne newspaper soberly summed up Australia's reasoning: "An act of support for our American allies, limited though it is by our resources, is the far-sighted course to take at this critical stage. It may have grave consequences, but it deepens the friendship we need."[9]

THE END OF AN ERA

On 10 January 1966, Prime Minister Robert Gordon Menzies retired. He was seventy-one years of age and had held office continuously since 1949, establishing an all-time record for any Australian leader. His opportunism had brought many Roman Catholic voters across to the coalition from the ALP, but his pursuit of short-term political gains was to leave his successors with a series of intractable headaches. Menzies had built on the foundations laid during World War II and had presided over an economic expansion almost as lengthy as the long boom of the nineteenth century. Where necessary for electoral popularity he could be a nondoctrinaire socialist as, for example, in extending state aid to the Roman Catholic school system; for the same reasons he could become completely reactionary on other issues.

It appeared to many that aside from keeping himself in power, he did not seem to have believed in anything very much. Even his anti-communism did not hinder good business when it came to selling Australian wheat to Communist China after 1961. Australians tended to admire him, respect him, but not to like him very much. During the war years, there had often been spontaneous applause when the figure of John Curtin appeared on the news reels. Nothing similar can be said about Robert Gordon Menzies, whose aloof and slightly patronizing air discouraged easy familiarity and whose often-repeated pride in his Britishness had made him something of an anachronism to young Australians by the time of his departure from public life.

10

Vietnam, People Power, and the Conservative Resurgence (1967–1983)

When Menzies retired, the Liberal Party amounted to a coalition of conservatives and liberals held together by opposition to the ALP and pragmatic anticommunism. Menzies had provided an administrative structure that ensured its survival, but the party had never committed itself to a belief that the state should play a lesser role in the daily life of the community. Menzies himself had been more than happy to use state power to advance liberal social policies and for his own electoral advantage. The innate tensions between liberals and conservatives within the party had been held in check by the towering figure of Menzies, and the years following his departure proved to be a testing time for the party he had created.

The Liberal Party chose Harold Holt as the replacement prime minister. He was friendly and personable, an avid sportsman who still swam and spear-fished whenever he could find the time. His basic decency and amiability of character made him popular with his colleagues in government and later in the year proved a strong electoral asset with the general public.

PRIME MINISTER HOLT

Harold Holt offered a more inclusive management style: "There is the leadership which can lead but at the same time, be close enough to the team to be a part of it and be on the basis of friendly cooperation. I will make that my technique of leadership."[1]

Changes in emphasis quickly emerged in attitudes to Asia and Southeast Asia. Menzies had always avoided Australia's northern neighbors, merely flying over them on his way to Europe or North America, but Holt actually seemed to like Asians and visited all of Australia's Southeast Asian neighbors in his first year of office. He made personal and friendly contact in this way with the heads of government in South Vietnam, Malaysia, Singapore, and Thailand.

Perhaps as a corollary, the last vestiges of the White Australia Policy were quietly disposed of during 1967, and the final barriers to skilled Asian immigration were removed. Holt's lack of racial prejudice also affected policies toward Aborigines. In May 1967, the government, with bipartisan support from the ALP, took a referendum to the Australian people that proposed to give the Commonwealth power to legislate for Aborigines. The intention was to put a stop to discrimination against Aborigines and to ensure that they would become full Australian citizens. Since federation, Aboriginal welfare had been a state concern, and by and large, the states had done very little for indigenous people. After all, they did not vote, so why waste money on them? Aboriginal health, housing, and education were scandals, and segregation was openly practiced in rural areas. Moreover, as workers on the northern pastoral stations Aborigines received rates of pay that were much lower than the wages paid to whites, and their working conditions were vastly inferior. This was clearly discrimination on the basis of color, and in September 1966, Aborigines at Wave Hill station in the Northern Territory had appealed to the United Nations for protection.

DEEPENING INVOLVEMENT IN VIETNAM

One of the legacies Menzies had left to his successors was Australia's involvement in the war in Vietnam, including the related questions of conscription and Australia's reliance on the United States for military protection. In March 1966, Holt announced that Australia would triple its commitment in South Vietnam to 4,500 men, who would constitute a self-contained task force under Australian command and would include conscripts. The opposition claimed that the government was cynically manipulating events for its own political advantage. If Communist China was really such a rogue state and a threat to world peace, then why promote trade with China? By accusing China of hostile intentions, Holt built up an advantageous electoral climate while simultaneously trading with China-won votes in rural areas.² Holt's government definitely seemed to have the best of both worlds.

THE AMERICAN ALLIANCE

The American alliance became inextricably intertwined with the Vietnam debate, because the coalition labeled all opposition to the war as anti-Americanism. Ironically, the ALP, which had initiated the turn to America against conservative opposition during World War II, became suspect for being opposed to the United States and its policies. Since the signing of the ANZUS pact, Liberal/Country Party governments had made the treaty with America the cornerstone of Australia's defense planning. They would do whatever it took to secure an American commitment to the defense of Australia, even if that meant sending conscripts to fight and die in Vietnam. The ALP vainly protested that it was opposed to American policy not to America, but it proved too subtle a distinction for most people, and the Holt government tapped into traditional Australian fears concerning the danger from Asia and the absolute need for a great and powerful ally with considerable success. The downside of such a policy, however, was an unthinking and automatic support of American policy on the war and Asia in general.

In June 1966, Prime Minister Holt visited the United States and in a speech before American president Lyndon Baines Johnson announced that Australia would go "All the way with LBJ." Many Australians shared Holt's affection for the president and gave Johnson a tumultuous welcome when he accepted Holt's invitation and toured Australia later that year. Johnson's visit also brought demonstrators into the streets, and antiwar activists jostled and scuffled with pro-Johnson supporters as the president's cavalcade drove past. It marked the escalation of a deeply divisive community debate on conscription for overseas service.

CONSCRIPTION AGAIN

Harold Holt called an election just one month after President Johnson's visit and focused the campaign squarely on the issues of the war, conscription, and the American alliance. The government won overwhelmingly, with eighty-two seats to the ALP's forty-one in the House of Representatives. Holt had read the country's mood and recognized that it would support the war against Asian communism in Vietnam and also conscription to fight that war. While Australia was involved in an Asian war, to be anti-American was tantamount to treason. American protection became even more significant in 1967, when Britain announced its intention to withdraw altogether from its bases in Singapore and Malaysia.

THE ECONOMY

Despite the effects of a prolonged El Niño drought cycle between 1964 and 1966, which impacted with particular severity in Queensland and New South Wales, costing producers hundreds of millions of dollars, the general strength of the Australian economy was demonstrated during 1967 when the Conciliation and Arbitration Commission replaced the concept of basic wage plus margins, established by the Harvester decision in the early years of the century, with a "total wage." The new approach absorbed the margins into a wage package for each industry, and future national wage increases would apply to this total wage.

An expectation of sustained economic growth was built into the new system, and similar optimistic expectations underlay the drive to bring married women into the workforce. Women had been liberated from their traditional roles of childbearing and housework by the arrival of cheap reliable contraception in the 1960s, and Australian women proved to be among the most enthusiastic in the world in their readiness to embrace the new opportunities scientific advances had made available. Spokeswomen began to argue that females were also entitled to expect a fair go in the workforce and that there was nothing gender specific in the concept.

THE LIBERAL PARTY: LEADERSHIP CHANGES

The government lost several by-elections and a Senate position in the Senate elections of 1967. ALP leader Gough Whitlam had begun to cause Holt enormous difficulties in the battles of parliamentary debate, and the prime minister had much on his mind on 17 December 1967 when he disappeared into the surf near his home in Melbourne never to be seen again. Despite an exhaustive search, no trace could be found, though a helicopter crew reported a huge shark in the area where the prime minister had last been sighted. A memorial service attended by President Johnson and the prince of Wales, the current and former prime ministers of England, and heads of state from South Vietnam, the Philippines, South Korea, New Zealand, Singapore, Malaysia, and Thailand attested to the popularity of Harold Holt with other world leaders. Never had so many Asian heads of state been in Australia at the same time; it was an obvious reflection of the changes in the country over which Holt had presided during his brief tenure in office.

Holt's party voted to replace him with Senator John Gorton, the minister for education and science. Gorton was the first prime minister to come from the Senate. He resigned his position in the upper house and won the by-election for Holt's seat in the House of Representatives. John Gorton marked a departure from the usual pattern of conservative political leaders in Australia. He was an unashamed Australian nationalist and possessed a streak of rowdyism that was to make him popular with the public but also an electoral risk. As government leader in the Senate he had acquitted himself well, while Holt had received a thorough mauling from Whitlam in the lower house. Gorton's supporters considered that he was one of the few Liberal members of Parliament capable of matching the formidable Whitlam. Gorton, a returned fighter pilot from World War II, possessed a combative nature, and Liberals hoped this aggression might curb the leader of the ALP, who was establishing an ascendancy in the House of Representatives that boded ill for the government.

PRIME MINISTERS GORTON AND McMAHON

The communal divisions caused by the war were beginning to tear the country apart. Thousands of young men refused to register for conscription, and when called up, they refused to be inducted into the army, either leaving the country, going into hiding, or developing a range of subterfuges to fail the medical. Public demonstrations against the war grew more violent as police and antiwar protesters confronted one another. Gorton and his successor floundered in office, and their reiterated statements of uncritical support for the United States palled as the war in Vietnam became increasingly unpopular.

Opposition to Gorton grew within his own party, exacerbated by his boorish and unacceptable behavior in private and his tendency to be autocratic and masterful in cabinet. Holt's leadership had relied upon persuasion and teamwork, while Gorton expected that the views of the prime minister must always prevail. This tendency ruffled the feathers of his ministers, as did his partiality for attractive women and his heavy drinking. Holt had similar proclivities but possessed a sense of decorum, whereas Gorton's indiscretions achieved rapid notoriety. Gorton's rival William McMahon, on the other hand, had such a well-deserved reputation as a disloyal leaker of ministerial secrets to the media that Whitlam described him in the House of Representatives as Tiberius with a telephone. Neither of the stopgap prime ministers established any significant ideological positions appropriate for conservatives in a rapidly changing world. They had run out of ideas and relied solely on vigorous anticommunism to maintain the government in office.

Meanwhile, Australia's trade figures began to decline as the bill for more than twenty years of unremitting coalition hostility toward China finally was presented. Canada extended diplomatic recognition to China and received an immediate reward in a large wheat purchase. Since by this time China took approximately one-third of Australia's annual wheat crop, the loss of such a market weighed heavily on rural producers. The fruit of decades of coalition vilification and abuse was a Chinese preference for wheat from countries that had extended recognition. The existing Australia/China wheat agreement expired in October 1970, and the Chinese did not renew it.

Gorton resigned in 1971 and was replaced by William McMahon. The new prime minister seemed destined for disaster. He came to office as the first effects of the world recession of the 1970s began to impact upon the Australian economy. Unemployment and inflation were steadily rising throughout the world, and after thirty years of prosperity, Australian electors showed little patience with a government manifestly unable to deal with the problems. For the rest of McMahon's term in office, inflation and unemployment proved to be intractable, although later in the decade his 2 percent unemployment and 6 percent inflation would have brought joy to the heart of any Australian government.

LABOR RETURNS FROM THE WILDERNESS

By the time of the next federal election in December 1972, McMahon had become a figure of ridicule saddled with the nickname "Silly Billy." A faction-ridden and dispirited government faced a buoyant and supremely confident ALP, which ran a very professional campaign on the theme that it was time for a change. Where the government vacillated, the ALP offered firm policies and a well-constructed program that had been carefully constructed by Gough Whitlam. On 2 December 1972, the first ALP government since 1949 was voted into office. The ALP secured a majority of seven in the House of Representatives, but with ominous overtones from 1931, the opposition retained control of the Senate. The Liberal Party voted McMahon out of the leadership and replaced him with Billy Mackie Sneddon.

A Labor government after twenty-three years raised expectations. But although the electorate had voted for change, seven seats did not constitute an overwhelming vote for innovation. It was Whitlam's failure to recognize the limited nature of his mandate that made the next three years so tumultuous. As leader of the opposition, Whitlam had presided over the formulation of a political program, and he was impatient to begin its implementation. Rather than wait for caucus to select the ministry, Whitlam and his deputy Lance Barnard had themselves sworn in as a two-man ministry, holding all the portfolios between them. This was unusual though constitutional, and thus it was that for the first two weeks in office the new executive consisted of two individuals who speedily set about inaugurating momentous change. The diplomatic recognition of Communist China and the speedy withdrawal of all Australian servicemen from Vietnam marked the first of many reversals of policy. Neither caused any surprise, as they had long been part of Whitlam's program.

CRASH THROUGH OR CRASH

The pace of change did not slacken appreciably after the election of the full ministry and the Christmas break, though the holiday afforded the public service some breathing space to adjust to a new and impatient style of government. Only three of the ministers had been members of Parliament back when the Curtin-Chifley governments had held office, and none had been ministers. The prime minister himself was without experience in government and had already displayed a temperamental impatience that came later to be described by journalists and political commentators as a "crash through or crash" approach. His earlier tendency as leader of the opposition to announce new developments or policy changes publicly and then to defy caucus to overturn them was translated into a tendency to ride roughshod over opposition in the cabinet and to throw tantrums when unable to get his own way. This characteristic antagonized some of the strong personalities in the cabinet, and the prime minister's lack of manipulative skills and cabinet diplomacy have been described as attesting to his managerial naïveté.[3]

The inexperience and ineptitude of the new administration was demonstrated by Attorney General Lionel Murphy, when on the morning of 16 March 1973 he actually mounted a police raid on the headquarters of the Australian Security Intelligence Organisation (ASIO) and seized documents and files. Since ASIO was under Murphy's own control, the resultant publicity brought no credit to the new government. The image of the attorney general raiding his own department and failing to produce any supporting evidence of a plot to withhold information from him proved to be very damaging. Whitlam himself later admitted that this fiasco was probably his government's greatest mistake.[4]

Murphy's raid does highlight a major difficulty encountered by the new government. The public service had become used to and comfortable with conservative administrations and sometimes proved obstructive or slow to implement the changes desired by the ALP government. Moreover, there is some evidence that public servants in some departments actively sabotaged and subverted the new administration. One senior civil servant commented: "If only the Labor Party knew how much the public service personnel in many areas deliberately undermine their programs they would not sleep at night."[5]

WAGES POLICY AND THE ECONOMY

The two-man government requested the Arbitration Commission to reopen the recently concluded National Wage case, to withdraw the submission made by the previous Liberal/Country Party government and replace it with a new submission. The Arbitration Commission agreed and handed down a historic wage decision making it mandatory that females in the workforce received equal pay for work of equal value. More than 50,000 female public servants received wage increases under this ruling, and it flowed through the rest of the economy during the next few years. The Whitlam government upset business by using the civil service as pacesetters for improved wages and conditions, which then could not be withheld from workers in other sectors of the economy. This reversed the tradition that the public service traded higher wages and improved conditions for the certainty of employment.

The structural effects of the new policy approach can be gauged by average weekly earnings. In 1973, average weekly earnings rose by 13.6 percent and were accompanied by an inflation rate of 13.2 percent. The following year, average weekly earnings jumped by 30.8 percent, and an inflationary wage/price spiral became inevitable. An across-the-board tariff cut of 25 percent on all imported goods in July 1973 meant that protected Australian industries began to shed labor. The combination of rising unemployment, rising inflation, and rising wages created severe economic dislocation. The economy collapsed into chaos in October 1973 when the Organization of Petroleum Exporting Countries (OPEC) of the Middle East suddenly quadrupled oil prices, causing economic disintegration and recession in all industrialized capitalist countries. Once again, the ALP found itself in office at a time of massive economic dislocation without a majority in the Senate.

Given the general international economic malaise, it has to asked, Did an inexperienced government with a determination to produce change as quickly as possible attempt to achieve too much too rapidly? When the pursuit of change endangered the economic security of the electorate, a more experienced administration might well have become more cautious. But the ALP was led by a man who believed in and practiced a crash through or crash philosophy of government, and caution did not come naturally to him. Besides, the Scullin government had opted for a policy of caution during the depression of the 1930s and had still been dumped unceremoniously from office.

WOMEN UNDER LABOR

Of all the changes embraced by the new government in 1973, probably the most symbolic was women's affairs and not just in the wages area. Feminists had become increasingly important in the late 1960s and the early 1970s as shapers and movers of established Australian attitudes toward women and their role in society. Behind the froth and ridicule meted out by a hostile media to female activists—who demanded that the ethic of the fair go be extended to include women, campaigned for changes in abortion law, for equal pay, and for a radical reappraisal of relationships between males and females within Australian society— there lay a slow shift in attitudes. Societal views were altering, and in recognition of this, Whitlam appointed a special adviser to the prime minister on women's affairs. Elizabeth Reid's brief was to examine all cabinet submissions and advise on their impact on women. The prime minister was far ahead of his party on the question of women's issues, and he was also out of step with majority opinion in the trade union movement. Real change, as opposed to rhetorical flourishes and symbolic gestures, was destined to take decades.

THE POLITICAL SCENE CHANGES

In April 1974, Sneddon forced an election when the Senate failed to pass the government's appropriation bills. The coalition fought the campaign on the issue of inflation and the government's incompetent handling of the economy, while Whitlam went to the people requesting that the ALP government be given a fair go. The opposition-dominated Senate had refused to pass four government bills in addition to supply. Despite a volatile electorate the ALP was returned to office with the loss of a single seat in the House of Representatives, but the party failed once again to gain a majority in the Senate.

Two aspects of the political situation changed dramatically as a result of the 1974 election. Firstly, the DLP lost all its seats in the Senate and disappeared forever. Second, as provided for in the constitution, the first joint sitting of both houses of the Federal Parliament took place in August 1974, and the ALP's disputed legislation was passed triumphantly into law.

Throughout the remainder of 1974 as the hapless Sneddon was systematically destroyed in Parliament by Whitlam, the Liberal heir-apparent Malcolm Fraser watched and waited. In March 1975, Sneddon's position had been sufficiently eroded for Fraser to stand against him for the leadership, and Sneddon was ignominiously deposed. The new leader of the opposition proclaimed his belief that a government that had been elected twice in less than two years was entitled to govern for its full term. Fraser promised that he would never force an election, as Sneddon had done, by denying the government passage of its budget in the Senate, unless extraordinary and reprehensible circumstances should occur. The hollowness of this undertaking would soon be demonstrated.

THE ARTS

Australian cultural life had benefited immensely from the large European infusion after 1947, and by the 1970s, the worlds of painting and literature reflected a lessening of the national sense of isolation. Whitlam, an intellectual by taste and inclination, proved enormously supportive to the creative arts and rode on a tidal wave of goodwill from this influential sector of the community. As prime minister, he supported and appreciated the work of local landscape artists like Arthur Boyd and Fred Williams and novelists like Morris West and Patrick White who extended literature's coverage by dealing with universal themes and a broader psychological canvas. He also took advantage of his good fortune in being in office when cultural events occurred in which he had played no part. For example, he presided over the opening of the Sydney Opera House by Queen Elizabeth II in 1973, amid a huge surge in national and international publicity. Similarly, when writer Patrick White received the Nobel Prize for Literature in 1973, some of the gloss rubbed off on the prime minister who was effusive in his congratulations. His support for modern art was demonstrated in his purchase of Jackson

Pollock's *Blue Poles* for the Australian National Art Gallery in Canberra, and the catholicity of his tastes emerged when he made a cameo appearance as himself in a raucous comedy film *The Adventures of Barry Mackenzie* written by comedian Barry Humphreys. Whitlam undoubtedly had become a major patron of the nation's cultural life, but it carried a high price as the economy collapsed.

THE LOANS AFFAIR

The second Whitlam government became the first Labor government ever to be reelected in the Federal Parliament, but the joint sitting marked the high point of its existence. The world economic climate continued to deteriorate, with the OPEC countries steadily increasing the price of crude oil and accelerating inflation in all industrialized countries. Domestically, unemployment and inflation posed serious problems, and the government lurched from crisis to crisis, while Malcolm Fraser searched for the "extraordinary and reprehensible circumstances" that would allow him to refuse to pass the budget in the Senate and force an election. Eventually, the government gave him the issue in the so-called loans affair.

The loans affair stemmed from the anxiety of Rex Connor, the minister for mines and energy, that Australia should regain control over its oil and mineral deposits, the rights to which had been cheaply passed over to foreign companies in the years of coalition rule. To "buy back the farm" would cost millions of dollars, and in the current economic climate, the only real source of such funds was the oil-rich countries of the Middle East. The government's intention of bypassing the formal apparatus for raising money overseas was leaked to the opposition and to an increasingly hostile media, and allegations of "funny money" began to be made. Despite the best efforts of the opposition, however, no evidence of substantial wrongdoing or criminality was uncovered until a dubious London-based broker named Tirath Khemlani was discovered still attempting to raise money on the government's behalf. Since both Whitlam and Connor had assured the House of Representatives that all authority to raise loans had been withdrawn, this resulted in the serious charge of deliberately deceiving Parliament. Connor resigned in disgrace, and Fraser had at last obtained the required circumstances in which the opposition could refuse to provide financing in the Senate. An election had become inevitable.

ADDITIONAL COMPLICATIONS

That the Senate would obey the behest of the leader of the opposition had been placed beyond doubt by the extraordinary behavior of the anti-Labor premiers of New South Wales and Queensland, who had both subverted political convention by filling ALP casual Senate vacancies with non-ALP senators. Strictly speaking, both premiers were entitled to make such appointments, but up to this time all political parties had permitted the party concerned to nominate senate replacements. Clearly, the deck was being stacked against Labor.

The Whitlam government also suffered from a series of smaller disasters culminating in the resignation of the deputy leader Lance Barnard, to take up the position of High Commissioner in London. Barnard's safe Labor seat of Bass in Tasmania was lost by the ALP in a massive swing against the government, which had lost its way and was drifting without purpose or direction from one disaster to another.

Nor was the Bass by-election the only electoral straw in the wind. In December 1974, Queensland held a state election, and the ALP received a heavy setback with a strong swing in favor of the Bjelke-Petersen coalition government. The following year, the popular ALP Premier Don Dunstan only just managed to hang on to office in South Australia and did so by pointedly disassociating himself and his government from the federal Labor government. The tide was running strongly against Labor and gathering momentum as 1975 progressed. Whitlam was doomed. It was no longer a matter of whether the opposition would win the next election but only of when it would be held.

CRISIS FOR THE GOVERNMENT

In this climate of opinion, Fraser used the loans affair as justification to deny supply and force an election. The government appeared to have cocooned itself from the world of everyday Australians. Millions of dollars expended on works of art like Jackson Pollock's *Blue Poles* for the National Gallery, or Whitlam's extensive trips visiting the ruins of classical civilization in Europe, did not sit well with people struggling to get by on the dole while inflation steadily eroded the value of their incomes.

The Senate withheld the budget in October 1975 and precipitated a major constitutional crisis. Without money the government would be unable to pay its bills or public service salaries by November. Fraser demanded a full general election to resolve the issue, but Whitlam believed the Senate's resolve would collapse before the money ran out. At this stage Governor General John Kerr intervened.

THE GOVERNOR GENERAL'S ROLE

Whitlam appointed Kerr as governor general in 1973, and he was well regarded by most people on both sides of politics. He had risen to the post of chief justice of New South Wales and was considered to be a sound constitutional lawyer.

This reputation proved to be unfounded, when Kerr breached constitutional convention and secretly consulted former Liberal Party Minister Garfield Barwick—then chief justice of Australia—over his proposed course of action. It is central to Australia's system of government that judiciary and politics are separated from one another, but the former chief justice of New South Wales and the current chief justice of Australia ignored the doctrine of the separation of powers and conspired together. Both Whitlam and Fraser received a summons from Kerr to visit the residence of the governor general on 11 November 1975. Fraser arrived first. His car was hidden from view, and he was taken to an anteroom where he waited while Kerr delivered the coup de grâce to the prime minister. When Whitlam arrived, he was shown into the governor general's presence and handed a letter removing him from office. Once the former prime minister had departed, Fraser was given a commission as caretaker prime minister to dissolve both Houses of Parliament and call a general election. The Senate immediately voted funds to support the caretaker government, and the country embarked upon one of the most divisive political campaigns of the twentieth century.

Labor supporters were furious that unilateral action by an unelected official like the governor general could ensure the demise of a properly elected government with two years of its term still to run and a comfortable working majority in the House of Representatives. On the other hand, Fraser and his supporters argued that the governor general had acted with complete propriety and legality. All they were doing was forcing an election at which the Australian people could express their opinion on the Whitlam government's performance. How could this be undemocratic? Fraser's stone-faced strength and stubborn refusal to admit that he had been responsible for unleashing a highly damaging crisis based upon a refusal to observe accepted political conventions contrasted with the frantic excitement of Labor supporters who made the slogan "Shame Fraser Shame" their theme for the election campaign.

Whitlam seemed transfixed by the events of 11 November and unable or unwilling to focus on wider concerns. Fraser, on the other hand, refused to concentrate on the constitutional issue and stubbornly fought to switch the emphasis to the government's ineptitude and fiscal irresponsibility. The result was a landslide win for Fraser and an overwhelming rejection of the ALP. The coalition won the biggest majority ever received since federation, collecting ninety-one seats in the House of Representatives to the ALP's thirty-six and gaining an absolute majority in the Senate.

THE AFTERMATH

Although the electoral arithmetic appeared to be overwhelmingly in Fraser's favor, the result should not overshadow the exceptional bitterness injected into Australian political affairs by the events of 11 November 1975. When the new Fraser government voted Kerr a salary increase of 171 percent in its first budget in 1976, ALP suspicions regarding the governor general seemed to be amply justified. Kerr's continuation in office constituted a persistent affront to the ALP and to many Australians who regarded his actions as quite improper. It also helped to stimulate the growth of republican sentiment, which had received a major stimulous from the dismissal. Moreover, Kerr's public behavior on occasions when he seemed to be the worse for liquor embarrassed the Fraser government, and he was mourned by no one in 1977 as he slipped out of the country and effectively into exile in Europe.

Malcolm Fraser, the new prime minister, must also accept a measure of responsibility for the acrimony he had helped unleash. The portents were for the Whitlam government to suffer a disastrous defeat when the next federal elections were held in 1976 or 1977. All Fraser had to do was to curb his eagerness and wait for the top office to drop into his lap like a piece of ripe fruit. Accession to power would then have been legitimate and unarguable. As it was, Fraser tainted himself and his government in the minds of many Australians by the indecent haste and overwhelming ambition the events of October and November 1975 demonstrated. For the next decade, Australian politics would revolve around the personalities of the protagonists in this great drama. Only after they had all departed the political scene would Australian federal politics shed some of the bitterness and personal animosity that characterized the next Liberal government; but permanent damage undoubtedly had been done to any sense of trust between either side of politics, and for the rest of the century mistrust and personal vilification became the norm and constituted Fraser's lasting legacy to Australian politics.

THE FRASER YEARS

The tone of Malcolm Fraser's time as prime minister owed much to his distaste for anything that carried reminders of the previous government. A great deal of effort was put into dismantling the elaborate apparatus of commissions and advisory committees through which Labor had sought to spread the message of centralism and increased Commonwealth involvement in many aspects of life. Severe cutbacks in expenditure in the fields of Aboriginal affairs, women's affairs, education, the arts, and social welfare were quickly put in place by a government intent on retrenchment in spending accompanied by selective financial incentives to its rural supporters and to businesses to increase production and assist the country to trade its way out of the economic morass into which it had strayed.

The previous Labor administration had antagonized many state governments by its use of tied grants to control developments in particular areas. The Fraser government took a different tack and under the label of "New Federalism" attempted to pass some income taxing powers back to the states. The system never actually came into operation, because the state premiers followed the lead of New South Wales Labor Premier Neville Wran, who insisted that any state government that introduced an additional income tax would be swept out of office by infuriated voters at the next election.

Malcolm Fraser also reversed the practice of using the federal public service as pacemaker for wages and conditions throughout the workforce. The new government quickly imposed staff ceilings on all federal departments and effectively limited the growth in the numbers of civil servants. In December 1976, the government introduced legislation allowing it to force redundancy on public servants on the grounds of excess numbers and to redeploy other staff to areas of greatest need. The following year further legislation permitted the government to remove without pay public servants who were unable to work due to any trade union industrial action in public or private spheres.

RISING UNEMPLOYMENT

The inevitable consequence of fighting inflation by rigorously pruning expenditure was rising unemployment. Government argued that a high level of unemployment was necessary in the short term in order to reduce inflationary wage expectations in the workforce and ultimately to curb inflation itself. The prime social effect was an increasingly demoralized and steadily growing pool of unemployed workers and eventually an assumption that the chronically unemployed really did not want to work. The term "dole bludger" entered the language at this time to describe someone who allegedly preferred to live in poverty rather than work for a living—an injustice, given the state of the economy that the government avidly perpetuated. The establishment of such a mentality meant that higher levels of unemployment than had ever been experienced outside the 1890s and the 1930s became acceptable. The Fraser government could effectively reduce living standards without incurring the blame such a policy would hitherto have earned. In 1961, an unemployment rate approaching 2 percent had almost caused defeat to the Menzies government. From the late 1970s onward, Australian governments could survive electorally with overall unemployment rates hovering around 10 percent and youth unemployment well into the 20 percent range. The measure of the Fraser government's achievement in this area is demonstrated by the increase in unemployment from 275,400 in December 1975 to 439,200 in January 1980 and 674,000 by the end of 1982.

A MULTICULTURAL SOCIETY

With unemployment running so high, immigration policies that added to the number of unemployed persons on social services came in for scrutiny, and care had to be taken to ensure that communal tensions were not aroused. Between 1950 and 1971, Australia's population had risen from 8 million to 12.7 million, and immigrants and their Australian-born children accounted for 53 percent of the increase. Migration patterns had also begun to produce fundamental changes in the Australian way of life. European and Middle Eastern migrants brought with them their national customs and found that for the most part these transplanted readily to their new country. Many of these exotic influences percolated through to the mass of the Anglo/Australian population. Foods became increasingly varied and imaginative, wine consumption grew, and footpath cafes, coffee bars, and exotic delicatessens added to the quality of Australian life, especially in the large urban centers.

In the capital cities themselves, entire suburbs slowly developed into ethnic neighborhoods in which English was a second language, and migrant language presses maintained a steady output of newspapers and magazines. Cultural and sporting clubs grew up that reflected the ethnic divisions within the different cities and locales, while suburban shopping centers demonstrated the changes in ethnicity by a plethora of multilan-

guage signs in shop windows. By the end of the 1970s government financed immigration was abolished, but a rising tide of refugee "boat
people" fleeing from communist-controlled Vietnam and Cambodia were
welcomed in Australia and added a further cultural complexity to an
already diverse Australian society.

While some opposition was expressed by small extremist groups, the
Whitlam government's Anti-Discrimination Act of 1975 ensured that a
resigned and occasionally sullen acquiescence seemed to be the usual
reaction of most Australians to the influx of non-Anglo-Celtic peoples.
The country could not isolate itself from international events and the
world community. Australia was no longer protected by distance.

FRASER IN DECLINE

In October 1980, the Fraser government stood once again for election,
and although the government was returned, the ALP picked up thirteen
seats from the coalition and was now within striking distance of victory.
The government had also lost seats in the Senate to a new party, the
Australian Democrats, led by former Liberal Cabinet Minister Don Chipp
who had been driven from the party by Fraser's conservatism. The Democrats held the balance of power in the Senate, and Chipp and the new
party had hit a nerve when they campaigned on the slogan "Keep the
bastards honest." Nobody was in any doubt that the "bastards" included
the members of all major political parties; and from then on, the Australian Democrats received consistent support from a voting public that
would vote for one of the major parties for the lower house, then cast a
restraining vote for the Democrats in the Senate.

Meanwhile, all was not well in the ALP, where Whitlam's replacement
Bill Hayden had come under sustained pressure from the followers of
an impatient rising star, the former president of the Australian Council
of Trade Unions, Robert James Lee Hawke. Although Hawke had only
been in Parliament since 1980, his supporters felt that they had to force
Hayden out before the next election because he might actually win it and
be impossible to remove as prime minister. Hawke's people argued that
while Hayden might win, only Hawke could guarantee to win because
of his extraordinary public profile. Hawke was widely known throughout Australia, especially for his abilities as a mediator between employers and unions during intractable industrial disputes. His conciliatory
abilities stood in marked contrast to Malcolm Fraser's confrontational
approach, and it was generally accepted that he was Australia's most
charismatic politician.

Malcolm Fraser, sensing the danger posed by Hawke, determined on a snap election before Hawke's supporters could marshal the numbers to overthrow Hayden. Fraser had anticipated preempting the move against Hayden and propping him up as leader of the ALP to ensure another three years in office. Hayden, however, seeing the writing on the wall, voluntarily withdrew as leader of the ALP in favor of Hawke, and where the government had hoped for savage internecine wrangling in the opposition, it found instead that it was confronted by a united party led by its nemesis Bob Hawke. Fraser had triumphantly announced in the press that he had caught Bill Hayden with his pants down, only to find himself publicly exposed in the same predicament. The government never recovered from this, and on 5 March 1983, the ALP won a resounding victory with a majority of twenty-five seats in the House of Representatives. Labor had campaigned on a policy of reconciliation and reconstruction after eight years of what was described as the most divisive government Australia had ever experienced.

When the result was announced, television cameras focused on a modest and magnanimous victor, then on a bitterly disappointed and weeping Malcolm Fraser. Would conciliation and consensus, personified by Hawke, bring the country together and bind up the deep wounds after the communal strife of 1975 and its aftermath? Would the departure of Malcolm Fraser finally allow the wounds to heal and a new start to be made? Kerr, Whitlam, and Fraser had all left the stage; there were new protagonists and different problems to be encountered. By rejecting Malcolm Fraser the electorate had also voted to put the events of 1975 behind it and to get on with the business of bringing Australia into the period of its bicentenary and thereafter into the twenty-first century.

Hawke had looked constructively to the future and had talked about his hopes of making Australia a better country to live in. He had come to personify the fair go, and the electorate perceived him that way and swept him into office on a wave of goodwill and national sentimentality. Whether any political leader could live up to those expectations and to what extent the substitution of consensus for traditional ALP policies would be acceptable to party and people in the long run provided the subtext for the next decade.

11

Deconstruction and Multiculturalism (1984–1996)

If ever a government came to power on a tide of optimism and goodwill, it was the first Hawke government. Hawke resisted the helter-skelter pace of reform that had been so exhilarating and so characteristic of the previous Whitlam administration. Consensus was to replace confrontation, and consensus required time to emerge. This was a reformist government, cautious in outlook and nonradical by temperament; this was no wild-eyed bunch of revolutionaries intent on overturning Australian society and abolishing capitalism but a sober-sided group of politicians who prided themselves on their professionalism and managerial competence.

HAWKE'S EARLY YEARS

The state of the economy and the performance of the government were inextricably meshed. The new treasurer Paul Keating devalued the Australian dollar by 10 percent and floated the currency before announcing with the prime minister their discovery that the country's finances were in a perilous condition. They used the precarious state of the economy and the high level of Australia's international debt as a justification for failing to honor their election promises. This admission that the country could not afford the policies the government had been elected to implement brought Hawke great kudos from Labor's traditional enemies. They saw it as evidence of firm and decisive leadership, whereas for many ALP supporters it merely demonstrated the new government's appalling readiness to jettison inconvenient promises once it had attained office. Fortunately, economic indicators soon brightened when within a few days of the election a prolonged El Niño drought cycle ended, and the rains brought renewed optimism to Australia's primary producers whose exports during the oncoming wet cycle were expected to reduce the high level of the deficit quickly.

IN SEARCH OF CONSENSUS

The prime minister did move promptly to call together summit meetings between employers and union organizations in 1983, and on taxation reform in 1984, as part of his plan to heal the deep wounds caused by the years of confrontation under Malcolm Fraser. These conferences produced little more than reformist rhetoric. The former Liberal leader facilitated consensus by quietly resigning as leader and retiring from Parliament to his farm Nareen where he watched as his successors—Andrew Peacock, the leader, and John Howard, the deputy leader—spent more time and energy fighting one another than in attacking the new ALP government.

The economic summit induced a plethora of patriotic and high-sounding generalizations about the partnership between capital and labor and the necessity for cooperation and better communication between management and workforce. On the other hand, once the conference moved to discuss specifics, old responses reappeared. The two major construction unions, the Building Workers Industrial Union (BWIU) and the Builders Labourers Federation (BLF), both announced that they had no intention of exercising wage restraint in the interests of the economy and the wider workforce. Their job was to maximize outcomes for their members, and they were determined to follow such a course, even if it left them outside the agreements brokered by the government and the ACTU. The following year, Paul Keating attempted unsuccessfully to reform the taxation system and introduce a tax on goods and services at another so-called summit on taxation.

THE ACCORD

The Prices and Incomes Accord, usually referred to simply as the Accord, dominated the whole period of the Hawke and Keating governments. In Hawke's time alone, it went through six versions that were ratified by the Industrial Relations Commission (IRC) and its predecessor the Arbitration Commission, and each of these became the centerpiece of the government's wages and incomes policy at that time. The Accords were designed to bring a measure of control over the economy and to give employers the advantage of knowing the policy framework and economic settings within which the government operated. They could not be taken by surprise by union claims that were artificially inflated for bargaining purposes because such claims would be outside the Accord and therefore unacceptable to the government and unratified by the IRC. Wage restraint was accepted by the ACTU, and improvements in workers' standards of living were pursued through alternative areas like taxation reform, improved social welfare, and superannuation (a retirement pension). The Accords not only secured a broad consensus over wages policy, but they made the ACTU a virtual partner with the government in establishing the structure of economic policy in general. This was one area where consensus appeared to enjoy a signal success, yet the question of how the Accords fitted into Australia's version of the Westminster System of government remained unclear. After all, parliamentarians could be called to account at elections, but what redress did those disadvantaged by the new system have against the ACTU?

CHANGING ECONOMIC ORTHODOXY

The innate financial conservatism of the Hawke-Keating government manifested itself once again in July 1984 at the ALP's national conference, where the treasurer sought and won approval to reverse years of ALP economic orthodoxy and to deregulate the banking system and welcome foreign banks to operate in Australia. Since the 1890s, Labor had been suspicious of the banks that it regarded as parasitical. But the party of controls had been taken captive by an even older ideology of free trade and economic deregulation. The primacy of market forces sat uneasily within the ALP, given the party's historic interests in regulation and industrial protection, yet despite misgivings, the conference endorsed the proposal to free up the Australian economy. It began a process that resulted over the following decade in the sale of all the government-run banks. Government banks had given the authorities the competitive ability to control banking charges and fees. Relinquishing any active role in banking by government left the community hostage to the greed of the private banking sector. The Accords fettered the workforce to minimum salary increases, while financial reconstruction set business and finance sectors free to pursue unlimited profit.

One consequence of the new arrangements was a serious downturn in the level of real wages paid to Australian workers that began in 1984 and ran consistently through to 1989. There was a clear and sustained decline in domestic household savings during these years, as falling real wages forced Australian families to consume disposable income for living expenses.[1] Yet the Hawke government managed to remain in office despite a state of affairs that in normal circumstances would have ensured defeat at the hands of an incensed and irritated electorate. This was partly due to the disarray and internal divisions within the coalition, as Peacock and Howard jostled for supremacy, but it was also due to the fact that the Accords trapped the ACTU into supporting a government that directly damaged the welfare and living standards of its members. It was no coincidence that this period of ALP government from 1983 to 1996 witnessed a continuing decline in the membership of both ALP and the trade union movement as disillusioned members withdrew from both organizations.

DEREGULATION AND OVERSEAS DEBT

The growing economic malaise eventually caused repercussions on overseas financial markets. Australia's increasing indebtedness indicated that the country was living beyond its means. The government's failure to reign in this rising level of debt stemmed from its inability to control the activities of large corporate buccaneers who took advantage of deregulation to borrow billions of dollars. These borrowings financed unproductive corporate takeovers and mergers. Early in 1986, the value of the free-floating Australian dollar suddenly collapsed by about 20 percent, which effectively raised the level of foreign debt by a comparable amount, leading the treasurer to declare on radio that Australia faced becoming a "Banana Republic."

Deregulation and *economic rationalism* became the watchwords of an essentially bipartisan policy framework at the national level, and the resultant consequences were a shared responsibility. The reduction of financial regulation and the reluctance of the Reserve Bank to intervene both meant that extensive credit was readily available. The so-called corporate excesses of the 1980s were directly attributable to an easy access to credit in a deregulated financial market. The Reserve Bank responded with rising interest rates, but these damaged productive enterprises that could no longer afford to expand. On the other hand, the corporate predators remained unperturbed and continued borrowing. Once again, large quantities of overseas capital flowed into Australia, attracted by the high interest rates, and the old but too familiar pattern of speculative boom followed by recession or depression seemed all too likely to reappear. Both sides of federal politics therefore must share accountability for the massive growth of Australian debt and for failure to preserve the national interest even if at the cost of unpopularity with the banks and the business interests. As unemployment grew and recession deepened, the prime minister and the treasurer kept assuring Australians that they were really better off than they had been before deregulation, but ordinary Australians had their doubts.

In the federal elections of July 1987, the ALP returned to office for a historic third term. No previous federal Labor administration had ever won a third mandate, and one of the reasons for this success lay in fiscal bipartisanship. The ALP under Hawke had pirated the traditional conservative ideology on free trade and economic deregulation, and with the electorate increasingly unwilling to swallow the old anticommunist fear campaigns, the opposition experienced considerable difficulty in establishing a distinct and separate identity for itself in a post–Cold War environment.

THE STOCK MARKET CRASHES

Hawke's timing proved fortuitous, as less than three months later, the international stock market collapsed. The value of Australian stocks and shares plummeted nearly 40 percent, and international central banks chose to promote international recovery by agreeing to work together and maintain business confidence by providing a high level of credit. While such a policy might well have been correct for the world at large, increasing credit for Australian entrepreneurs was the financial equivalent of pouring gasoline on a fire. The collapse of the stock markets provided only a temporary interruption to their incessant borrowing. Soon, bigger and bigger corporate takeovers occurred, financed by huge loans both domestic and foreign, as banks seemingly flung money at dubious businessmen. Bank lending to business grew by 24 percent during 1986–1987 and by 29 percent during 1987–1988. When high interest rates finally did begin to slow down the economy, they not only affected the corporate paper-shufflers but also destroyed many orthodox and productive enterprises. Good and bad companies collapsed and asset values plummeted.[2]

SCANDALS AND DISASTERS

During its transition from a party of the lower orders to a party more representative of the bourgeoisie, the ALP at both state and federal levels had formed close links with some disreputable denizens of the corporate sector and had indulged in questionable business practices designed to retain business support for ALP administrations. During the third Hawke government a number of scandals came to light that caused serious affront to the party's traditional constituency and cast grave doubts on ALP claims to superior managerial ability and competence. These were not short-lived political emergencies but long-running cancers that by the end of the decade were to bring down ALP state governments in Western Australia, Victoria, and South Australia. The prime minister's enthusiastic acknowledgment of his friendships with failed and eventually incarcerated entrepreneurs such as Alan Bond or Laurie Connell, or his continuing relationships with businessmen with daring reputations like Sir Peter Abeles and Kerry Packer, kindled a quickening uneasiness as public inquiries in several states brought to light associations between ALP functionaries and businessmen that were unwise, sometimes improper, and occasionally illegal. Moreover, the prime minister and the federal government became tainted with guilt by association when these financial irregularities were exposed.

Just as financial policy was bipartisan during these decades, so too was the prevalence of corruption at the state level; and Queensland and Tasmania provided ample illustration that coalition politicians were as well practiced in criminal activities as were their ALP counterparts in the other states. In Queensland, the National Party government, led by Premier Joh Bjelke-Petersen, became notorious for the irregular activities of ministers and premier and for the venality of the police. Bjelke-Petersen's admission to a Commission of Inquiry that businessmen seeking favorable treatment from his government would sometimes leave brown paper bags containing thousands of dollars on his desk aroused disgust and repugnance; while in Tasmania, the Liberal leader was found guilty of offering a $100,000 bribe to an ALP member of Parliament. The conservative forces in Australia were irretrievably tainted by the seemingly endless revelations of malpractice, and this robbed complaints of ALP corruption and incompetence of much of their force. At the same time, bipartisan corruption also increased the contempt and hostility many Australians felt for politicians of all persuasions.

DEREGULATION AND PRIMARY INDUSTRY

Deregulation also flowed through to primary industry, as many Australian farmers succumbed to tumbling returns. The price of wool collapsed to the point where foreign buyers made up only 10 percent of purchasers, and the government-funded Wool Corporation actually purchased and stored the bulk of the annual wool clip. That Australia was selling its wool to itself was a comedic situation that could not be permitted to continue. In the deregulatory climate of the 1990s, Australian primary producers were forced to compete on the open market or go under. The declining contribution of wool to the country's export earnings was dramatic. By October 1991, wool prices had fallen to their nadir, regressing to below the level of 1890, and more than $3.5 billion in overseas income had been lost.

Since the nineteenth century Australian wool had been competitive with the rest of the world, and there seemed little doubt that after reconstruction the wool industry could once again resume its primacy in the rural exports of Australia. The same could not be said, however, for the wheat industry, and therein lay an anomaly. Australian wheat could compete successfully on an open international market if other countries played by the deregulation rules. In such circumstances the terms of trade favored Australia's wheat growers. But in 1991, Australian growers lost market share to subsidized wheat sold by the United States, Canada, and the European Common Market. Australian wheat farmers faced a serious crisis as the Australian government refused assistance to them and their chief competitors refused to compete without subsidy. It made little difference that in June 1991 Treasurer Paul Keating resigned from the ministry after an unsuccessful attempt to dethrone Bob Hawke and was replaced by former Minister for Primary Industry John Kerrin. By this time the ideology of free trade and economic rationalism had become an article of faith with all the mainstream political groups in Australia. The rider might change, but the horse continued to gallop in the same direction.

In the outback, as in the cities, the chief villain was the banking sector. It was not just corporate Australia that had been corrupted by financial deregulation and the flood of speculative capital that flooded into Australia during the 1980s. When the corporate collapses began, the banks looked for ways to recoup their losses. High interest rates and ruthless foreclosures in rural Australia became policy as the financial institutions attempted to cover the losses they had incurred during the years in which they had funded the corporate raiders. The managers of country bank branches pointed the finger of blame at top management and claimed that they no longer had authority over bank lending and repossession policy at ground level.[3]

Estimates of farm debt varied between $300,000 and $500,000 per property, and as farm incomes declined precipitously the banks declined to extend more credit and the value of rural properties plunged. The rising generation of young farmers began to sell up and leave the land, and traditional family properties fell into the hands of large agribusinesses involved in corporate farming. The move was to ever larger properties in pursuit of economies of scale. The historic desire of white Australians to own a piece of rural Australia and to wrest a living from it came openly into conflict with the new economic reality that innovative agricultural technology had become too expensive for most individual farmers. The statistics of the rural decline of the early 1990s indicate the stark reality:

> Farm incomes slashed by 67 per cent with 38 per cent of farmers receiving no income at all, 75 per cent of farmers owing $225,000 or more, financial returns per hectare down 92 per cent, farm sector spending cut by $5 billion, total losses to the economy totalling $10 billion, the margin for wheat growers between costs and prices down to 2 per cent.[4]

The ALP government and the economic institutions that unleashed this financial reign of terror managed to escape the consequences because the opposition espoused the same policies and an identical ideology. As the former prime minister and farmer Malcolm Fraser pointed out, deregulatory bipartisanship meant that the Liberal Party stood by and applauded as the ALP initiated policies that were to cause so much damage.[5] In November 1991, the Hawke government was forced to alter welfare regulations to enable primary producers to go on the dole without having to sell their farms.

ABORIGINAL POLICY

Such concerns were far from the minds of most Australians, however, on 26 January 1988 when the nation celebrated the bicentenary of white settlement. It was a day of patriotic pride and goodwill for most Australians, though descendants of the Aborigines held a day of mourning and a large pro-Aboriginal demonstration and march at the end of which they castigated both federal and state governments for 200 years of neglect and racial prejudice.

Aboriginal rights and ALP policy came into conflict over the question of mining in Northern Australia. When some Aboriginal groups wanted to open uranium mines on their land, they soon ran into ideological opposition from the ALP. The irony of Aboriginal support for increased uranium mining, and the royalty income it promised them, grew even richer when the Hawke government refused to consider reopening the mine at Coronation Hill on the fringes of Kakadu National Park.

Coronation Hill had been a successful uranium mine during the 1950s and 1960s, and recent geological exploration had shown it possessed deposits of platinum and gold that could easily be mined and would earn Australia hundreds of millions of dollars. Reopening mining there was opposed vociferously by the Greens on the grounds of ecological damage to Kakadu and by the local Jawoyn Aborigines who first agreed that mining could take place but later on reversed their decision. Aborigines believed mining would disturb Bula, a local deity said to be asleep beneath the surface. Bula had the reputation of being capable of enormous mischief and destruction. The mining industry, for its part, demanded access to Coronation Hill and pointed out that it had already been extensively mined without awakening Bula. The deposits of platinum and gold carried high international earning potential, and Australia could ill afford to turn its back on such a considerable sum of money. The mining industry and the opposition reacted to the refusal with great bitterness and complained that a decision permitting the religious rights of a very small number of people to override the welfare of the entire nation might well drive potential investors to other countries that were more self-interested and less self-indulgent.

MULTICULTURALISM

One of the great defining issues that separated the ALP government from the opposition during the Hawke years was the symbolic area of immigration. The Liberal leader John Howard attempted to stem the growth of a multicultural and cosmopolitan Australia by stressing that incoming migrants should assimilate into the mainstream community, and this became the policy position of the coalition under the rubric "One Australia." Howard abandoned the bipartisan tradition on immigration that had marked all administrations since 1947 and attempted to tap into a core of dissatisfaction and unhappiness revealed by the Fitz-Gerald Report on Australian Immigration Policy that had been presented to Parliament during 1988. The FitzGerald Report had demonstrated that genuine consensus did not exist over multiculturalism, and it was this underlying uneasiness that Howard attempted to exploit for the Liberals.

Howard plunged into this emotional vortex when he proclaimed "One Australia" and was caught in an impossible position. His concern lay in those wider community tensions to which FitzGerald Stephen had alluded, and he worried about the nation's ability to absorb large numbers of Asian migrants. But the migrant lobby was too strong to ignore, and the Liberals quickly disposed of Howard in favor of Andrew Peacock. Peacock held more liberal views on immigration and multiculturalism, and at his first press conference after the coup, he announced the restoration of bipartisanship in this area. When Peacock lost the 1990 election, the Liberals—in an effort to replace the endless recycling of Howard and Peacock—replaced him with former professor of economics John Hewson.

HAWKE VERSUS KEATING

Reconciliation and healing were also sorely needed within the Labor government from 1988 onward, as the rivalry between prime minister and treasurer began to impact upon government performance. The relationship between the government's two main performers became so poisoned that in November 1988 they met at the prime ministerial villa in Sydney, Kirribilli House, where Hawke—before witnesses called by both men—promised to retire as prime minister and leader of the ALP in favor of Keating after the 1990 elections. The blatant impropriety of such a compact in a democratic country and in a democratically based party seemed not to concern either man. The promise, when it came to light in 1991, proved that Hawke had lied throughout the 1990 election when he promised specifically that he would stay on as prime minister. If he had meant to keep that undertaking, it could only have been done by violating the pledge he had made to Keating in 1988. One way or the other, the prime minister had been exposed as a liar, which did little to restore the credibility of politicians from the abyss into which it continued to sink.

The whole sordid mess emerged in 1991 when Hawke reneged on his promise to Keating, and the treasurer challenged him before the ALP federal caucus. At first glance, it would seem nonsensical that any party member should challenge the most successful leader the ALP had ever produced, especially when that person was still the incumbent in the highest office in the land. But Paul Keating was a paradox in Australian politics. His economic policies of deregulation and economic rationalism had brought undoubted hardship to countless ordinary Australians and impacted heavily on the traditional working-class constituency of the ALP. By mid-1991, he had caused the Hawke government to be eighteen points behind the opposition in public opinion polls, and yet he was also the dynamo of a tired Hawke administration and far and away its best parliamentary performer. Keating as a teenager had spent a great deal of time around the former depression premier of New South Wales, Jack Lang, and Lang had influenced the young man's development. He had become, like his mentor Lang, a warrior whom the opposition rightly feared for the ferocity of his enmity and for his capacity in Parliament to leave them speechless and demoralized. Menzies had dominated Parliament with his wit and intellect, whereas Keating dominated it with his scalding invective and contempt for conservative social policies and politicians. The cynicism of his views on political leadership in Australia had been revealed in September 1990 when he responded to a suggestion that he could never hope to reverse his huge personal unpopularity, by commenting: "If the day comes that I have to throw the switch to vaudeville, I'll do it, understand? I mean, if one has to be all-singing, all-dancing, that's what we'll be. But all in due time. There's a more substantial agenda."[6]

So the challenge to Hawke in June 1991 was not one that the party took lightly, and when that challenge failed and Keating retired from the ministry to the back bench, the government, lacking anybody on its front bench of comparable ability, floundered badly in Parliament.

Keating continued his campaign to destabilize the prime minister from the back bench by publicly calling for a revision of policies he himself had formulated and for a return to a traditional ALP concentration on the provision of jobs for the unemployed. The ALP under Hawke showed all the signs of a tired and out-of-touch administration, and the "them and us" double standard of the government toward its supporters was reflected in an enormous decline in party membership. When Hawke led the ALP back into office in 1983, ALP membership rose Australia wide to around 50,000. By 1991, this had dropped to below 40,000 and was falling steadily. In that year, the party's national secretary attributed the fall-off in morale and numbers to a growing perception among blue-collar members that they had become irrelevant to the new-look ALP and they had become increasingly alienated from the party and its policies.[7]

The figures starkly mirror this alteration in the structural basis of the ALP. In the 1940s, 1 in 40 manual workers was a member of the party;

by the 1980s this had become 1 in 275. By the middle of 1991, the ALP had been transformed into a party in which the dominant group consisted of professionals and college students who had not joined the ALP to fight the evils of capitalist exploitation but to pursue an interest in implementing the policy ideals of the new social movements for feminism, peace, and the environment.[8]

The opposition recognized that Hawke was vulnerable on this issue, and their new leader John Hewson exploited his advantage in Parliament with telling effect, when he accused the Hawke administration of finally extinguishing the "light on the hill," that beacon of idealism that had activated Ben Chifley's Labor government. Hewson's charge was that Labor under Hawke had forfeited any legitimate claim to be the party of ordinary Australians. " 'People don't want any more special deals to help Labor's rich mates', he told Parliament. 'They want a realistic plan to make this country prosperous again.' "[9]

HAWKE'S LAST DAYS

In August 1990, Hawke decided—without even bothering to call a cabinet meeting—to commit three warships of the Royal Australian Navy to support an American-led international blockade of Iraq. The blockade would interdict all shipping to Iraq as a punishment for that country's invasion and occupation of Kuwait. The ensuing war caused no Australian casualties and brought a short-lived boost to the prime minister's fading popularity, as had his decision in 1989 to permit Chinese students marooned in Australia after the Tienanmen Square massacre to stay on as residents. But it was short-lived popularity, and when John Hewson announced the details of the coalition's new taxation package, which included sweeping reductions in personal income tax, the abolition of all wholesale tax, and the imposition of a new goods and services tax, the government found itself in real danger. Hawke and his front bench proved quite incapable of responding to Hewson's challenge, and the ALP found itself in the position of having to run a scare campaign against a policy it had itself supported and attempted to introduce at the ill-fated taxation summit. The government's chances of surviving the elections due in 1993 seemed next to impossible, and in desperation on 19 December 1991 the federal caucus of the ALP made the only decision available to it, if the malaise was not to prove terminal, and voted by a margin of five votes, fifty-six to fifty-one, for Paul Keating to replace Bob Hawke as leader of the ALP and prime minister. The vote was yet another historic first for Hawke, as it marked the first time the ALP had unseated a sitting prime minister. Hawke departed most unwillingly to the back bench, publicly shedding tears as he officiated at his final function as prime minister.

THE KEATING ASCENDANCY

Paul Keating's assumption of power in 1991 seemed to many to be a poisoned chalice, with the ALP dead in the water at both state and federal levels. The Hawke government had given the impression that it expected to be defeated in 1993, and its ministers were said to be actively canvassing alternative career options for the postelection years.[10]

At the state level, ALP governments fell like dominoes, beginning with Tasmania in February 1992, then Victoria in October 1992, then Western Australia early in 1993, followed by South Australia in December 1993. It seemed more than clear that at the state level the electorate—ravaged by recession—was intent on punishing ALP administrations for the corruption and incompetence they had demonstrated during the 1980s. It was in this unfavorable climate of opinion that Keating cemented his place in ALP mythology by reversing the trend of events and reinvigorating and inspiring a government that had appeared to be in the terminal stages of decay.

The first major response to John Hewson's "Fightback" taxation package came in February 1992, when Keating launched his "One Nation" alternative. One Nation effectively robbed the coalition of its major attraction of income tax cuts in return for a GST (goods and services tax) by offering broadly the same income tax cuts without an unsettling adventure into the unknown.

Keating also fused the twin themes of idealism and nationalism into a potent appeal to the younger members of the electorate. This was nowhere better demonstrated than in the furor over the visit of Queen Elizabeth to Australia in February 1992. Keating, in his speech of welcome, enunciated a vision of two countries once very close but now drifting apart as each pursued a regional destiny, Great Britain's in Europe and Australia's in the Asia-Pacific region. The opposition overreacted, attacking the prime minister for being undignified and disrespectful to Australia's head of state. Three days later Keating addressed them directly and painted an unequivocal picture of the differences between Labor and the coalition on the issue of nationalism and the British.

I was told that I did not learn respect at school. I learned one thing: I learned about self-respect and self-regard for Australia—not about some cultural cringe to a country which decided not to defend the Malaysian peninsula, not to worry about Singapore and not to give us our troops back to keep ourselves free of Japanese domination. This was the country that you wedded yourselves to, and even as it walked out on you and joined the Common Market, you were still looking for your MBEs [Members of the Order of the British Empire] and your knighthoods, and all the rest of the regalia that comes with it. You would take Australia right back down the time tunnel to the cultural cringe where you have always come from.[11]

The speech galvanized the ALP and delighted the dispirited parliamentarians who had hoped for just such leadership when they had disposed of Bob Hawke. It had been a long time since ALP back benchers had cheered their leader's sallies in debate, and they found plenty of occasion to cheer over the following weeks and months, as Keating established an undoubted ascendancy over the coalition front bench. But it was done at a heavy cost in terms of the destruction of personal civility and respect in Parliament and the complete eradication of the formerly clublike atmosphere that had been characteristic of Federal Parliament since 1901.

REGIONAL TIES

The other allied area in which the Keating-ALP outshone the opposition was in the enunciation of a clear vision of an Australian future inevitably linked with Asia. Keating saw the dynamism of Asian economic development as an exciting opportunity for Australia, and he visited Indonesia and Japan very early in his term of office, and well before he traveled to Europe or to Britain. In so openly embracing an Asia-focused future, the prime minister antagonized many Australians who were skeptical about migration and many older Australians who were nostalgic for the days of their youth and for an overwhelmingly white Australia that no longer existed outside of their memories. While the new policy setting might well have appealed to the idealistically inclined generation of younger Australians, it was risky in a time of massive unemployment. It was very easy for minority groups opposed to any Asian immigration to portray their opposition in terms of protecting the jobs and job opportunities of "real" Australians. The problem with Keating's new direction was that while it certainly inspired some Australians, it also proved deeply divisive.

THE FIRST GST ELECTION

The election in 1993 was bitterly fought, with considerable personal animus on both sides. The new coalition state government in Victoria had embraced standard coalition industrial policies to abolish the system of industrial awards and the centralized system for setting wage levels and working conditions. It had also abolished annual leave loadings (a higher pay rate) and holiday pay, plus penalty loadings in all state awards. The result had been demonstrations and street protests the like of which had not been seen since the days of the Vietnam War. Keating was quick to point out that the policies being implemented in Victoria would apply nationally if the coalition won the election in March 1993. As if the prospect of a GST were not enough, a victory for the opposition would also involve the possibility of an out and out war between the incoming government and the ACTU.

The primary focus of the campaign, however, remained the GST, and most political watchers forecast a close election with a coalition victory. In the event, they were wrong. The Keating government not only won the election but actually increased its majority in the House of Representatives. On election night, Keating described the win to celebrating party workers at campaign headquarters as "the sweetest victory of all." The press, which had been extraordinarily hostile to the government and had touted for a coalition victory throughout the campaign, saddled Hewson with complete personal responsibility for the defeat:

> The Election victory by Mr Keating and the Labor Party is one of the most remarkable in Australia's political history. It was achieved against the gravity of history and most of the conventional wisdom about elections. . . . A million people unemployed had been supposed, in another mantra of conventional wisdom, as an impossible leg-iron on any government. But voters around Australia showed that they were prepared to accept the terrible troubles and problems of their current situation rather than undertake a leap in the dark over the massive restructuring of the tax regime.[12]

In the aftermath of the election, Keating set about repairing some of the damage the decade of ALP government had inflicted on the fabric of the party. Economic rationalism could not be jettisoned in an increasingly global economy, and there could be no returning to the comfortable pattern of inefficient industries sheltering behind a tariff wall and providing safe employment for the community. What could be done, however, was to put in place policies that would ensure that when economic recovery did occur, the unemployed would not be left behind. The prime minister was determined to avoid the creation of an underclass of impoverished workers and their families, and the new ALP administration set about establishing a framework whereby unemployed workers would be offered retraining and education to upgrade existing skills or to acquire new ones. The traditional ethic of the fair go was resurrected, the light on the hill reignited, and the government promised that those currently unemployed would not be left to stagnate. The success of this policy could be seen as early as the end of 1994, when the number of unemployed had dropped under the million mark, the economy had a growth rate of between 4 and 5 percent, and an economic upturn had already produced more than 320,000 additional jobs.

NATIVE TITLE

It was in the area of Aboriginal affairs, however, that Keating applied the fair go ethic in its most radical form. Hitherto, the ideal that every Australian was entitled to a fair go had not applied to Aboriginal Australians. They had no title to the country in which they had lived for millennia that was recognized by the courts until the Mabo Judgment handed down by the High Court of Australia in June 1992. That decision recognized for the first time that a form of native title did exist still in certain parts of Australia and that the indigenous inhabitants had been the legal owners of the soil when European settlement took place. How was the government to respond to this new situation?

In Keating's view, the Mabo Judgment offered a priceless opportunity to break the mold and to rethink and rework the relationship between Aborigines and the rest of the community and base it—for the first time—on the principles of justice and fair dealing. Accordingly, in June 1993, the government released a set of principles that it hoped might produce an acceptable compromise between the rights of indigenous people to native title and the need to protect pastoral and mining operations on contested land. It was proposed that national legislation to secure mining and pastoral leases be introduced and that compensation be paid to Aborigines who had lost title to land by the issue of such leases. In contested areas it was proposed that a nonadversarial system of tribunals be established to determine where legal title lay and, finally, that the government would establish a national land acquisition fund that would provide money to assist Aborigines who had lost their traditional links with the land to obtain freehold land of their own.

The mining industry attacked the proposals as unwieldy and unworkable, and the newly elected coalition governments in Western Australia and Victoria refused to cooperate in any national system. At the federal level, the coalition found itself trapped by the mining companies and some of the more extreme pastoralists who were its natural constituency and who demanded nothing less than complete and untrammeled opposition. The necessity of implementing the High Court judgment and giving Aboriginal Australians a belated recognition as the original possessors of the soil might conform to abstract notions of justice, but when such desires came into conflict with established interests that were traditional supporters of the coalition, then justice for Aborigines took second place. The government's Native Title Act contained provisions to validate existing land titles placed in doubt by the Mabo Judgment, to set up the tribunals to adjudicate in contested claims for native title, and to set guidelines for compensation payments where these were appropriate. The key principle that underlay the legislation was the unambiguous recognition that native title did exist and had to be protected in law. When the government first introduced the Native Title Bill to the House of Representatives, the coalition declared that it was a day of shame in Australia's history.

Aboriginal groups generally responded favorably, and the National Farmers Federation supported the legislation because of the protection it extended to pastoral leases. The mining industry and the Business Council of Australia maintained that it would render the country's land tenure system unworkable and inhibit investment. Tim Fischer, the federal leader of the National Party, and some prominent Liberals called for a referendum to overturn the High Court's decision. In Keating's view, this was a moral, not a political, issue. The prime minister declared that the legislation embodied "an unashamed appeal for justice—a 'fair go'—for Aboriginal Australians. . . . We owe it to Aboriginal Australians, to all Australians, we owe it to our fair and democratic traditions and to future generations of Australians to recognise this native title."[13]

The Native Title Act illustrated one of the major characteristics of Keating's time as prime minister, in that he held the view that there was no point in the ALP being in power if it did nothing with it. His government had all the reforming zeal of a new administration, and by 1993 he had sacked or disposed of nearly all of Hawke's ministers. This was anything but a tired administration, and the fatalism of the final Hawke years had been left far behind. Keating led a proactive government that shrewdly blended idealism and nationalism into a formidable and heady brew. It did not just respond to the drift of events but provided firm and decisive leadership.

Most Australians accepted without demur that the Native Title Act was a significant move in the reconciliation between black and white Australians, and the prime minister had successfully tapped the idealism of the rising generation who generally seemed happy to see a historic injustice addressed in this fashion. Moreover, in the process, the government had maneuvered the opposition into a position where it was seen to be implacably destructive.

THE REPUBLIC

The republican issue provided a further example of the essentially re-active nature of the coalition in national politics. In April 1993, the prime minister—in keeping with his election pledge—announced the establishment of a broadly based committee of eminent Australians to consider the options for a change to a republican form of government before the bicentenary of federation in 2001. Although the former Liberal premier of New South Wales, Nick Greiner, agreed to serve on the committee, along with prominent media personalities, academics, and the chairperson of ATSIC, the coalition refused to participate and to nominate a representative to the committee. From this point onward, coalition policy toward the issue of a republic placed the opposition out of step with the rising generation where support for the republic was strongest and locked it into the age group of fifty-five and over where support for the monarchy was at its most enthusiastic. This remained the coalition leader's position right through until the referendum on the republic in 1999, no matter who held the office.

THE COALITION STAGGERS

By May 1994, Hewson's tenuous hold on the leadership slipped as a result of a rapid decline in the party's financial position. Business withheld donations as a way of pressuring the Liberal Party to dispose of so unsuccessful a leader, and eventually the party's administrative officers, including the federal president, orchestrated a move against Hewson by a combined leadership team of Alexander Downer from South Australia and Peter Costello from Victoria. The dynamic duo failed to bring about the destruction of the Keating Labor government, and after a series of extraordinary gaffes and errors of judgment from Alexander Downer over the next year, in desperation the Liberals turned to the only man with the staying power to match Keating in Parliament and, in 1995, elected John Howard leader of the Liberal Party for the second time. An ebullient Howard described himself as being like Lazarus with a triple bypass, but he had demonstrated grit and determination to stage a come-back from political oblivion, and time would show that he had what it took to turn Labor out of office.

THE BIG PICTURE IN ASIA

One of the hallmarks of the Keating government was its policy of integrating the Australian economy into Asia, where two-thirds of its exports already went. When Keating became prime minister, there had been no meeting between the heads of government of Australia and In-donesia for almost a decade. He speedily set about changing that, and the depth and warmth of his personal contacts with President Suharto of Indonesia over the next few years became legendary. He also estab-lished close bilateral relations with the governments of South Korea, Ja-pan, China, Vietnam, and Australia's neighbors in the South Pacific. Keating had convinced U.S. President Bill Clinton in 1994 that it was in that country's interest to support his move to establish the Asia Pacific Economic Cooperation (APEC) forum, and a number of very successful leaders' meetings had been held to begin the demolition of trade barriers between the countries of the region. Australia, as a foundation member of APEC, had begun to exercise a powerful influence to move the region into a progressive embrace of free trade that would be completed by the decade 2010–2020.

The prime minister's dictum that Australia had to find its security in Asia rather than from Asia was soundly based in economic realities, but it was deliberately misrepresented by the coalition in Australia as a pol-icy to make Australia a part of Asia and to reconstitute Australians into Asians. In December 1993, the prime minister responded in a speech where he made his position crystal clear: "Australia is not, and can never be, an 'Asian nation' any more than we can—or want to be—European or North American or African. We can only be Australian and we can only relate to our friends as Australian."[14] Only in the case of Malaysia did this move meet opposition, and there Prime Minister Mahathir Mo-hamad's rejection was largely caused by his contempt for Australia's claim to be considered a legitimate participant in the region's affairs. Mahathir held that Australia's European culture and history disqualified the country from full participation.

The Malaysian media echoed the Mahathir line that Keating's alleged bad manners were the result of his descent from convict stock, and the Malaysian government orchestrated a campaign against Australia's increased role in the region. Mahathir went on to argue that only Asian countries could rightfully participate in regional forums like APEC, and his government did everything in its power to ensure Australia was excluded. Keating was incensed and responded in kind. If Australians were to be excluded on racial grounds from a full participation in the region's affairs, then Australia would feel obliged to reconsider its defense relationship with Malaysia. Australia would also reimpose dormant exchange controls on Malaysia to stop capital flows from this country being used to underwrite Malaysian development. Faced with such a damaging prospect, Mahathir backed off, but his resentment against Australia continued to smolder and was reignited when Keating incautiously described him as "recalcitrant." By his appeal to history and his economic pressure, Keating had amply demonstrated that Australia had a right to claim a role in the region and the strength to back up the demand if necessary. After all, more than 500 Australian servicemen and women had met their deaths in protecting Malaysia from Chinese communist insurgents during the 1950s and from Indonesian invasion during the 1960s, and if it was good enough for Australians to die for Malaysia, then it should be good enough for them to be accepted as equal partners.

THE KEATING STYLE

In the meantime, the attacks on Keating became more hysterical and vituperative than ever. The prime minister's personal jibes at the opposition in Parliament for its old-fashioned and backward-looking attachment to England and the empire resulted in a sustained reaction of character assassination that undermined his reputation for honesty and accused him of arrogance in his public and private conduct. The fact that he wore stylish Italian suits, collected antique French clocks, and preferred classical music to popular bands was said to demonstrate his alienation from the common people. The costs of upgrading the prime ministerial residence "The Lodge" in Canberra were alleged to indicate his profligate nature, as was the allegedly extravagant cost of a $23,000 teak dining table that the prime minister desired to purchase. Untruths were peddled that Paul Keating and his family wished to air-condition a kennel for their dog and to waste copious amounts of money in renovating and improving the Sydney harborside residence known as Kirribilli House. News reports concentrated on these claims and on the prime minister's fighting performances during Question Time (a daily session whenever Parliament is sitting wherein members of Parliament can question any minister on any aspect of their ministry) in the House of Representatives, to reinforce the view that he was both profligate and unduly combative.

The coalition had decided to focus opposition almost entirely on the personality of Paul Keating, and their new leader John Howard gave a public assurance that he would improve the standard of parliamentary behavior, would establish a code of ethics to ensure that all ministers behaved with propriety, and would lead an honest and transparent administration. Howard, as treasurer in Malcolm Fraser's governments, had presided over some very questionable transactions in the area of tax avoidance schemes for the rich and influential. In recognition, he had been tagged with the ironic nickname of "Honest John" by the media, but public memory had faded of the ironic intent of the nickname. Being "Honest John" Howard became a real electoral advantage and a way of distinguishing himself from the tainted Keating. For his part, Howard assured the Australian people that the lesson of 1993 had been learned by the coalition and that it would never—ever—contemplate trying to implement a GST again.

12

Mutual Obligation and the Conservative Revival (1997–2001)

The election of 2 March 1996, provided a landslide victory for the opposition with a majority of twenty-nine seats. Paul Keating suffered a massive personal rejection after a campaign in which Howard had made the prime minister the key issue. Globalization and the economic integration with Asia, the move toward a lasting peace with the Aborigines, and the economic recovery that had taken place during the three years between 1993 and 1996 all counted for little. Keating became the victim of a revulsion by the community against the rapidity and extent of change. He had also—like his old mentor Jack Lang—become a paradox in that he was simultaneously loathed by a majority of the electorate and yet loved and admired by a substantial minority. The comprehensive reaction against thirteen years of Labor government could no longer be held at bay. Howard had rejected a GST, he had offered a better-behaved Parliament, a willingness to continue the reconciliation with the indigenous people, and an acceptance of a multicultural Australian community. He had even promised a constitutional convention on the question of the republic. In other words, Howard offered reassurance on all the issues that were acknowledged strengths in the Keating program, and by doing so he provided an opportunity for an angry electorate to scapegoat an unpopular prime minister. Keating resigned from Parliament, and the job of rebuilding the ALP fell to the deputy leader from Western Australia, Kim Beasley.

THE COALITION IN GOVERNMENT

Howard was a conservative, and the party he led looked back nostalgically to the Menzies Era. The new government established a lasting reputation for hypocrisy very early in its term, when Howard announced that there had been "core" promises and ordinary promises made by him during the election campaign. The core promises were those that he intended to keep, while the other promises might prove more difficult to attain.

Insofar as restoring integrity to government had been one of the core promises that had brought him to power, Howard moved quickly to introduce a new ministerial code of conduct, under which ministers were required to make a declaration of their ownership of shares and properties. In the next three years, a series of ministers and staffers failed to pass Howard's integrity test and were consigned to political oblivion, but Howard reacted very badly when his code of conduct threatened to end the careers of two old friends: Warwick Parer, who was caught with a significant holding of coal shares that he had neglected to declare, and Queensland Liberal Warren Entsch, who similarly transgressed the code of conduct. The attrition had to stop, and Howard declared that the code amounted only to guidelines and that henceforth proven criminal activities alone would result in ministers being forced to resign.

THE HOWARD LIFESTYLE

The 1996 election campaign had concentrated on the degree to which Keating had become "arrogant" and out of touch with the lives and aspirations of ordinary Australians. Howard had identified the "battlers" as a constituency to which he could successfully appeal. Battlers were former ALP supporters who had been left behind by the pace of change and had become frightened and resentful of an ALP that had so clearly abandoned them to their fate. In casting their votes for the coalition, they had looked for an end to extravagances like $23,000 dining room tables for the prime ministerial residence when they were suffering economic hardship.

But Howard's concern for the views of the battlers seemed to disappear soon after the election, when he announced his intention to move his family into Kirribilli House in Sydney rather than live in Canberra on a full-time basis. The coalition advocated that the unemployed should move to areas where work was available or lose their dole, but this was a rule for the battlers, not for the prime minister, who had no intention of moving to his place of employment in Canberra. Kirribilli House had been originally designed to house visiting heads of state and foreign dignitaries, but Howard appropriated it for his own use so as not to disrupt his family or the education of his children. The misappropriation included an additional upgrade of the security arrangements at a cost of well over $1 million. Nor did his occupation of the residence end once his children had completed their education; he retained Kirribilli House as his primary residence while also making use of the Lodge in Canberra when Parliament was in session. The alleged extravagance of Keating paled to relative insignificance alongside Howard's self-indulgence. In the first four years of his occupancy, Howard spent over half a million dollars in renovations and improvements to Kirribilli House. By the end of the year 2000, Howard seemed likely to be remembered as the Marie Antoinette of Australian politics for his incorrigible use of public monies to support the Howard family's personal comfort.[1]

PAULINE HANSON AND ONE NATION

During the 1996 election campaign, a little-known female candidate for the Liberal Party named Pauline Hanson stood for the Queensland seat of Ipswich. A former proprietor of the local fish and chip shop, Hanson represented the small business wing of the Liberal Party. She made some prejudiced and racist remarks during the campaign about Aborigines and Asians, and the Liberals reacted quickly and in damage-control mode expelled her from the party. This engendered enormous public sympathy for her, and she won the seat as an independent.

Her maiden speech in the House of Representatives touched on the problems of a multicultural Australia with particular reference to alleged special treatment for racial minorities at the expense of mainstream Australia. An enormous furor erupted, with most of the press and Labor politicians taking a hard line of opposition to what they regarded as a worrisome revival of Australian racism. On the other hand, the coalition government gave tacit support to Hanson's views, and the prime minister revisited his earlier statements of concern about the pace of multicultural change and suggested that people who opposed Hanson were seeking to impose their own brand of "political correctness" on her and were endangering free speech in Australia. Howard's tendency to follow a populist course rather than show leadership on the racial issue reflected the opinion polls that showed that there was considerable sympathy for Hanson in the wider community. Howard refused to condemn her views, and the result was an explosion of bigotry as Aborigines, Asians, and other migrant minorities came under open attack. The residue of Australia's historic racism seemed to be stirred into life by the prime minister's inactivity, which provided covert support for Hanson and her followers.

Later in 1996, Pauline Hanson formed a new political party known as One Nation, which launched a populist campaign based on Australians' increasing distrust of professional politicians. The new party was a paradox in that it garnered support from an electorate on the basis that it was an antipolitical political party and could therefore be trusted, whereas the other parties composed of professional politicians could not. One Nation won considerable support throughout rural and urban Australia by attacking welfare payments to Aborigines, the "Asianization" of Australia, gun-law reforms that outlawed automatic and semiautomatic firearms, and economic rationalism. Party branches opened in all states, and Hanson developed into an articulate, though sometimes incoherent, media performer. Still Howard and the coalition in Canberra did nothing, though Liberal state leaders like Jeff Kennett, the premier of Victoria, recognized the danger Hanson posed and actively campaigned against her. The ALP, on the other hand, had opposed Hanson and One Nation from the outset and announced that whenever state or federal elections might be held, One Nation candidates would automatically be placed last on all ALP How-to-Vote leaflets, whatever the political cost. Beasley and the ALP won great kudos from this decision, but Howard and the coalition remained steadfast in their refusal to condemn the One Nation party or its policies.

Early in 1998, a state election in Queensland shocked the coalition, when eleven One Nation candidates won seats in the Legislative Assembly, largely at the expense of Liberal and National Party members. The depth of electoral disillusionment with conventional politics was demonstrated by the success of the new party, and the National Party in particular began to fear the loss of many of its federal seats. In order to win back its waning support, the Howard government began to espouse policy positions that had more in common with One Nation policies than the normal bill of fare of Liberal-led coalitions since the time of Menzies. Aboriginal affairs was one area where Howard made an unashamed appeal to recapture conservative rural votes from One Nation.

RECONCILIATION, RACISM, AND *WIK*

Following the 1992 Mabo Decision of the High Court, and the Native Title Act, the Aboriginal people had continued to explore the new law, especially the limited criteria under which a successful native title claim could be made. It had been generally understood that the Native Title Act ruled out overlapping titles and that wherever leases or freehold had been given to settlers, native title had been effectively extinguished. Nevertheless, when the High Court handed down its judgment in the *Wik Peoples v. Queensland* case in 1996, the whole area was thrown open to question, for the judges ruled that native title and pastoral leases could coexist and that a pastoral lease did not necessarily extinguish native title. The National Party was the major partner in the coalition in Queensland, and the northern pastoral interests had become a vital ingredient of the coalition support base. The *Wik* judgment became the cause of great concern to northern pastoralists who argued that if native title had not been extinguished by the issuing of a pastoral lease, then it might not have been extinguished by other forms of alienation either. Perhaps native title might be found to coexist with mining leases or other forms of leasehold, or even freehold title? Scaremongers suggested that suburban backyards were now in danger of native title claims. The mining industry feared that the earlier difficulty over Coronation Hill could provide a template for a future that involved endless confrontation between mining companies and Aboriginal people; and the Howard government took the extremist position that the economic consequences of the *Wik* judgment could prove ruinous to all involved in pastoral and mining enterprises.

The One Nation Party's well-known anti-Aboriginal prejudice meant that the National Party's support had begun to hemorrhage in rural districts, and the coalition had to act promptly if it was not to lose more seats to the new party. The government spent the next two years in dealing with the *Wik* decision and brought in legislation to provide certainty to the holders of pastoral and mining leases by legislating native title out of existence on all land that had ever been the subject of any form of leasehold tenure. Howard commented that "the pendulum had swung too far towards Aborigines and had to be reset."[2] Aboriginal people and the ALP opposed this eradication of native title, but National Party leader Tim Fischer had promised his rural supporters that the government's bill would provide "buckets of extinguishment," and the *Wik* debate in the Senate generated enormous controversy throughout Australia. Fischer denigrated Aboriginal culture as being so backward that it had not even developed a wheeled cart.[3] The final compromise between the government and the independent Brian Harradine from Tasmania in the Senate in July 1998 was in favor of the coalition and provided the certainty pastoralists had demanded at the expense of the indigenous people. The enactment also stretched beyond the *Wik* decision and limited native title legislatively to land that had never been alienated. Furthermore, the government's attacks on native title and its determination to win back the rights granted to Aborigines by the High Court won the coalition important support in the country areas and urban districts where people were feeling the pinch of privation, and it weakened the growing appeal of One Nation.

Relations with Aboriginal people continued to decline throughout the Howard government's time in office, and the coalition's intransigence over the *Wik* issue was echoed during the government's second term by Howard's inability and unwillingness to issue an apology to the nation's indigenous people for the injustices and policies of forced assimilation that had been inflicted upon them since 1788. The kidnapping of Aboriginal children had been government policy in most states of Australia until the second half of the twentieth century, and Aboriginal people mourned the loss of what they termed the "stolen generations." The trauma of forcible removal took an enormous toll both mentally and physically on the kidnapped children and their families and was held partly to explain the high rates of suicide brought to light by the Royal Commission into Aboriginal Deaths in Custody, which delivered its report in 1995. Very few Aboriginal families were unaffected by the abduction of children, and most Aborigines in modern Australia could point to at least one missing family member. The sense of outrage, therefore, was almost palpable when Howard's personal appointee as minister for aboriginal affairs, Senator John Herron, in May 2000 affirmed in Parliament the government's view that there was no such thing as a stolen generation, because no more than 10 percent of any generation of Aboriginal children had ever been kidnapped. Howard and Herron stuck to this position, despite a chorus of complaint from Aborigines and academic professionals who argued that the real figure was much higher than this and that even a 10 percent abduction rate was totally unacceptable in any free country. Australian Democrat Senator Aden Ridgeway—himself of Aboriginal descent—accused Howard of deliberate provocation of Aboriginal people for his own political gain.[4] When it later turned out that Herron's submission had actually been written in Howard's office, and that its intention had been to minimize any potential liability for compensation claims from the victims of the kidnappings or their families, Howard's credibility on the race issue was in shambles. When, on 28 May 2000, well over 200,000 people led by community leaders, politicians, and clergy, and including former prime ministers from both sides of politics, marched across Sydney Harbour Bridge to show support for reconciliation between Aboriginal people and the rest of the community, Howard refused to walk and continued to withhold the apology that most Aboriginal people maintained was an essential prerequisite to any process of reconciliation. His position on an apology had been described by the conservative *Sydney Morning Herald* twelve months earlier as "so obtuse as to defy reason."[5]

THE GOODS AND SERVICES TAX

Howard's statement that he would never, ever revive the question of a goods and services tax only lasted about halfway into his first term as prime minister. Clearly, his undertaking had not been a "core" promise, and the cynicism regarding politicians and their promises received a further stimulus, when he revived the issue and made it the centerpiece of the next election campaign. His twenty-nine-seat majority gave Howard a comfortable cushion of risk, and he revisited the Hewson model for a GST with some confidence that even if it did frighten the electorate, no government had ever lost an election with such a huge majority under its belt. Moreover, the level of the new tax was set at only 10 percent, significantly lower than Hewson's attempt to set it at 15 percent, and the abolition of wholesale taxes accompanied by large reductions in the rates of income tax would sweeten the package.

The difference between introducing the new tax with the advantages of incumbency rather than from opposition emerged in the election campaign, when Howard's government appropriated a $70 million Federation Cultural and Heritage Projects scheme for community projects to celebrate the bicentenary of federation in 2001. To ensure transparency, an independent assessment process existed to decide which of the hundreds of applications should receive funding. When 60 proposals had been selected, two ministers, Senators Robert Hill and Richard Alston, then intervened to include 16 projects that had not appeared in the list of winners. At least 114 other applications had been ranked ahead of these 16. The intervention occurred three days before Howard called the election, and its overall effect was that three-quarters of the funding for projects in marginal seats went to seats held by coalition members. During the election campaign, 39 winners were announced, 33 of them in coalition seats. On the other hand, most of the successful applications from ALP seats were not announced, and the losers were not informed until after the election. Since the government's majority was reduced from twenty-nine to six as a result of the election, and since it won the election with a minority of the total votes cast, this unethical use of patronage might well have secured its return.

The electoral arithmetic shows how perilously close to losing Howard came. The coalition drifted within 1,500 votes of losing office in the marginal seats and could well have done so, had it not been for the money doled out via the federation fund. In national terms, after the distribution of preferences Howard lost the popular vote by more than 200,000 votes. The promise of large tax cuts for the middle and upper classes probably got Howard over the line, but the parties opposed to a GST actually won a majority of the votes cast. The Australian Democrats, however, opted to negotiate with Howard for improvements in the GST, and after the coalition agreed to exempt fresh food from the tax, the Australian Democrats supported the government's legislation in the Senate and voted the GST into law. The new tax system came into operation on 1 July 2000, and in the run-up to its imposition Howard and his treasurer Peter Costello spent well over $400 million of public money to fund a media campaign that presented the GST as a positive achievement for the government and the nation. Ironically, despite the barrage of advertising, it was the possibility of war with Indonesia rather than the introduction of a new tax that attracted most attention in the six months prior to the GST's scheduled starting date.

RELATIONSHIPS IN THE ASIA/PACIFIC REGION

Australia's good relations with Indonesia dated back to World War II when Indonesian nationalists worked in Australia to help the Allied war effort throw the occupying Japanese out of their country. Once the war was over, Australia supported the establishment of an independent Indonesian state and resisted the reimposition of colonial rule by the Netherlands. Indeed, Australia was seen by Indonesia as its strongest supporter in its four-year struggle to achieve independence from the Dutch, and Indonesian appreciation of Australian support during their nationalist liberation period provided the basis for Keating's policy of constructive engagement with Australia's largest northern neighbor. When the coalition came to power in 1996, Australia had a security pact with Indonesia, and the two countries undertook joint military exercises together. Indonesian soldiers were trained in Australia, and the close personal relationship between Indonesian President Suharto and Prime

Minister Keating was reflected by similarly close professional and personal relationships between the senior military personnel in both countries.

The incoming coalition administration wasted no time in assuring Indonesia that it wished for a similarly close rapport between the two
nations. Deputy Prime Minister Tim Fischer traveled to Indonesia soon
after the election and crowned his first official visit to that country by
acclaiming President Suharto at an official reception as "perhaps the
world's greatest figure in the second half of the century."[6] Unfortunately,
the cozy relationship was destined to founder on the rocks of Indonesia's
annexation of East Timor back in 1975.

The East Timorese had suffered terribly under Japanese occupation
during the war, but this had not stopped them from offering substantial
aid and assistance to Australian commandos operating behind the Japanese lines. An estimated 60,000 East Timorese had met their deaths at
the hands of the Japanese for their support of Australian forces, and most
Australians felt that they owed East Timor a debt of gratitude. When
Indonesia invaded East Timor in 1975, and when the East Timorese resistance movement continued to resist incorporation into the Republic of
Indonesia through a campaign of guerrilla warfare, an irritant had been
injected into the relationship between Australia and Indonesia. As long
as President Suharto and the Indonesian armed forces remained firmly
in control, East Timor remained a small irritant. But in 1998, Suharto's
grip on power began to slip, and eventually he was replaced by an in-
terim civilian, President B.J. Habibie. It was the decline of Suharto and
Indonesia's military that encouraged the East Timorese to agitate with
renewed intensity for independence, and eventually, after considerable
stalling from Indonesia and a great deal of thuggery and murder from
Indonesian-funded militias in East Timor, the people voted overwhelmingly for an existence outside Indonesia.

Descriptions from Australian commentators and observers of Indonesia's violent attempts to retain East Timor as a province had raised considerable sympathy for the plight of the East Timorese, and the fall of
Suharto made a change in Australian policy toward Indonesia impera-
tive. The existing accommodation with Indonesia had delivered considerable benefits to Australia in the form of increased trade, expanding
educational and business links, and political stability between Australia
and a nation of over 210 million people to its north. The rising tide of
public support for East Timor and the hostility directed toward Indonesian military violations of human rights in East Timor required careful
management at the Australian end if these gains were not to be placed

in jeopardy. Unfortunately, East Timor collapsed into anarchy, and the coalition found itself forced by public opinion into the leadership of an international peacekeeping force known as INTERFET (International Force for East Timor) and comprising mostly Australian soldiers that landed in East Timor to protect the people from the violence of the Indonesian-backed militias. The Interfet force deployed rapidly, and for the next three months, in a magnificent display of discipline and proactive soldiering, it held the militias at bay until a UN peacekeeping force could be assembled and transported to East Timor to relieve the Australians.

The effect of Interfet on relations between Australia and Indonesia was disastrous, and Howard's use of the crisis to improve his political position in Australia became the immediate cause of a diplomatic crisis. Howard announced that Interfet was in East Timor to defend what Australia thought was right. The Australian public demanded a military involvement for reasons of morality, and Howard provided it; but the solution finally had to be found in a political outcome. Australia, with 19 million people, could not afford a military conflict with Indonesia's 210 million people. Australia's best interests were served by peace and stability in the region, but Howard's enunciation of the conflict in cultural and moral terms of right and wrong was designed for a domestic Australian audience. Howard also described Australia as a deputy sheriff for the United States, and Indonesia resented this description of the situation as a form of cultural arrogance involving a veiled threat. When Howard went further and pointed out that in his opinion previous Australian governments had been too interested in promoting a special relationship between Australia and Indonesia at the expense of what we knew to be right, the response was swift. Indonesia abrogated the security treaty, and a relationship based on years of careful diplomacy was lost. Mobs in Jakarta stoned the Australian embassy, and the Australian flag was ceremonially burned and trampled upon in the streets of Indonesia's capital. One effect of the special relationship had been that Australia's expenditure on defense had fallen to the lowest proportion of gross domestic product for sixty years, so one immediate outcome from the fallout with Indonesia was a dramatic increase in military expenditure in the budget for 2000, with a similar increase projected ahead for at least the next four to five years.

Relationships with Indonesia declined dramatically, with the newly elected Indonesian President Abdurrahman Wahid refusing to visit Australia until June 2001, and the Indonesian Airforce scrambling warplanes to intercept and confront four unarmed Australian jet fighters and a refueling tanker in midair over the ocean off East Timor in May 2000. What

Indonesians viewed as Australia's humiliation of the Indonesian military produced a combustible situation, so that despite the Australian fighters having the necessary clearances from Jakarta, they were within a hair's breadth of a disaster. Howard's depiction of the disagreement as a cultural one in which only he of all Australia's leaders, both Labor and Liberal, was prepared to do what was right played into the hands of Australia's inveterate rival in the region, the prime minister of Malaysia, Dr. Mahathir, who described Australia's attitude to non-European societies as belligerent. In June 2000, President Wahid gave tacit endorsement to Mahathir's accusation when he pointedly informed Howard that it was Indonesia's belief that Asian countries needed to develop a common cultural identity and to act collectively. Indonesian policy remained unchanged when President Megawati Sukanoputri replaced the sacked Wahid in July 2000.

From 1996 to mid-2000, Australia's hitherto successful engagement with its East Asian neighbors faltered and collapsed in the hands of a prime minister whose focus on short-term domestic politics seemed to take precedence over any sense of vision concerning the country's long-term needs for stability and peace in a potentially dangerous part of the world. In June 2000, Howard and President Wahid met on neutral ground in Japan as they each attended the funeral of the Japanese prime minister, and the Indonesian president had expressed a cautious desire for the relationship to be improved. The fragility of the former friendship between the two countries, and Indonesian suspicions concerning the coalition's attitude to the Indonesian province of Irian Jaya (formerly Netherlands New Guinea), was demonstrated at this meeting by Howard having to reassure President Wahid that his government did not desire to destabilize Indonesia and did not support the local independence movement in that troubled province. [7] This obvious mistrust contrasted markedly to the warmth of the welcome extended by President Wahid to the ALP leader Kim Beasley, when he had visited Jakarta the previous month.

SCUTTLING THE REPUBLIC

In 1995, when John Howard was resurrected as leader of the Liberal Party, he found himself facing a prime minister who was an avowed republican and who had promised an indicative plebiscite if reelected in 1996 on whether Australians wanted an Australian national as head of state or to retain the British monarch in that role. Howard accepted the idea of a people's convention to discuss the republican issue that his predecessor, Alexander Downer, had made Liberal policy; and he promised that if the coalition won office, he would call such a convention into being, and if it came up with a majority in favor of a republic, he would place the issue before the public in a referendum. In February 1998, a half-elected, half-nominated constitutional convention met in Canberra and eventually resolved in favor of a republic with a president who was to be elected by a joint sitting of the members of the Federal Parliament. Because it was an essentially undemocratic body, the convention's recommendation was flawed from the start.

Howard determined to bypass the simple plebiscite favored by the ALP on whether a change to an Australian head of state was desired and insisted that voters had to say either yes or no to a head of state appointed by politicians only. Howard knew that in the political history of Australia no referendum had ever been passed that had been opposed by the prime minister of the day. In the event, the prime minister's tactics worked well, and the referendum failed in all states, attaining about 45 percent support nationally. Howard permitted some of his ministers to mount a campaign of opposition to the referendum that focused on the untrustworthiness of politicians. The "No" case, which Howard supported, only increased the mistrust and discredit of politicians in Australia. Public opinion seems clear that a republic is probably inevitable, either at the hands of Howard's successors as coalition leader or from an opposition government.

13

Advance Australia Where?
(2001 and Beyond)

ENTERING THE THIRD MILLENNIUM

As we begin the third millennium of the current epoch, there appears to be very little common wealth left to be shared by the members of the Commonwealth of Australia. The signs seem to be of division and decline. In 1901, liberals, country folk, and members of the labor movement shared a common belief in the future of the new nation that made them essentially optimists. A century later, the optimism has gone, and the golden soil and wealth for toil that are celebrated in the national anthem seem a cruel dream to many in the community. Australia's 19 million people are more divided than they have been since the convict days, and the easy egalitarianism that rode on the back of national abundance has been replaced by a fearfulness about a future in which the class divisions of the old world, that many had hoped had been left behind in 1901, have been replicated and even strengthened in the deepening economic and social fragmentation in the contemporary one. In June 2000, the national weekend newspaper the *Australian* led with a banner headline that announced the "Death of the Fair Go" and highlighted the despair and alienation of those sectors of the community like the rural population and the urban working poor that had become casualties of change and fallen behind the mainstream in the new privatized and economically rationalized economy.[1]

Rural Australia is in a perilous state, and a huge divide has opened between urban and rural Australia. Many regional and outer suburban areas are in danger of collapse as incomes and assets have declined rapidly in real value. In one region that covers a third of New South Wales, the average value of the family farm had slumped from $500,000 in 1990 to less than $200,000 at the end of the century. A decline in wool and commodity prices, the ravages inflicted by the cycles of El Niño, and large-scale land degradation and salination caused by inappropriate farming methods and tree clearances have devastated rural communities in all states. Many farmers have been forced into negative incomes by the decline, and foreclosures will force many of those still hanging on to walk off their properties. Nationally, over the past thirty years the number of families able to wrest a living from a farm has dropped by 10,000, and a further 20 percent are expected to give up the struggle in the next decade.

The devastation of the farm sector has been reflected in the destruction of the social and economic infrastructure that is essential to maintain viable communities in the bush. In New South Wales alone, in the past decade of economic rationalization, over 100 towns and communities outside Sydney have lost their last bank branches in a process that has resulted in the disappearance of almost a quarter of the state's rural bank branches. The twelve postcode areas with the lowest average personal income are all in rural New South Wales, whereas the five top areas are all in Sydney. From 1988 to 1995 rural New South Wales lost more than 5,000 hospital beds, and thirty hospitals were closed, downgraded, or privatized. Schools, public transport, and other businesses are all affected by the decline, and they too scale back or even discontinue services. Internal migration bleeds the younger and more mobile population off to the larger towns and cities, and the average age of Australian farmers is now fifty-six and still rising. The stress of living in rural Australia is reflected in the rising assault rates that are now outstripping those of the capital cities. For example, in Sydney in 1998 there were about 40 sexual assaults per 100,000 people; in the far west of New South Wales there are now 160 sexual assaults per 100,000 people.

Even within the capital cities, the economic chasm between the haves and the have-nots is closer to nineteenth-century figures than to those that applied for most of the twentieth. In the well-to-do areas and those affected by high-tech investment and industries, average household incomes have continued to rise; but in those other parts of the cities that have relied on small-scale manufacturing, textiles, and metal products— the so-called rust bucket industries—household incomes have barely moved in the last ten years. In 1999, the Australian Local Government Association issued a comprehensive report covering all 628 local government areas of Australia, and the story was the same throughout the nation. The loss of services and facilities affected cities as well as rural areas, and the falling morale and demoralization were spread from one side of the country to the other. In all, since 1993, about 1,800 bank branches have closed across Australia, with the concomitant loss of about 40,000 jobs. Most of these branches and jobs came from the cities. Similarly with the Telstra corporation, where in March 2000 the chief executive of the partially privatized corporation announced that a further 10,000 jobs would be shed by the telecommunications giant in addition to the 20,000 to 30,000 jobs that had already gone. Distrust for politicians of all parties is one of the by-products of a situation like this, as is the rising support in urban as well as rural Australia for the scapegoating of easy targets like Aborigines and Asians as bearing responsibility for people's suffering.

PACIFIC SOLUTION OR PACIFIC PARIAH, THE 2001 FEDERAL ELECTION

These themes were amply demonstrated in the run up to the federal election in November 2001. Back in March, the coalition had been twenty points behind the Beasley led ALP in the opinion polls and seemed destined for a heavy defeat. Things changed dramatically, however, in August when a Norwegian container ship the MV *Tampa* rescued 234 Afghan and Middle Eastern boat people from their sinking vessel in Indonesian waters. They had been part of a growing flood of illegal immigrants attempting a surreptitious entry into Australia.

The Norwegian captain elected to sail into Australian waters and to land the refugees at Christmas Island off the northern coast of Western Australia. A major political and diplomatic emergency followed as a result of this decision, and it permitted the coalition to reverse completely the trend of political events and to snatch victory from a seemingly impossible position.

The context within which this miraculous recovery took place, was an increasing tide of hostility in the previous decade in Australia's largest cities directed against immigrants of Islamic background. Much of this had been caused by criminal gangs of young Muslim men who stood accused of a long list of antisocial behaviors, including aggressively engaging in the drug trade, deliberately targeting non-Islamic girls for pack rape attacks during which they were taunted with being "Aussies," and subjecting the police, school teachers, Asians, and ordinary Australians to physical violence and attack.

The arrival of the *Tampa* crystallized and focused this rising tide of concern because the refugees were all followers of Islam, and the government linked its harsh anti-boat people policy to the revulsion of the wider community for what was perceived as Muslim lawlessness, into a so-called "Pacific Solution" to the problem of illegal immigrants. So strong had public opinion become on this issue, that the ALP meekly offered full bipartisan support to the government for its Pacific Solution. Briefly, the *Tampa* boat people and all boatloads thereafter, would not be permitted in any circumstances to land even temporarily in any Australian territory. Rather, Australia would search for small Pacific islands that would agree to take the refugees in barbed-wire internment camps until their claims for refugee status had been fully investigated. Only then would they be permitted to request entrance into Australia.

To enforce the new policy, ships of the Royal Australian Navy were ordered to patrol the oceans to Australia's north to intercept illegal migrant vessels and persuade them to turn back to the Indonesian ports from which they had come. The *Tampa* was boarded by Australian Special Air Services commandos, and the ship sailed to the island of Nauru, which had agreed to become the first Pacific holding camp in return for a payment amounting to many millions of dollars. Meanwhile, the government began to sound out other similar island states like Fiji, the Solomon Islands, and Kiribati, to ascertain whether they too would be willing to follow Nauru's lead. Beasley, the ALP leader, followed every turn and twist by Howard in this episode, and both coalition and Labor were as one in seeking a Pacific Solution.

When Muslim terrorists attacked the United States on 11 September 2001, it took little effort to add the threats posed by the international terrorist organization run by Osama Bin Laden to the already combustible mix of anti-Islamic sentiment in Australia. Islamic terrorism abroad, Islamic crime within Australia, and illegal Muslim refugees came together in the most timely fashion on the eve of an election that Howard had appeared earlier to have no chance of winning. Howard immediately offered America the "unequivocal support of Australia and a promise of full military assistance to the extent of our capabilities." Beasley supported the policy on behalf of the opposition.

The election campaign formally began in October, and Beasley found it virtually impossible to campaign on domestic issues like education, public health, and aged care while a war was going on in Afghanistan to which Australian combat forces had already been committed. The newspapers concentrated the front pages on reporting the progress of America's War Against Terrorism, and Howard made frequent reference during the campaign to the possibility that there would be Australian casualties once our troops arrived in the war zone and engaged the enemy soldiers of the Afghan Taliban.

On 10 November 2001, Howard and the coalition secured a third term in office. It was a wonderful endorsement of Howard's gritty determination and refusal ever to admit the inevitability of defeat. Not only did the coalition retain government, but it enjoyed a nationwide upswing in its support of just under two percent, while the ALP endured a similar erosion. Labor's primary vote fell to the lowest level since the defeat of the Scullin government in the Great Depression of the 1930s, as many Labor supporters—disgusted at Beasley's policy of fully supporting the coalition on boat people and the war—gave their first preference to minor parties and independents, and only delivered their second preference to the ALP.

Howard had proved to be a formidable and ruthless campaigner, who deliberately used the issues of race and war to his electoral advantage. The coalition's final week of advertising had saturated the media with images of the prime minister with a clenched and raised fist announcing that "We will decide who comes to this country and the circumstances in which they come!" The policy approach was deplored by two former prime ministers, the Liberal Malcolm Fraser who commented that Howard's use of the race issue had put Australian politics back a century, and the ALP's Keating who claimed that Howard had stained the soul of the nation.

The election result and the policy of the Pacific Solution on which the coalition had campaigned, and to which Beasley had made the ALP an accessory, was greeted with considerable reserve in some parts of the world. The *Financial Times* in London editorialized that Howard's victory was "squalid," and a top adviser to the Indonesian government commented that for the nations of South East Asia, the Howard win bore witness to the fact that Australia had revealed itself to be a deeply racist country that risked becoming a pariah throughout the region.[2]

TWO NATIONS?

Australia's division into two nations of haves and have-nots may result in a process of decline in the legitimacy of governments. Economic rationalization has been practiced by both sides of the political divide, and it has entrenched an underclass of working poor together with cynicism and disengagement from the political system. Add to that the questionable behavior of John Howard as prime minister and ALP predecessor, Paul Keating, and the disenchantment with electoral politics becomes more understandable. The dislike of the community for the established political parties can be seen in the November 2001 federal election, when both government and opposition suffered a decline in their reputations and the ALP in its primary vote, and in the continuing fall off in party membership. The two largest parties seem to be literally dying on their feet. Liberals are beset with a rapid decline in members, and the situation in New South Wales mirrors developments in the other states. In May 2000, more than 80 percent of Liberal Party members in New South Wales were aged over fifty-five, and almost two-thirds of the membership was sixty-five or older. In 1975, the state branch had a membership of about 50,000, which by the turn of the next century had fallen to only 6,000 active members. When the Liberal Party held its national convention in Melbourne early in the year 2000, it was so short of money that it permitted the tobacco company Philip Morris to sponsor its convention dinner. Nor was the ALP in much better shape. The grassroots of the party lie in the trade union movement, but that now represents merely 25 percent of the workforce. The branch structure (party divisions at the electorate level) has been corrupted by wholesale branch stacking so as to produce private factional fiefdoms and safe preselections for favored candidates. The rampant use of ethnic groups to stack a branch has angered and alienated traditional members who actually did the hard routine work of manning polling booths on election days and door knocking and letter boxing on behalf of Labor candidates. They have withdrawn their labor, and the party has increasing difficulty in manning its polling booths. Moreover, the ALP has long ceased to be a political party in which a coal miner or a train driver might one day become prime minister, and in the millennium year, there were only three Labor members of the House of Representatives who had not previously worked as union officials, political staffers, or public servants, and two of them had been lawyers with well-established trade union practices.

Of the smaller parties, the National Party has been losing members to the One Nation movement as the party's representatives in Canberra embrace the economic rationalist dogma despite the enormous human cost in rural areas; and the Australian Democrats and the Greens still retain a large number of members who engage in democratic consultations before policy changes can be undertaken. It is rumored, however, that the Australian Democrats' cooperation with the coalition to bring in the GST cost the party dearly in terms of membership numbers and support. It lost one Senate positions in the 2001 federal election.

As the nation approached the centenary of federation and the beginning of the twenty-first century, there was a sense of impatience with the status quo and a feeling that the country had begun to stagnate. Kim Beasley resigned as ALP leader, and commentators are beginning to call for John Howard to resign and make way for a younger and more dynamic generation of leadership. Australia is at a crossroads, and there is little faith in any of the country's institutions. Both political parties have presided over a process of increasing disenchantment, disengagement, and cynicism, and a great deal of repair work needs to be done. The question of who is to undertake the task remains unclear, and a sense of directionless drift characterizes society. These are hardly auspicious signposts for the new millennium, and it is clear that the Australian people will have to change their ways. History provides one possible model, and Australia needs quite consciously to recapture the free-flowing, radical, and inclusive self-confidence of 1901 and lose the arthritic conservatism and corrosive self-doubt of 2001. Whether it can do so remains to be seen.

The picture is not entirely without hope, however, and the basic strengths of Australian society and the inherent decency of its people cannot be overlooked. It is a strongly democratic country with a population that still responds to appeals to its idealism and generosity of spirit. The rising generation is well educated, sophisticated, and well aware of what needs to be done to actualize the potential of a land that according to the national anthem, "abounds with nature's gifts, of beauty rich and rare." Renewal, when generational change finally occurs, may well unleash an explosion of energy that will burst the log jam and permit the nation to resume its interrupted progress toward the vision of a tolerant, fair-minded, and decent society for all its citizens, that energized and activated the men and women of the six colonies who brought the country together in the aptly named Commonwealth of Australia in 1901. The power to bring about such a transformation lies latent, but potent beneath the surface of an apparently hedonistic, and self-satisfied society. It needs to be reawakened.

Notable People in the History of Australia

Barton, Edmund (1849–1920). Protectionist politician, federation leader, and first prime minister; resigned in 1903 to become a judge on the High Court.

Bonner, Neville (1922–2000). Liberal politician and first Aborigine to be elected to Federal Parliament; Liberal senator for Queensland (1971–1973).

Buckley, William (1780–1856). Soldier, convict escapee; lived with Victorian Aborigines (1803–1835).

Chifley, Ben (1885–1951). Labor politician; prime minister (1945–1949); defeated over bank nationalization.

Chisholm, Caroline (1808–1877). Social reformer, immigration advocate; she pioneered free female immigration to Australia in the nineteenth century.

Clark, Charles Manning Hope (1915–1991). Historian; Australia's most prolific and influential twentieth-century historian.

Cowan, Edith (1861–1932). Nationalist Party politician; she became the first elected female in an Australian parliament when elected to the Western Australian Legislative Assembly (1921–1924).

Curtin, John (1885–1945). Labor politician; prime minister (1941–1945); led Australia with distinction during darkest days of World War II.

Deakin, Alfred (1856–1919). Protectionist politician, federation advocate, Australia's second prime minister (1903–1904, 1905–1908, 1909–1910); fused protectionists and free traders into the Liberal Party in 1909, thereby introducing two-party politics into Australia.

Dunlop, Edward (Weary) (1907–1993). Doctor, soldier, humanitarian; he won undying fame for his selfless heroism in protecting Australian prisoners of war captured by the Japanese in World War II.

Florey, Howard (1898–1968). Doctor, scientist; pioneered development of penicillin with Ernst Chain in 1945.

Gilmore, Mary (1865–1962). Poet, social reformer; she became the first female member of the Australian Workers' Union; her poetry is notably sympathetic toward the plight of Aborigines and shows great appreciation of Aboriginal culture.

Goyder, George (1826–1898). Surveyor general of South Australia, he became the first to plot rainfall patterns to establish an area's suitability for development and to link rainfall with viability of permanent settlement.

Greenway, Francis (1777–1837). Convict architect responsible for the construction of some of Australia's most famous and memorable colonial buildings.

Griffin, Walter Burley (1876–1937). American architect whose design for the new capital city of Canberra won first prize in an international competition in 1912; he came to Australia to supervise construction of the city but was systematically sabotaged by a provincial and petty public service until his resignation in 1920.

Hannan, Patrick (1842–1925). Prospector and miner, he found Kalgoorlie, the country's richest goldfield, in 1893.

Hargraves, Edward Hammond (1816–1891). Prospector, he claimed credit for discovery of Australia's first commercial goldfield near Bathurst in 1851 and triggered a gold rush.

Heysen, Hans (1877–1968). Artist renowned for his realistic depiction of Australian landscapes.

Isaacs, Isaac (1855–1948). Lawyer, politician; justice of the High Court; he became the first Australian-born governor general in 1930.

Keating, Paul (1944–). Labor politician, prime minister (1991–1996); championed the deregulation of the economy and Australia finding a regional rather than a European destiny.

Kelly, Edward (Ned) (1855–1880). Bushranger, murderer, social bandit, he was regarded as a hero by impoverished free selectors for his attacks on wealthy landowners and the banks; famous for his homemade armor, for his bravery during the siege at the Glenrowan Hotel, and for his composure at his execution.

Lalor, Peter (1827–1889). Miners' leader at the Eureka Stockade in 1854; lost an arm from wounds received; politician; speaker of Victorian Legislative Assembly.

Lawson, Henry (1867–1922). Novelist, poet, journalist, alcoholic; his writing espoused Australian nationalism and represented the aspirations of federationists for the formation of an Australian nation.

Lawson, Louisa (1848–1920). Suffragist, feminist, publisher; she founded and edited *The Dawn* (1888–1905) to educate and empower women via their own journal.

Lyons, Enid (1897–1981). Liberal politician, teacher, the wife of Prime Minister Joseph Lyon; after his death entered Parliament in 1943 to become the first female cabinet minister in a federal government.

Macquarie, Lachlan (1761–1824). Soldier and fifth governor of New South Wales (1810–1822); he is regarded as the father of Australia because of his humane concern with the welfare and advancement of the convicts.

Mawson, Douglas (1882–1958). Antarctic explorer, geologist, sole survivor of 1912 expedition to cross King George V land; his work laid the basis for Australia's claimed mandate over part of Antarctica.

Menzies, Robert Gordon (1894–1978). Liberal politician and longest-serving prime minister (1939–1941, 1949–1966); he founded the Liberal Party in 1944 and dominated political life until his retirement in 1966.

Mitchell, Helen (Nellie Melba) (1861–1931). Opera singer and entertainer, she became internationally famous as one of the best singers of her generation and sang in most of the world's great opera houses.

Monash, John (1865–1931). Soldier, commander of the Australian Army Corps in France in 1918; he developed a reputation as a brilliant strategist and won the trust of his men for refusing to waste their lives needlessly.

Nolan, Sidney (1917–1992). Artist; produced the famous series of Ned Kelly paintings between 1945 and 1947 that melded Kelly into a bush legend and became artistic cultural icons.

Paterson, Andrew (Banjo) (1864–1941). Poet, writer, journalist; the author of Australia's best-known and most loved bush ballads, including *The Man from Snowy River, Clancy of the Overflow*, and *Waltzing Matilda.*

Penfold, Mary (1820–1896). Winegrower; founder of Penfolds Wines; she arrived in South Australia in 1844 and began making wine from her own vines shortly thereafter, continuing until her retirement in 1884; to preserve respectability, she kept her wine making a secret for many years.

Phillip, Arthur (1738–1814). Naval officer, spy, Australia's first governor; he commanded the First Fleet, which arrived in 1788, and administered the embryo colony until his departure in 1792 to seek medical attention and to return to active service.

Roberts, Tom (1856–1931). Artist and founder of the Heidelberg School, Australia's first impressionists; he painted several classic and much reproduced works including *Shearing the Rams, Bailed Up*, and *The Big Picture* in which he commemorated the opening of the first Federal Parliament.

Smith, Charles Kingsford (1897–1935). Pioneer aviator; with Charles Ulm became the first to fly across the Pacific in 1928; founded Australian National Airways in 1929 and crashed in Bay of Bengal in 1935 while on a flight from England.

Spence, Catherine (1825–1910). Suffragist, journalist, tireless agitator for women's rights; she helped win the vote for women in South Australia in 1894 and became Australia's first female political candidate when she stood unsuccessfully for election to the Federal Convention in 1897.

Stuart, John McDouall (1815–1866). Explorer, surveyor; he led an expedition from Adelaide to Chambers Bay in the Northern Territory in 1861–1862; privation destroyed his health.

Sturt, Charles (1795–1869). Explorer; discovered the Darling River in 1828 and used a collapsible boat to travel down the Murrumbidgee and Murray Rivers to the sea in 1830; in 1844–1845 discovered Sturt's Stony Desert in South Australia.

Wentworth, William Charles (1792–1872). Politician, lawyer, journalist; he became leader and spokesman for the emancipists and the native-born in New South Wales from the 1820s to the 1840s and drafted the constitution for the introduction of Responsible Government; he attempted to introduce a hereditary aristocracy into colonial politics.

Notes

CHAPTER 1

1. *Sun-Herald*, 15 July 2001.

CHAPTER 3

1. William Dampier, cited by C.M.H. Clark, *Sources of Australian History* (London: Oxford University Press, 1971), pp. 24–27.

2. Leslie Marchant, *France Australe* (Perth: Artlook Books, 1982), p. 64.

3. Keneth Gordon McIntyre, *The Secret Discovery of Australia* (London: Souvenir Press, 1977), pp. 196–97.

4. Watkin Tench, cited by Clark, *Sources*, p. 69; and David Collins, *An Account of the English Colony in New South Wales* (London: A.W. Reed, 1798), 1:53, 496.

5. Noel Butlin, *Our Original Aggression* (Sydney: George Allen & Unwin, 1983), p. 20.

6. Monica Perrot, *A Tolerable Good Success: Economic Opportunities for Women in New South Wales 1788–1830* (Sydney: Hale & Iremonger, 1983), p. 23.

7. Arthur Phillip to Lord Grenville, 17 July 1790, *Historical Records of Australia, 1914–1925* Series 1, vol. 1 (p. 195).

8. Watkin Tench, cited by Clark, *Sources*, p. 100.

9. Malcolm Ellis, *John Macarthur* (Sydney: Angus & Robertson, 1973), p. 260.

10. Lachlan Macquarie to Lord Bathurst, 27 July 1822, *Historical Records of Australia, 1914–1925*, Series 1, vol. 10.

11. Lloyd Robson, *The Convict Settlers of Australia* (Melbourne: Melbourne University Press, 1976), chapter 5.

12. John Hirst, *Convict Society and Its Enemies* (Sydney: George Allen & Unwin, 1983), pp. 57–69.

13. C.M.H. Clark, *Occasional Writings and Speeches* (Melbourne: Fontana/Collins, 1980), pp. 94–143.

14. *Australian*, 19 January 1826.

15. *Australian*, 12 January 1826.

CHAPTER 4

1. Figures from Peter Burroughs, *Britain and Australia 1831–1855: A Study in Imperial Relations and Crown Lands Administration* (London: Oxford University Press, 1967), appendix 2.

2. F.G. Clarke, *The Land of Contrarieties: British Attitudes to the Australian Colonies 1828–1855* (Melbourne: Melbourne University Press, 1977), p. 124.

3. *Sydney Gazette*, 28 April 1835.

4. F.G. Clarke, *The Land of Contrarieties: British Attitudes to the Australian Colonies 1828–1855* (Melbourne: Melbourne University Press, 1977), p. 30.

5. Lord Glenelg to Richard Bourke, 30 November 1835, *Historical Records of Australia*, Series 1, vol. 18.

6. Gawler to Glenelg, 22 January 1839, *Despatches of the Governor of South Australia to the Secretary of State for the Colonies*; British Colonial Office Papers.

7. Lord Glenelg to Richard Bourke, 13 April 1836, ibid.

8. Lord Stanley to George Gipps, 5 September 1842, *Historical Records of Australia, 1914–1925*, Series 1, vol. 22.

9. Geoffrey Serle, *The Golden Age* (Melbourne: Melbourne University Press, 1963), p. 168.

CHAPTER 5

1. *Empire*, 21 October 1861.

2. *Sydney Morning Herald*, 16 September 1861.

3. C.M.H. Clark, *A History of Australia* (Melbourne: Melbourne University Press, 1979), 4:138–142.

4. F.G. Clarke, *The Big History Question: Snapshots of Australian History* vol. 1 (Sydney: Simon & Schuster, 1998), pp. 43–46.

5. For a full account, see Ken Inglis, *The Rehearsal: Australians at War in the Sudan 1885* (Adelaide: Rigby, 1985).

6. Clarke, *Big History Question*, pp. 72–76.

7. N.G. Butlin, *Investment in Australian Economic Development 1861–1900* (Cambridge: Cambridge University Press, 1964), p. 6.

8. Michael Cannon, *The Land Boomers* (Melbourne: Nelson, 1966), p. 34.

CHAPTER 6

1. Cited by J.A. La Nauze, *Alfred Deakin: A Biography* (Melbourne: Melbourne University Press, 1965), p. 131.

2. Henry Parkes's speech at Tenterfield, cited by C.M.H. Clark, *Select Documents in Australian History 1851–1900* (Sydney: Angus & Robertson, 1973), p. 468.

CHAPTER 7

1. Peter Coleman and Les Tanner, eds., *Cartoons of Australian History* (Melbourne: Nelson, 1967), p. 120.

2. F.G. Clarke, *The Big History Question* vol. 2 (Sydney: Simon & Schuster, 2000), pp. 5–9.

3. W.M. Hughes, *Policies and Potentates* (Sydney: Angus & Robertson, 1950), pp. 242–43.

4. W.M. Hughes, *The Splendid Adventure* (London: E. Benn, 1929), p. 236.

CHAPTER 8

1. Justice Pike's Report on Soldier Settlement 1929, cited by F.K. Crowley, ed., *Modern Australia in Documents 1901–1939* (Melbourne: Wren, 1973), 1: 449.

2. John Robertson, *J.H. Scullin: A Political Biography* (Nedlands: University of Western Australia Press, 1974), pp. 103–5.

3. *Labor Daily*, 27 August 1930.

4. *Labor Call*, 11 December 1930.

5. *Australian Worker*, 27 August 1930.

6. Cecil Edwards, *Bruce of Melbourne: Man of Two Worlds* (London: Heinemann, 1965), p. 208.

7. F.G. Clarke; *The Big History Question* vol. 1 (Sydney: Simon & Schuster, 1998), pp. 131–35.

8. *Age*, 27 April 1939.

9. *Sydney Morning Herald*, 4 September 1939.

CHAPTER 9

1. Cameron Hazlehurst, *Menzies Observed* (Sydney: George Allen & Unwin, 1979), p. 138.
2. Ibid., p. 140.
3. *Australian Worker*, 25 October 1939.
4. *Sydney Morning Herald*, 27 December 1941.
5. *Courier Mail*, 3 April 1943.
6. F.K. Crowley, ed. *Modern Australia in Documents 1939–1970* (Melbourne: Wren, 1973), pp. 284–88.
7. F.G. Clarke, "Loaves and Fishes: The Financial Difficulties of the Democratic Labor Party in WA," *Politics* (May 1971), pp. 82–84.
8. *Sydney Morning Herald*, 3 March 1951.
9. *Herald*, 20 April 1965.

CHAPTER 10

1. *Age*, 21 January 1966.
2. *Commonwealth Parliamentary Debates*, House of Representatives, 8 March 1966, p. 240.
3. James Walter, *The Leader: A Political Biography of Gough Whitlam* (St. Lucia: University of Queensland Press, 1980), p. 154.
4. Fred Daly, *From Curtin to Kerr* (Melbourne: Sun Books, 1977), p. 198.
5. Cited by Lorna Lippman, "The Aborigines," in A. Patience and B. Head, eds., *From Whitlam to Fraser: Reform and Reaction in Australian Politics* (Melbourne: Oxford University Press, 1979), p. 177.

CHAPTER 11

1. Michael McGrath, "Economic Review," *Australian Quarterly* (Autumn 1989): 123.
2. *The Independent*, May 1991.
3. *Sydney Morning Herald*, 30 March 1991.
4. *Weekend Australian*, 29–30 June 1991.
5. *Sun-Herald*, 15 September 1991.
6. *Sydney Morning Herald*, 1 June 1991.
7. *Weekend Australian*, 23–24 March 1991.
8. *Australian*, 22 May 1991.
9. *Weekend Australian*, 11–12 May 1991.
10. *Sydney Morning Herald*, 20 August 1994.
11. *Commonwealth Parliamentary Debates*, House of Representatives, Question Time, 27 February 1992.
12. *Sydney Morning Herald*, 15 March 1993.

13. *Age*, 16 November 1993.

14. Paul Keating, *Engagement: Australia Faces the Asia-Pacific* (Sydney: Macmillan, 2000), pp. 20–21.

CHAPTER 12

1. *Sydney Morning Herald*, 12 February 2000.
2. *Age*, 9 June 1997.
3. *Sydney Morning Herald*, 10 July 1999.
4. *Sydney Morning Herald*, 4 April 2000.
5. *Sydney Morning Herald*, 7 June 1999.
6. *Sydney Morning Herald*, 10 July 1999.
7. *Sydney Morning Herald*, 9 June 2000.

CHAPTER 13

1. *Weekend Australian*, 17–18 June 2000.
2. *Sydney Morning Herald*, 16 November 2001.

Bibliographic Essay

The most readable and accessible general histories of Australia are David Day, *Claiming a Continent: A New History of Australia* (Sydney: HarperCollins, 2001); and F.G. Clarke, *Australia: A Concise Political and Social History* (Sydney: Harcourt Brace, 1992). The doyen of professional historians Charles Manning Hope Clark's magisterial six-volume opus *A History of Australia* (Melbourne: Melbourne University Press, 1962, 1968, 1973, 1978, 1981, and 1987) is still the most comprehensive and useful of the multivolume histories, although the prose is dense and the style literary. A more recent but less satisfactory series is *Australians 1788–1988: A Historical Library* (Cambridge University Press, 1988), a ten-volume multiauthored offering prepared for the celebration of the bicentenary. Its five volumes of sources, lists, and maps are extremely useful, but its other five volumes amount to a failed attempt at innovative history. Also readily available is Robert Hughes's *The Fatal Shore: The Epic of Australia's Founding* (New York: Vintage, 1988).

Readers interested in environmental history could start with Tim Flannery, *The Future Eaters* (New York: George Braziller, 1995); William Lines, *Taming the Great South Land: A History of the Conquest of Nature in Australia* (University of California Press, 1992); and Tim Low, *Feral Future: The Untold Story of Australia's Exotic Invaders* (Ringwood: Viking, 1999). The complexity of European Australians' relationship with the land is beautifully dealt with by Peter Read, *Returning to Nothing: The Meaning of Lost Places* (Cambridge: Cambridge University Press, 1996).

Women's history and studies of gender relations in the nineteenth century are superbly dealt with by Portia Robinson, *The Women of Botany Bay: A Reinterpretation of the Role of Women in the Origins of Australian Society* (Ringwood: Penguin, 1993); and by Trevor McClaughlin, ed., *Irish Women in Colonial Australia* (Sydney: Allen & Unwin, 2000). Twentieth-century developments are covered by Kay Daniels and Mary Murnane, eds., *Uphill All the Way: A Documentary History of Women in Australia* (St. Lucia: University of Queensland Press, 1980); and Jill Matthews, *Good and Mad Women: The Historical Construction of Femininity in Twentieth Century Australia* (Sydney: Allen & Unwin, 1984).

In the area of Aboriginal history and culture, it is hard to go past Heather Goodall, *Invasion to Embassy: Land in Aboriginal Politics in New South Wales, 1770–1972* (Sydney: Allen & Unwin, 1996): and Henry Reynolds, *The Other Side of the Frontier: Aboriginal Resistance to the European Invasion of Australia* (Ringword: Penguin, 1990). The best specialized study on the primacy of place in Aboriginal culture is Tony Swain, *A Place for Strangers: Towards a History of Aboriginal Being* (Cambridge: Cambridge University Press, 1993).

Race relations in Australia have received extensive coverage, but perhaps the best work is still A.T. Yarwood and M.J. Knowling, *Race Relations in Australia: A History* (Sydney: Methuen, 1982); Charles Price, *The Great White Walls Are Built: Restrictive Immigration to North America and Australia 1830–1888* (Canberra: ANU Press, 1974); and Eric Rolls, *Sojourners: The Epic Story of China's Centuries-Old Relationship with Australia* (St. Lucia: University of Queensland Press, 1992). The venerable study by Myra Willard, *History of the White Australia Policy* (Melbourne: Melbourne University Press, 1923; reprint, Fairfield, NJ: Augustus M. Kelley, 1968), still remains useful as a brief but comprehensive treatment.

The area of religious history is well serviced with histories of the various Christian denominations and the major non-Christian religions, but the most recent and inclusive scholarly work is Hilary Carey, *Believing in Australia: A Cultural History of Religions* (Sydney: Allen & Unwin, 1996), whereas New Age religiosity is covered by David Tacey, *ReEnchantment: The New Australian Spirituality* (Sydney: HarperCollins, 2000). The contributions of esoteric and occult religions are recognized in Nevill Drury and Gregory Tillet's *Other Temples Other Gods: The Occult in Australia* (Sydney: Hodder & Stoughton, 1982).

Cultural history is comprehensively traversed in John Rickard, *Australia: A Cultural History* (Harlow: Longman, 1988); art in Australian history by Bernard Smith, *Australian Painting 1788–1970* (Melbourne: Oxford University Press, 1971); music by Roger Covell, *Australia's Music: Themes of a New Society* (Melbourne: Sun Books, 1967); and literature by Leonie Kramer, ed., *The Oxford History of Australian Literature* (Melbourne: Oxford University Press, 1981).

Australia has a long tradition of political and labor history, and there are many publications dealing with the histories of the various political parties and individual biographies. Wider themes have been dealt with by Bede Nairn, *Civilising Capitalism: The Labour Movement in New South Wales 1870–1900* (Canberra: ANU Press, 1973), and R.W. Connell and T.H. Irving, *Class Structure in Australian History* (Melbourne: Longman, 1980). The role of class and ideology is studied in Tim Rowse, *Australian Liberalism and National Character* (Malmsbury: Kibble Books, 1978).

For other topics, one may consult the bibliography *Australians: A Guide to Australian Historical Sources*, published as part of the bicentennial series; the *Australian Dictionary of Biography* (Melbourne: Melbourne University Press, 1961–   ); or Kay Daniels, Mary Murnane, and Anne Picot, eds., *Women in Australia: An Annotated Guide to Records* (Canberra: AGPS, 1977).

Index

About the Author

FRANK G. CLARKE is Professor of History at Macquarie University in Sydney, Australia and the author of six books and many articles and book reviews in the area of Australian History. He is also a regular broadcaster on the Australian Broadcasting Corporation (ABC) national radio programs.